TUCHMAN

THE INTERNATIONAL
♦ KOSHER COOKBOOK ♦

The International Kosher Cookbook

BY THE 92ND STREET Y COOKING SCHOOL

Edited by
Batia Plotch
and
Patricia Cobe

◆

FAWCETT COLUMBINE
NEW YORK

A Fawcett Columbine Book
Published by Ballantine Books
Copyright © 1992 by The 92nd Street Young Men's Young Women's
Hebrew Association and Patricia Cobe
Illustrations copyright © 1992 by Lauren Jarrett

Library of Congress Cataloging-in-Publication Data
The International kosher cookbook / by the 92nd Street Y Kosher
Cooking School ; edited by Batia Ploch and Patricia Cobe. — 1st ed.
p. cm.
Includes index.
ISBN 0-449-90366-4
1. Cookery, Jewish. I. Plotch, Batia. II. Cobe, Patricia, 1949–   .
III. 92nd Street Y Kosher Cooking School.
TX724.I57 1992
641.5'67—dc20   *91-73146*
CIP

Designed by Beth Tondreau Design

Manufactured in the United States of America
First Edition: March 1992
10 9 8 7 6 5 4 3 2 1

This book is dedicated to the memory of my parents, Ninette Dina and Joseph Louzon. Cooking was one of my mom's passions. I remember her silhouette bent over her culinary utensils with delicious aromas permeating the air. Mom's philosophy of life was all about love of people and keeping them well fed. In my family, dinner was a celebration of good cheer and exotic, traditional food. Dad, as well, appreciated Mom's creative cuisine, and this love of gastronomic fare was passed on to me and my own family. My kitchen became a testing lab for the cooking creations of our 92nd Street Y chefs. My husband, Stephen, and my children, Adam and Dina, were the beneficiaries and judges of all these wonderful new recipes.

Batia Plotch

♦

I dedicate this book to my mother, whose delicious meals inspired my love of cooking, and my father, whose way with words inspired my love of writing; to both my parents, who encouraged me to try everything. My husband, Elliott, and my children, Josh and Matthew, also contributed their never-ending patience, support, understanding, and willingness to eat.

Patricia Cobe

Contents

Menus

FRENCH

MENU I—PROVENCE

Sea Bream with Spinach and Mustard Sauce—*Filets de Dorade sur Lit d'Épinards à la Sauce Moutarde*, 9
Chicken with Forty Cloves of Garlic—*Poulet aux Quarante Gousses d'Ail*, 10
Asparagus with Morels—*Asperges et Morilles*, 12
Pears Poached in Wine Scented with Pepper and Bay Leaf—*Les Poires au Vin de Poivre et de Laurier*, 14

MENU II—ALSACE

Cream of Carrot Soup—*Potage Lorraine*, 16
Veal Chops with Mustard Sauce—*Veau au Moutarde*, 18
Alsatian Noodles, 18
Red Cabbage with Chestnuts and Wine—*Choux Rouge aux Marrons*, 20
Apple Tart—*Tarte aux Pommes*, 21

MENU III—PARIS

Salmon with Olive Butter en Papillote—*Saumon au Beurre d' Olive en Papillote*, 23
Braised Artichokes with Beets and Beet Greens, 24
Gratin of Fresh Peaches and Bananas—*Gratin de Pêches et Bananes*, 26

Okra with Mustard—*Bhindi-Subzi*, 74
Chicken and Bamboo Curry with Coconut, 75
Puffy and Flat Indian Breads—*Parathas and Pooris*, 76
Indian Pareve Dessert—*Suji Halwa*, 79

MOROCCAN
JEWISH-STYLE MENU

Hot Cigars—*Garros*, 85
Fish in Saffron Sauce—*Hout Metbuch*, 88
Pumpkin Soup—*Mark del Gar'a*, 89
Chicken Tagine with Potatoes, Olives, and Tomatoes—*Bel Btata*, 90
Grated Carrot Salad—*Salada de Chizo*, 91
Eggplant Salad, 91
Shortbread—*Ghriba*, 92

ARABIC-STYLE MENU

"Pigeon" Pie—*Pastilla*, 94
Fish in Red Sauce—*Hout Metbuch*, 96
Moroccan Lentil Soup—*Harira*, 97
Chicken Stew with Semolina—*Chicken Couscous*, 98
Harissa, 100
Raw Tomato Relish, 101
Cooked Carrot Salad—*Salada de Chizo Metbucha*, 102
Stuffed Dried Fruit—*Noix et Dates Fourées*, 102

TURKISH
MENU I

Chicken Turkish Style—*Gayina à la Turka*, 109
Cracked Wheat with Chickpeas—*Bulgur*, 110
Rice with Pine Nuts—*Pilaf Piñones*, 111
Celery with Carrots—*Apio con Zanahorias*, 112
Leek Pancakes—*Keftes de Prasa*, 113
Nut Cookies—*Korabies*, 114

Spicy Coconut Milk and Chicken Soup—*Tom Kha Gai,* 153
Sautéed Rice Noodles with Beef and Broccoli—*Pad See-um,* 154
Black Soy Sauce, 155
Sweet Rice Pudding with Apricots—*Khow Neeow Sum,* 156

MENU II

Corn Fritters—*Khao Pud Tod,* 157
Ground Beef Salad—*Lap Nuea,* 158
Chile Steak with Mint—*Nuea Pad Prik,* 160
Stir-fried Bean Threads—*Pad Woon Sen,* 160
Marinated Chicken in Coconut Milk—*Gai Yang,* 162
Gai Yang Dipping Sauce—*Nam Jim Gai Yang,* 163
Curried Rice—*Khow Phat Pong Kali,* 164
Bananas in Coconut Milk—*Khrow Buad Chi,* 165

TUNISIAN
MENU I

Complete Couscous with Meat and Meatballs—*Couscous
Complet avec Viande et Boulettes,* 171
Marinated Vegetable Salad—*Torchi,* 174
Vegetable Ragout—*Marmouma,* 175
Stuffed Dates—*Dattes Farcies,* 176

MENU II

Puffy Tunisian Omelet—*Maakoude de Poisson,* 177
Chicken and Okra Casserole—*Ganaouia au Poulet,* 178
Pine Nut Confections—*Bouchées aux Pignons,* 180

HUNGARIAN
MENU I

Caraway Soup—*Köménymagos Leves,* 186
Chicken Paprikas—*Csirke Paprikás,* 187
Cucumber Salad—*Uborka Sálata,* 189
Hazelnut Torte—*Mogyoró Torta,* 190

VIETNAMESE

Lime Chicken Brochettes—*Ga Nuong Voi*, 276
Soybean and Ginger Sauce—*Nuoc Tuong*, 277
Vietnamese-style Barbecued Veal Chops—*Thit Be Nuong*, 278
Pickled Cabbage or Mustard Greens—*Dua Cai*, 280
Crisp-fried Bean Curd in Tomato Sauce—*Dau Phy Sot Ca Chua*, 281
Rice and Black Mushrooms in a Clay Pot—*Com Nam Huong*, 282
Black Bean Dessert—*Che Dau Den*, 283

RUSSIAN-POLISH
MENU I—MEAT MEAL

Mushroom-Barley Soup, 289
Chopped Liver—*Gehakte Leber*, 290
Chicken Fat and Cracklings—*Schmalz and Gribenes*, 291
Pot Roast, 292
Groats and Noodles—*Kasha Varnishkes*, 293
String Beans with Garlic, 294
Noodle Pudding—*Lokshen Kugel*, 295
Apple Cake, 296

MENU II—DAIRY LUNCH

Beet Soup—*Borscht*, 298
Vegetarian Chopped Liver, 299
Little Pies—*Pirogen or Piroshki*, 300
Potato Kneidlach, 301
Rugelach, 302

CELEBRATIONS
MEDITERRANEAN APPETIZER BUFFET

Nice-style Salad—*Salade Niçoise*, 307
Vegetable Omelet—*Frittata or Tortilla Espanola*, 308
Marinated Anchovies with Dill and Pimiento, 310
Spanish Sausage Stew—*Cazuelo de Chorizo*, 311

HOLIDAY MEALS

Acknowledgments

I t takes the hard work of many people to give birth to a cooking school and cookbook. We'd like to thank Rabbi Mark D. Angel of Congregation Shearith Israel, who gave his full support to the creation of the cooking school. It was through his efforts and those of Arnie Goldfarb and his staff that our cooking program became a reality. Rabbi Marc Schneier and Toby Einsidler of the Park East Synagogue were instrumental in extending the program to the east side of Manhattan. Our thanks, too, to Rabbi David Gorelick, formerly of Park East Synagogue and currently rabbi of Congregation Keneseth Beth Israel in Richmond, Virginia. He carefully read over the text and recipes that follow to make certain all the material was in accordance with Jewish law.

More thank-yous go to Counsellor Henry Cohn for his legal assistance; our enthusiastic agent, Carla Mayer Glasser, for bringing it all together; Joëlle Delbourgo, our editor at Ballantine Books, who provided us with expert guidance all along the way; Helaine Katz, Melissa Golub, Sol Adler (executive director), and Dan R. Kaplan (president) of the 92nd Street Y for their cooperation and encouragement on this project; all the cooking teachers at the 92nd Street Y Kosher Cooking School, who filled the pages of this book with their lively anecdotes and wonderful recipes; and all the students who tasted and tested the delicious results.

Introduction

Throughout history, the Jews have been an itinerant people, sometimes by choice, other times by dictate. These frequent wanderings limited the material goods they could transport from one home to the next, so as they moved from land to land they often took only what they could carry on their backs. But there was always plenty of room in Jewish hearts and minds to carry their most cherished possessions—their religious beliefs and family traditions. No cruel governing body could restrict the Jews from transplanting their spiritual and cultural baggage.

Wherever Jews settled, they preserved and perpetuated their rich heritage, and a major part of this heritage seemed to revolve around religion and food. As one generation passed into the next, the religious aspects of Jewish life stayed fairly stable. The strict teachings of the Torah and Talmud remained the foundations of Jewish religious life, whether that life was being lived in France, Turkey, Argentina, or Africa. Through persecutions and expulsions, wars and famines, the Jews have made a supreme effort to keep their religious beliefs intact, forming a strong spiritual bulwark against a hostile world. At times, this has meant practicing Judaism underground.

Jewish culinary traditions, on the other hand, have emerged somewhat differently. True, observant Jewish cooks have always tried to adhere to the kosher dietary laws, often in the face of great adversity. But the foods that crept into their repertoire naturally made use of locally available ingredients. As a result of their vast travels, Jewish cooks have developed a diverse and colorful cuisine—a cuisine in which local dishes were adapted and adopted, and new ones invented, all within the framework of the dietary laws. At the same time, they have enriched the cooking of their host countries with distinctly Jewish culinary customs and recipes.

Today, Jewish cuisine is still evolving, as curious and creative Jewish cooks embrace other ethnic cooking styles. Sophisticated modern Ashkenazic Jews know there's a lot more out there than gefilte fish and chicken soup. Increased travel abroad, trendy contemporary restaurants, and the current boom in home cooking have combined to spark an intense interest in adapting the dishes of different nationalities to the kosher guidelines.

Through the 92nd Street YM-YWHA, a mecca for Jewish cultural life in New York City, aspiring and accomplished cooks can learn how to prepare fascinating foreign foods in accordance with the Jewish dietary laws. As sponsor of the only kosher cooking school in the metropolitan New York area, the Y offers classes in cuisines as diverse as Japanese, Cajun, French, Indian, Turkish, Chinese, Iraqi-Syrian, Moroccan, and Thai. There is also instruction for those who wish to learn more about traditional Eastern European cooking and holiday dishes.

Teachers for these classes are carefully chosen for their expertise in these distinct cooking styles. Each brings his or her background, teaching techniques, and personalized approach to the cooking school. Nevertheless, every one of the instructors must scrupulously follow the dietary laws. For example, the Chinese cooking teacher substitutes veal or turkey for pork in her mu shu recipe; coconut milk is used instead of yogurt or regular milk in an Indian chicken curry; and nondairy creamer replaces cream in a rich French carrot soup. All the classes are conducted in synagogue kitchens under strict rabbinical supervision.

These restrictions might seem inhibiting to cooks who are accustomed to choosing and combining ingredients freely in their homelands. But once the teachers realize the extent and variety of permitted foods, their creativity soars. Those who are not Jewish start thinking kosher, inventing new pairings of foods and flavors, while the Jewish teachers from other parts of the world enthusiastically share their treasured cooking secrets. All the instructors take extra care to make the kosher recipes as authentic as possible, never sacrificing the ethnic nuances that made them so special in the first place. The changes they do make often work to advantage, resulting in a dish that is more healthful and interesting than the original.

Unfortunately, there are large numbers of observant homes across America that are nowhere near the Y cooking school. Until now, cooks in other areas of the country were either totally unfamiliar with the Jewish components of certain foreign cuisines or were unable to convert their favorite ethnic recipes to kosher ones. Since most American Jews are of Russian or Eastern European ancestry, they know little or nothing of the rich culinary history of the Sephardic and Far Eastern Jews.

With the publication of *The International Kosher Cookbook,* these problems can be solved. This comprehensive cookbook is a collection of the best recipes taught and cooked through the 92nd Street Y—a representation of many different cuisines and all the major Jewish holidays. The moment has come when imaginative kosher cooks everywhere can discover the excitement of "eating ethnic" and rediscover their own culinary roots.

Rabbi's Note

The laws of kashrut are prescribed as a diet to maintain one's spiritual being—not merely a diet for the body, but a diet for the soul as well; a medium to attain holiness and to draw us closer to God. The Bible does not link the dietary laws to healthiness, but to holiness, another element of a distinctive life for the Jewish people. Therefore, it is most appropriate that the laws of kashrut are recorded in Leviticus, the book of sacrifices. These and other rituals remind the Jew that without a spirit of sacrifice and dedication, little can be achieved.

Throughout history, Jews have endangered their lives by their relentless sacrifices for kashrut observance. During the period of the Maccabees, Hannah and her seven sons chose martyrdom rather than transgress the dietary laws. Josephus spoke of the Essenes "who were racked and twisted, burnt and broken, and made to pass through every instrument of torture in order to induce them to blaspheme their lawgiver and to eat some forbidden thing; yet they refused to yield to either demand, nor even once did they cringe to their persecutors or shed a tear."

A Jewish survivor of the Crusades wrote, "It is fitting that I should recount the praises of those who were faithful. Whatever they ate or drank, they did at the peril of their lives." And so throughout the ages, despite the difficulties and even dangers during periods of severe persecution, the Jewish people remained steadfast in their loyalty to the laws of kashrut.

Today, when keeping kosher is acceptable and even in vogue, when kosher foods are available to satisfy a variety of ethnic tastes, when kosher products are readily accessible to a multitude of consumers, let us remember this legacy of kashrut—the countless examples of dedication and sacrifice even at great personal peril. Let us recall the sacrifices that were made to preserve this element of holiness so that we, the privileged generation, can enjoy a diverse menu of kosher foods while preserving our rich heritage and noble traditions.

—Rabbi Marc Schneier
Park East Synagogue, New York

The Kosher Kitchen

Each of the cuisines presented in this book has its own unique blend of cooking styles and ingredients. But while techniques and seasonings vary from country to country, all our recipes adhere to the same set of dietary principles—the laws of kashrut.

The word *kashrut* actually translates to "kosherness," and generally means all the laws, rules, and regulations that govern the traditional Jewish household; more specifically, what foods can and cannot be eaten by observant Jews.

The Jewish dietary laws originated from passages in the Bible, then were further elaborated upon in the Talmud. They cover many aspects of food preparation and cooking, including the ritual slaughter of animals, the type of vessels in which cooking takes place, and the amount of time that should elapse between meals, as well as all the permitted and prohibited foods. What follows is a simplified summary of the laws of kashrut.

♦ PERMITTED FOODS ♦

- All fresh fruits and vegetables
- All nuts and grains

- Four-footed animals that chew their cuds and have parted hooves (cows, sheep, deer, and goats are the most common)
- Domesticated fowl (chickens, turkeys, geese, ducks, and the like)
- Fish having both scales and fins

- Four-footed animals that do *not* chew their cuds or do *not* have parted or cloven hooves (pigs, rabbits, horses, dogs, camels)
- All insects, rodents, reptiles, and related species
- Most creeping animals
- Fish that do *not* have fins and scales (all shellfish, catfish, shark, eel, and puffers; swordfish and sturgeon are kosher according to some Conservative authorities but are not permitted in Orthodox households)
- Products derived from prohibited animals, such as gelatin and bone meal
- Animal blood
- Certain sinews and fat from kosher animals
- Any animal that has died of natural causes or has been killed by another animal; all animals must be slaughtered in accordance with the laws of kashrut (see below)
- Any mixture of milk and meat

Ritual Slaughter and Koshering of Meat

The laws of kashrut detail the specific rules by which an animal or bird is slaughtered for its meat. Kosher slaughter *(shechitta)* can only be performed by a shochet—a pious Jew who has been meticulously trained and authorized by a rabbi to carry out the procedure. The shochet must use a razor-sharp knife, free of all nicks and dents, that can cut through the windpipe, esophagus, and arteries of the neck in a single swift stroke. This action causes the animal to lose consciousness instantly and die a quick and painless death. Shechitta is thought to be the most humane method of killing an animal, and exemplifies the Jewish concern for preventing the suffering of all living beings.

After the slaughter, the animal or bird is hung upside down so the arterial blood drains out. Next, the shochet examines the body to make sure there are no signs of disease, discoloration, or ulceration of the organs.

The carcasses are then sent to a kosher butcher who removes certain arteries, veins, and sinews, as well as the intestines from poultry. Since the sinews from the hindquarter are very difficult to remove, this portion of the animal is generally not used by kosher cooks. However, some butchers do make the effort to take out the sinews, and there is a market among Sephardic Jews and some kosher restaurants for leg of lamb, filet mignon, and similar cuts of meat.

Kashering the meat or eliminating the capillary blood is the final step in the process. This procedure starts by rinsing the meat or poultry, then soaking it in cold water for about thirty minutes. Next, it's salted on all surfaces and placed on a grate or perforated tray for about one hour to permit the blood to drain off. Finally, the meat is thoroughly rinsed. To kasher liver, which is so rich in blood that it cannot be drained completely, the meat is placed on a grate and broiled.

Guide to Kosher Meats

The cuts of meat, poultry, and fish used in this cookbook are all kosher. However, if you would like to adapt other international or ethnic recipes to the Jewish dietary laws, the following list can help you. It's best to substitute a cut of meat that's similar in texture and tenderness to the original, such as round steak in place of flank steak and veal rib for veal loin.

BEEF	
Permitted	*Not permitted*
Brisket	Loin
Chuck (ground, steak, pot roast)	Rump
Flanken	Shank
Rib top	Flank

BEEF

Permitted	Not permitted
Short rib	
Standing rib roast	
Shoulder roast	
Rib eye, rib steak	
Round (ground, steak, London broil, pot roast)	
Minute steak or cube steak	
Skirt steak	
Tongue	

VEAL

Permitted	Not permitted
Breast	Loin
Cutlets	Flank
Shoulder	Leg
Rib (chops and roast)	Hind shank
Brisket	
Tongue	

LAMB

Permitted	Not permitted
Neck	Loin
Shoulder chops	Leg
Shank	
Rib (chops, roast)	
Breast (roast, brisket)	

POULTRY

Permitted
Chicken
Cornish hen
Duck
Goose
Pigeon
Turkey
Capon

Separation of Meat and Milk

According to the Jewish dietary laws, milk and meat must never be cooked or eaten together. This means that meals must center around either meat and meat products or dairy foods. Furthermore, observant Jews typically wait six hours after a meat meal before consuming any milk or milk products. After a dairy meal, some kosher households require a wait of thirty minutes before eating meat, while others consider a rinse of the mouth and a few minutes' wait sufficient. Throughout history, these waiting times have been altered by individual congregations or communities. Therefore, it's best to rely on your own rabbi or spiritual community for guidance in these matters.

The prohibition against mixing milk and meat extends to cooking utensils and serving dishes as well. A separate set of pots, pans, flatware, dishes, knives, and other equipment for food preparation and eating is needed for dairy, meat, and Passover (Pesach) foods. Kosher homes must have at least three sets of china and flatware, and many have six or more to suit various occasions.

◆ PAREVE ◆

Foods that do not fall into the meat or dairy categories are classified as pareve, or neutral. The pareve group represents a large assortment of edibles, including fruits, vegetables, nuts, grains, fish, eggs, flour, sugar, tea, coffee, spices, oils, and most condiments. These foods can generally be used in combination with either meat or milk products, and cooked in or eaten from either set of utensils.

◆ SHOPPING FOR ◆ KOSHER FOODS

These days, grocery shopping can be a complicated task for kosher families. While it's fairly simple to choose fresh kosher foods—meats, fish, dairy products, fruits, vegetables, nuts, and grains—sorting out the acceptable from the prohibited in the large array of packaged foods is a bit more difficult. Shopping becomes even more complex if you're searching for foreign or ethnic ingredients to authenticate a particular recipe.

In general, a shopper may identify canned, frozen, and other processed food as kosher by reading the list of ingredients printed on the label. In order for a product to be certified kosher, the manufacturing process must be supervised by a rabbi. If it passes inspection, the food package can then be printed with a kosher label. At times the Hebrew letters כשר appear along with the ⓚ , or another type of symbol is used. Here are the most common registered symbols or seals printed on food packages:

ⓤ The symbol of the Union of Orthodox Jewish Congregations, this is the best-known and most widely used kosher seal across America.

ⓚ The symbol of the Organized Kashrut Laboratories, Brooklyn, New York

Certain areas of the country have their own local kosher symbols:*

🅼 K.V.H. Kashrut Commission of the Vaad Horabanim (Rabbinical Council) of New England, Boston, Massachusetts

ⓑ Kosher Supervision Service, Teaneck, New Jersey

Ⓥ Vaad Hoeir of St. Louis, St. Louis, Missouri

☆ Vaad Hakashrus of Baltimore, Baltimore, Maryland

♦ THE QUEST FOR PERMISSIBLE ♦
ETHNIC INGREDIENTS

Preparing authentic international dishes can be a challenge to the kosher cook—it's a little trickier finding foreign foods certified with a kosher symbol. In fact, many ethnic products are imported from their country of origin, and may not even list recognizable ingredients on their labels. Although some may be printed with a ⓤ or similar seal, others do not have any familiar labeling language.

The first step in determining whether or not a foreign food product

---

*Taken from Blu Greenberg's *How to Run a Traditional Jewish Household.*

conforms to the dietary laws is to look over its ingredient list. Such items as shortening, gelatin, stearic acid, lactic acid, and mono- or diglycerides are questionable, since they can be derived from non-kosher animals or dairy products. The next step is to try to figure out the composition of the product. For example, the traditional fish sauce nam pla, used in Thai cooking, is made from a combination of fermented fish, including shrimp. Since this is not acceptable in a kosher kitchen, a substitute must be used, as has been done in our Thai chapter. In other instances, it may be necessary to discover where and under what conditions the product was manufactured. While the food itself might be strictly kosher, the processing machinery used to manufacture it may be used for nonkosher foods as well.

If there's still a doubt about the purity of an ingredient, it's best to check it out with your rabbi, or a rabbi who specializes in certifying kosher foods. All the ingredients used in this cookbook were carefully scrutinized before they were used in the cooking classes sponsored by the 92nd Street Y. Before each class, the cooking teachers took their grocery orders to either Rabbi Angel at the Spanish-Portuguese synagogue or Rabbi Schneier at Park East Synagogue. These learned men carefully evaluated questionable products before endorsing them as kosher. Occasionally, it was necessary to call overseas and check with a foreign processing plant before approval could be granted.

These days, it's possible to find a large assortment of ethnic ingredients in most large supermarkets and kosher food stores. But if you do hit a few dead ends in your search for the exotic, we've supplied a list of shopping sources at the end of the book to help you out.

A Primer on Kosher Wine

Wine in the Garden of Eden—yes! But that was only the beginning. Since then, wine-making has blossomed, and production of kosher wines is now budding as never before.

Today, wine lovers who keep kosher can choose among wines almost as various as the nonkosher wines on the shelves. Kosher wine is being made from grapes grown in virtually all the great wine-growing regions of the world—Bordeaux, Burgundy, Champagne, Italy, Spain, California, and New York are all represented. Turnabouts have occurred in those regions that have traditionally provided vast amounts of kosher wines and have earned poor reputations for their efforts. New York is the outstanding example, having become a high-quality producer of fine, dry kosher wines after generations of churning out sweet wine from Concord grapes—for too long thought the only grape suitable for the climate.

Let's return for a moment to the Garden of Eden, where the climate was benign and the wine-making process simple. The grape itself did all the work, and the result was similar to Beaujolais. Actually, the hand of man need not touch the grape at all to produce wine—the juice starts fermenting within the unbroken grape itself. Wherever ripe grapes hang on the vine, there is bound to be such wine, fermented through enzymatic action. This process is known as carbonic maceration. As it proceeds, the ripe and fermenting grapes burst their skins, the yeasts that exist throughout the vineyard do their thing, and the process accelerates. Evidence of the efficacy of this natural action can be seen in any vineyard at harvesttime—bees buzzing excitedly around the dripping grapes, flying erratically away to spread the good news at the hive, and often failing to reach home, falling stupefied to the ground to sleep it off.

Wine-makers who are kosher have not been such busy bees until recent years, when the boom in technology has made improved grape varieties and methods of production available throughout the world. It is probable that the wines produced for religious purposes and consumed by Jews for centuries were young and simple, much like the wine that virtually makes itself in the grape.

That does not necessarily mean poor wine. Standards have been set for a long time. Ernest Herzog, the noted scholar and wine-maker of the Royal Wine Company, which produces Kedem, dates Jewish wine connoisseurship to Maimonides, which connotes a long history of wine-making. Herzog sums up Maimonides on fine wine: "The wine had to be red, it couldn't be ameliorated with water, it couldn't be sweetened with sugar, it couldn't have any off-taste, off-odor, vinegar, bacteria, oxidation. It had to be the perfect wine, a high-quality, pure, dry wine."

Some four hundred years ago, Rabbis Joseph Caro and Moses Isserles led the effort that put together the dictates of the Rambam, the Talmud, and the needs of the Jewish people into that code of law called the Shulchan Aruch. Technically, the thinking behind the criteria for kosher wine was advanced. Just as with the portions pertaining to food, good sanitation was requisite. As just one example, it was required that each barrel must be cleaned three times. Diving into a barrel or tank with a mop or brush is difficult and time-consuming but, at that time, was most necessary. Although it was not until Pasteur's discoveries that bacteria were understood, it was obvious that something was always in the neighborhood of wine, ready to spoil it; cleanliness became of prime importance. Steam jets and purifying chemicals have made the barrel-cleaning job easier and more effective, but the injunction to clean thrice remains in force.

The practice of boiling wine came about for different reasons. The sages figured that wine that was to be drunk in the company of gentiles should be limited, so as to discourage prolonged association and possible intermarriage. They decided that the wine should be boiled. In those days, as the saying goes, "boiled was spoiled," and the niceties of commercial hospitality with gentiles could be concluded without encouraging any party to linger.

The word for boiling in Hebrew is transliterated as *mevushal* or *m'vushal*. This word is displayed on wine bottle labels in English, Hebrew, or both. Wine that is mevushal may be poured by anyone, Jewish or not, without losing its standing as kosher. Kosher wine that is not mevushal can only be poured by a Jew.

The rest of the kosher wine-making procedures are carried out in normal fashion, care being taken not to use certain ingredients in the finishing treatments. Some fining and filtering agents are derived from animal products and are banned in kosher wine-making, as are commercial yeasts, which are not kosher for Passover. Nonkosher wine-makers use specialized yeasts that are not available in kosher form. Most kosher wine-makers use the natural yeasts present on the grapes and in the air to start fermentation; these yeasts are then scooped up from the top of the juice (known in wine-making as *must*), multiplied quickly, and returned to the slowly fermenting must to invigorate the process.

Most kosher wines are also kosher for Passover. Visits to virtually all kosher wineries will show all the prohibitions attendant to the holiday strictly observed year round within the winery, or at least in those parts where the wine is produced and bottled. Mevushal or not, kosher l'Pesach or not, an astonishing array of high-quality kosher wines is being produced in the world and the number keeps rising.

Talented kosher wine-makers are found from California to Casablanca, from the Hudson Valley of New York to the Haute Côte de Nuits of France. Kosher wines are available from most of the great wine-growing regions of France, Italy, Spain, and Israel and the administered territories. If they cannot be found on the spot in a local store, they can be ordered and delivered to the store in a matter of days, such is the distribution system in effect in most of the urban United States.

World-class kosher wines are being produced in California mainly by Royal Kedem, Gan Eden, Weinstock, and Hagafen in so many varieties and styles that it is often necessary when buying Kedem's Herzog wines to differentiate between Herzog and Baron Herzog; between reserve and regular. Even Carmel has raised its level of sophistication, its better line being labeled Carmel Vineyards.

Which brings us to the place where it all begins—the vineyards. Such care is taken in producing kosher wine today that it would be normal to think that the same attention is given to growing the grapes themselves. That is not wholly the case. Carmel wine-maker Alfred Stiller explains that wine-growers in the land of Israel follow the agricultural commandments. But kosher wine-makers in other countries are free to buy their fruit from any grape-grower, asking no questions other than those pertaining to the quality of the grapes themselves. Stiller emphasizes that only in Israel are the vineyards given a rest once every seven years, according to the Biblical injunction: "Six years thou shalt sow thy field and six years thou shalt prune thy vineyard and gather in the fruit thereof; but in the seventh year shall be a sabbath of rest unto the land, a sabbath for the Lord . . ."

Israeli grape-growers also adhere to the commandment: "And when ye shall come into the land and shall have planted all manner of trees for food, then ye shall count the fruit thereof as uncircumcised: three years shall it be as uncircumcised unto you: it shall not be eaten of. But in the fourth year all the fruit thereof shall be holy for a celebration to the Lord. And in the fifth year shall ye eat of the fruit thereof, that it may yield unto you the increase thereof . . ."

Also in Leviticus is the commandment: "And when ye reap the harvest of your land, thou shalt not wholly reap the corners of thy field, neither shalt thou gather the gleanings of thy harvest. And thou shalt not glean thy vineyard, neither shalt thou gather every grape of thy vineyard; thou shalt leave them for the poor and stranger . . ."

There are other rules as well. Producing vineyards may not be torn up. Even if the grape variety falls out of favor and to grow it is not economical, the vineyard must be left standing. Nor can anything be planted between the rows of vines. This is interpreted as leaving enough space between the vines and anything else so that the roots do not touch. There are definite separations, therefore, between vineyards and orchards, and between fruit-bearing land and vegetable plots, for example.

The complaint that kosher wine is always higher priced than nonkosher is answered by the realities implicit in observing these laws. Years must go by before the kosher Israeli wine-maker can taste the fruit of his vineyard, and even then not every grape may be used and the produce from each succeeding seventh year may not be sold at all. Outside of Israel, in California, for example, where kosher wine may come from any vineyard with fewer religious sanctions in effect, the necessity of adhering to the religious rules of production can still add considerably to already higher personnel costs. Kosher wine companies tend to pay their employees more than do others, as it is recognized that living as a Sabbath-observing Jew is inherently more expensive.

Rabbis who oversee and certify production also add considerably to the bottom line. It is necessary here to correct a widespread misapprehension of the role of such rabbis. Many people think the rabbi utters a prayer over the wine and poof!, it is kosher. Not so. There are no such blessings. The rabbi must make sure that the wine is handled according to the law of kashrut, from the time of the separation of the grape juice from the pulp through to the corking of the bottle.

Despite these additional costs, kosher wineries and wines are proliferating. As a rule, modern techniques and technology are acceptable for kosher production. Since these make the growing of finer grape varieties possible in areas where they have not been planted before, drier wines to go with food have become more available and acceptable at the kosher table. Fine wines made for cellaring, that is, for improving with age, are still rare, but are becoming less so. For example, Herzog Reserve Cabernet Sauvignon 1986, Gan Eden Cabernet Sauvignon 1986, and Hagafen Cabernet Sauvignon 1987—all

California wines—are exceptional by any standards; filled with fruit, massive of body, luscious in the bouquet, and firm in structure. These are surely wines to mature over several years.

In that great citadel of French wine, Bordeaux, wine is again being produced under the Rothschild banner. Baron Eric de Rothschild has confided that kosher wine was made at Chateau Lafitte-Rothschild at the very beginning of its tenure under the family's control. Now, Baron Edmund, Eric's uncle and a major stockholder in the Lafitte enterprises, has converted a Bordeaux pig farm into a modern wine property, part of which is set aside as a kosher facility. Such is the power and pride of the Rothschilds that the wine has been offered in futures—before it is finished or delivered—at a price that could make one gasp!

Wines sold at such superpremium prices generally have a track record that indicates their aging ability; that remains to be seen with some of the newer kosher wines. Yet such is the appetite for kosher wines throughout the world that more than several French chateaux are establishing separate operations and are producing both kosher and nonkosher wines, with only slight changes of the label to indicate the difference.

The most popular wines in America are the varietals, wines known for the type of grape from which they are made—Chardonnay, Cabernet Sauvignon, and Pinot Noir, for example. The least expensive category of wine are generics—those identified as to class or type. These include Yarden Mount Hermon red and white or "Chablis," "Burgundy," and the like that do not claim to be from those areas of France but signify some vague type or style.

These lower-priced wines are most worthy of exploration. Sometimes they will fill the bill as no expensive wine could do. A delightful little rosé, fresh and fruity and perhaps with some sweetness, can wash down a turkey sandwich or a turkey dinner much better than a big red meant to be put away for aging, and better still than a Chardonnay, drunk more because it is fashionable and a known quantity than because it complements the food. In fact, price and quality often have no bearing on one another. With dozens upon scores of such wines to investigate, some heady experiences await the wine lover.

These developments are quite positive for the kosher cook and oenophile. Boeuf bourguignon with real Burgundy; Alsatian choucroute made with real Alsace wine; a true Moroccan wine to complement couscous from nearby Tunisia, and so on. Not only is there wine to cook with, but the same wine now is palatable enough to go with the meal and, if better is desired, it is available. About the only type of wine not readily available in the United States market as this is written is a true, dry kosher sherry.

Even without dry sherry, wine will enrich a dish as it can enrich our lives. It is only in recent years that the kosher cook has been able to follow the old precept of cooking with the same kind of wine that will fill the glass on the table. This is not a bad rule to follow, although with moderation. For instance, it would be too expensive to cook with a Gevrey-Chambertin, but a lesser Burgundy, perhaps a Bourgogne Pinot Noir, would do just as well in the pot, giving the full Burgundian flavor and leaving the vastly more expensive Gevrey-Chambertin to be savored as an accompaniment to the meal.

Wine is usually added to the pot toward the end of cooking and even then, judiciously. The exceptions are those dishes in which the main ingredient is partly or totally immersed in the wine for the entire cooking period. Heat vaporizes most of but not all the alcohol in wine, leaving the taste constituents of the wine in the food and a richness brought by no other ingredient.

In buying, it's better to tote the wine home days, even weeks before serving it. Wine when shaken doesn't taste half as good as wine given a chance to rest and regain its composure, as it were. Few wines need much airing—a few minutes in the glass will let the aroma or bouquet rise.

Old red wines need decanting, if just to separate the sediment that has formed naturally over the years. Let the bottle stand upright for a day or more; then, without shaking it, gently peel off the capsule, pull the cork, and, with a flashlight or candle shining through the tilted bottle from underneath, let the liquid run into decanter, carafe, or pitcher. When you can see the dark sediment approaching the lip of the bottle, stop pouring. That wine left with the sediment isn't worth bothering about and certainly won't taste very good.

To discover what *will* taste good, take note of the fine wines I have suggested after the recipes and/or menus in this cookbook. When no wine is suggested, wine is probably not complementary to the dish. Beer, for instance, will partner very hot and spicy dishes better than most, or perhaps any, wine. And coffee or tea is often the best choice for dessert.

At times, you might want to try all the suggestions that go with a particular menu; at other times, just one. And there's no reason not to substitute a similar favorite label of your own choosing, or forgo wine altogether. Above all, indulge, in moderation, and enjoy!

—*M. David Levin*

M. David Levin

*A*n educational background in journalism and a personal interest in wine have led M. David Levin into the type of work he does today. For the past twenty-one years, he has been employed as a writer or producer for WCBS radio in New York City. He started out using his journalistic skills to create news and feature stories for the station. Along the way, he developed an appreciation and knowledge of wine. It wasn't long before he thought up the idea of combining the two in a radio segment called "News from the Grapevine."

The successful show eventually went off the air, but M. David's interest in wine remained strong. He began free-lancing for other media, becoming a wine columnist for Vineyard and Winery Management Magazine *and* Jewish Week. *Through his travels, M. David grew very familiar with the New York State wineries, including Kedem, the kosher winery that is one of the largest producers in the country. After tasting many wines at Kedem, he felt it worthwhile to look further into the burgeoning kosher wine market. Much to his pleasure, he discovered that fine kosher wines are now being produced in California, Oregon, France, Italy, and Spain, as well as New York and, of course, Israel.*

In addition to his free-lance writing assignments and duties at WCBS radio, M. David is currently the chairman of the Wine Media Guild, an organization of some forty prominent wine writers. He also has taught several popular kosher wine classes at the 92nd Street Y. A born and bred New Yorker, M. David still lives in Manhattan with his wife, Glenis. He has one grown son, Thunder, who recently made his debut as a movie director.

THE INTERNATIONAL
◆ KOSHER COOKBOOK ◆

French

*f*rom both a geographic and gastronomic point of view, France is divided into several regions. In the sunny south, the gentle climate and rich soil are perfect for growing tomatoes, olives, and garlic, and the Mediterranean Sea is teeming with all kinds of seafood. To the northeast, onions, cabbage, and root vegetables proliferate, and the cooking is a bit more robust. Every province in between has its own breads, cheeses, stews, sausages, pastries, and other specialties, all of which capitalize on the availability of fine local food products and the innate skill of French cooks. In Paris, France's culinary center and capital, many of these ingredients have come together and been refined into what the world calls haute cuisine.

The regions of Provence, Alsace-Lorraine, and Ile-de-France, the province that includes Paris, show the scope and character of French cooking to its fullest. Let's begin our culinary journey in the sun-drenched fields of Provence.

Bordering on the Mediterranean Sea and situated as it is between Italy and Spain, Provence has always shown strong Italian, Spanish, and Mediterranean connections in its cooking. It is also justly famous for its herbs. Rosemary, basil, sage, lavender, fennel, thyme, and savory grow everywhere, perfuming the air with their lovely aromas.

The fruits and vegetables of Provence are among the juiciest and sweetest in all of France. While French cooks in other parts of the country eagerly await spring, when the first tomatoes, melons, peaches, oranges, asparagus, and artichokes arrive from Provençal farms, the open-air markets of this southern province are in full swing year round, selling succulent fresh sun-ripened produce.

The people of Provence are descended from a mix of Mediterranean ethnic groups, each bringing its own customs to the Provençal food heritage. Inhabitants have included Romans, Greeks, North Africans, Spaniards, and Portuguese, many of whom became fishermen and farmers. During the Middle Ages, Provence was a separate country, and when the Jews were first banned from France in 1306, many migrated south and settled there. These Jewish settlers remained until the beginning of the sixteenth century, borrowing from the Provençal culinary style and adding a bit of their own. One significant contribution they made to the cuisine was the introduction of artichokes.

Like the Provençal Jews of past centuries, you should have little problem creating dishes that evoke the flavors and feeling of this region. Pareve olive oil, not butter, is the cooking fat of choice, and other dairy products, such as cream, are rarely used in combination with meat. Although some Provençal seafood specialties contain a lot of shellfish, a firm-fleshed fin fish, cut into chunks, can be substituted.

Moving to the opposite corner of the country, we come to the northern provinces of Alsace and Lorraine. Bordered by Germany, this section has always been swayed by its neighbor's culture and customs. Alsace, which is physically separated from the rest of France by the Vosges Mountains, is the most dramatically Germanic in its cuisine, language, dress, and architecture. Today, more than a million Alsatians still speak a German dialect.

Alsace is the only part of France in which the Jews have lived continuously since the twelfth century, the time from which documentation exists. In fact, the Jews of Strasbourg were mentioned by the famous Jewish traveler Benjamin of Tudela in the 1170s. The Crusades and subsequent riots against the Jews that swept Europe in the mid-1300s destroyed the once-powerful Jewish settlements in Alsace, Lorraine, and Champagne. But while the latter two provinces never recovered, the Alsatian Jews eventually rebuilt and revitalized their community.

Until the French Revolution democratized France, Alsace was the only region there with a Jewish population. But all was not rosy—the Alsatian Jews suffered their share of discrimination and harassment. Nevertheless, they endured until World War II, when the German invaders forced the community to disperse. After the war, a number of Jewish families returned to Strasbourg and rekindled the community. Today, these Alsatian Jews have been joined by Jews from North Africa and Eastern Europe, each group having its own congregation and preserving its own traditions.

Although the cooking of Alsace bears some resemblance to that of Germany, it takes full advantage of local farm products and livestock. These are ingeniously combined to create a tasty and hearty peasant cuisine. In addition, many of the dishes reflect the Jewish presence in the province; some go as far as to include the term *à la Juive* (in the Jewish style) in their names.

Fresh produce that goes into sturdy Alsatian fare includes cabbage (often cured into sauerkraut), root vegetables such as potatoes and turnips, chestnuts, pears, apples, plums, and cherries. A variety of grains grow in the fertile Alsatian fields; geese and pigs are the primary sources of meat; the streams and rivers yield trout, salmon, and other choice fish.

It's not too tricky to adapt the foods of Alsace to the dietary laws. Goose fat, used for cooking many dishes, is acceptable in kosher meat recipes. And since Jews have continuously lived in Alsace for many centuries, some of the regional specialties have already been translated to kosher. Bacon and other pork products can be eliminated or replaced fairly easily in most recipes, and pastries, tarts, and cakes can be baked with pareve margarine instead of butter or lard.

While Provence, Alsace, and the other French provinces can boast of fresh-tasting and inventive peasant dishes, Paris is where haute cuisine reigns supreme and new food trends take hold. Situated near two rivers—its own Seine and the nearby Loire—Paris is strategically located to receive the choicest food products from the French countryside.

After the French Revolution in 1789, the great chefs moved from the castle kitchens of the king and lords to the restaurants of Paris. Here classic cooking flourished, eventually evolving into the artfully

sauced, beautifully presented cuisine familiar to connoisseurs everywhere. In the past decade or two, some young French chefs have
begun to update the classics to better suit today's tastes. Their contemporary French dishes are usually cooked with a lighter hand,
allowing the natural flavors of the ingredients to shine, and the
calorie count to diminish.

It is generally believed that Jews lived in and around Paris before
the Franks did. Up until the late 1300s, the Jews owned all the
great vineyards and operated the wineries in Champagne and some
of the other growing areas. Surprisingly, by the time of the Crusades, the Frank and German communities were the hub of Jewish
life in Europe. Then the Jews were banished from all of France
except Alsace, many going east to Poland and Russia. It wasn't
until after the French Revolution that some Jews officially returned
to France and Paris. Most Parisian Jews became well assimilated
into the cosmopolitan life-style until the Nazi persecutions during
World War II again drove them from Paris. Some left for the
United States and other countries offering refuge, some were
herded off to concentration camps, and others went underground
until the war was over.

As we near the end of the twentieth century, Paris again has a
significant Jewish population. A number of Jews have emigrated
from Morocco, Algiers, and Tunisia, while others have shifted west
from the Eastern European countries. A visitor to present-day Paris
would find it relatively easy to eat in a kosher restaurant or deli, or
shop at a kosher butcher's. And it wouldn't be difficult to enjoy a
wonderful French meal prepared with care and finesse according to
the Jewish dietary laws.

Brian Engel

Brian Engel's love of food began at an early age. In the Youngs-
town, Ohio, home where he grew up, both of his parents were
accomplished cooks. Brian's father loved to bake, and originally
thought about getting a degree in hotel and restaurant management.

Instead, the elder Mr. Engel became a social worker, but continued to turn out baked goods at home. Mrs. Engel, whose family (like her husband's) was of Hungarian-Jewish descent, cooked many foods that reflected her heritage. But she also liked to create new dishes, some of which had a definite Hungarian twist.

All this activity in the kitchen generated an interest in a culinary career for Brian. So in 1980, after completing a college degree in liberal arts, he came to New York City to get some on-the-job restaurant training. He started by working in the kitchen of the Hotel Pierre, then moved on to Le Petit Robert, a small French restaurant in Greenwich Village. Here he was able to refine his classic French techniques and innovate a bit with new combinations of ingredients. These days, Brian is working as the sous chef at Docks, an inventive seafood restaurant on Manhattan's Upper West Side.

Although Brian's formal training has been mostly in French, Italian, and fish cookery, he still enjoys preparing the foods he ate as a child. These include chicken soup, chopped liver, cholent, gefilte fish, and a good old-fashioned chicken paprikas—made in the kosher way without sour cream. He also takes pleasure in preparing authentic, wonderful-tasting French food according to the Jewish dietary laws. "It's easy enough to separate milk and meat, and I never find it necessary to use nondairy creamers or similar products," he says.

Brian Engel currently lives with his wife, Susan, in Manhattan.

Gil Marks

G il Marks is a multifaceted man—he trained and practiced as a social worker, historian, and teacher, and has even been ordained as a rabbi. These days, he combines these diverse experiences with his lifelong passion for food and writing in his job as founder and editor-in-chief of Kosher Gourmet magazine.

Kosher Gourmet is unique in a field that's flooded with cooking publications. It is the only food magazine that devotes itself entirely to kosher cuisine, printing recipes, stories, news items, personality profiles, restaurant and cookbook reviews, and other information of interest to the burgeoning and increasingly sophisticated audience of kosher cooks. Gil recognized the need for such a product and enthusiastically launched it, first as a thin black-and-white magazine, then as a four-color glossy publication that's double the size and scope of the original.

Gil learned to cook while growing up in Richmond, Virginia, home to one of the oldest continuing synagogues in the United States. Along with his four siblings, he learned from his mother how to hold his own in the kitchen. Mrs. Marks's repertoire included traditional Jewish dishes from the family's Eastern European–Russian background, as well as southern specialties adapted to the dietary laws. Since the family lived close to lush southern farmland, the freshest ingredients were always available to enhance the cooking.

Gil Marks left Virginia to study at Yeshiva University in New York City. It was here that he earned his master's degrees in both social work and history, as well as his rabbinical certificate. While running a high school guidance department, he moonlighted as a kosher caterer, working mostly as a dessert baker. Gil so enjoyed puttering around the kitchen and expanding the horizons of kosher cooking that he decided to do it full-time.

In the pages of his magazine and in the cooking classes that he teaches, Gil capitalizes on his varied background to introduce readers and students to the many dimensions of kosher cooking. He brings both a social and historical perspective to the different cuisines he cooks and writes about, showing if and how the Jews have influenced that particular cooking style. And he uses his teaching and catering expertise to demonstrate how effortless it can be to make traditional ethnic dishes kosher. In addition to teaching French cuisine at the 92nd Street Y Kosher Cooking School, Gil Marks gives popular classes in low-calorie, seasonal, and holiday cooking, the latter including Passover, Purim, Rosh Hashanah, and Shavuot specialties.

◆ ◆ ◆

For biographical note on André Balog, see page 183.

Sea Bream with Spinach and Mustard Sauce—
Filets de Dorade sur Lit d'Épinards à la Sauce Moutarde
Chicken with Forty Cloves of Garlic—
Poulet aux Quarante Gousses d'Ail
Asparagus with Morels—*Asperges et Morilles*
Pears Poached in Wine Scented with Pepper and Bay Leaf—
Les Poires au Vin de Poivre et de Laurier

Sea Bream with Spinach and Mustard Sauce

Filets de Dorade sur Lit d'Épinards à la Sauce Moutarde

MAKES 4 SERVINGS

This recipe calls for a species of fish native to the Mediterranean Sea, but you may substitute snapper, flounder, or sole fillets.

 2 egg yolks, at room temperature
 3 tablespoons freshly squeezed lemon juice
 1 rounded teaspoon Dijon mustard
   Salt
 $\frac{3}{4}$ cup peanut oil or olive oil
 1 shallot, peeled and finely chopped
   Hot pepper sauce to taste
 1 teaspoon melted margarine
 $1\frac{1}{2}$ pounds fish fillets (sea bream, snapper, flounder, or sole)
   Freshly ground black pepper to taste
 $\frac{2}{3}$ cup dry white wine
 1 pound fresh spinach, stems removed
   Additional olive oil (optional)

1. In medium bowl, blend egg yolks, 1 tablespoon lemon juice, mustard, and a pinch of salt with wire whisk. Gradually add oil, a little at a time, beating mixture constantly with whisk until it thickens. Gradually whisk in remaining 2 tablespoons lemon juice. Add shallot and hot pepper sauce to taste; set aside.

2. Preheat oven to 425°F. Brush bottom of baking dish with melted margarine. Sprinkle fish fillets with salt and pepper to taste. Place fillets, skin side down, in baking dish; pour in wine. Bake fish 10 minutes, or until it flakes when touched with a fork. Remove from oven; skin fillets.

3. Meanwhile, in large saucepan over high heat, bring 8 cups water to a boil. Add spinach; return to boiling. Cook spinach, uncovered, for 1 minute. Drain and cool under cold running water; squeeze spinach leaves to remove excess water. Coarsely chop spinach; transfer to small bowl and season with salt and pepper to taste.

4. To serve, spoon some mustard sauce on each plate, arrange a round bed of spinach on top, and place a fish fillet in center of spinach. Sprinkle fish with a few extra drops of olive oil.

Wine note: Standard fish wines apply here. First choice would be a Riesling from Alsace; second choice, a Sancerre. Chablis would be fine, as would Macon-Villages, Pinot Blanc, Pinot Grigio, Gavi, Sauvignon Blanc, and Chardonnay. Each is different and will bring varying harmonies to this dish.

Chicken with Forty Cloves of Garlic
Poulet aux Quarante Gousses d'Ail

MAKES 4 TO 6 SERVINGS

A simple but succulent roast chicken is as much a part of the French Sunday dinner as it is of the Jewish Shabbat meal on Friday night. Provençal housewives often cook their chicken with garlic and herbs to reflect the flavors of their region. Although this recipe calls for 40 cloves of garlic, it isn't at all overpowering—the garlic loses its pungency during the long roasting period. In fact, it turns out mellow and creamy enough to spread on the sliced chicken.

ROASTED GARLIC

2 tablespoons olive oil

$\frac{1}{2}$ teaspoon sugar

Salt to taste

Freshly ground black pepper to taste

40 large cloves garlic (about 4 large heads), separated but unpeeled

CHICKEN

One 3-pound chicken, cleaned

Salt to taste

Freshly ground black pepper to taste

$\frac{1}{2}$ cup olive oil

2 tablespoons finely chopped parsley

2 tablespoons finely chopped fresh chives

2 teaspoons finely chopped cilantro (Chinese parsley or coriander)

2 teaspoons finely chopped fresh basil leaves

1 teaspoon chopped fresh thyme leaves

Chopped fresh chervil (optional)

$\frac{1}{2}$ bay leaf

1. Prepare garlic: In shallow dish, combine olive oil, sugar, and salt and pepper to taste. Roll garlic cloves in oil mixture until thoroughly coated.

2. Preheat oven to 425°F. Generously sprinkle chicken inside and out with salt and pepper.

3. In roasting pan or dutch oven, heat $\frac{1}{2}$ cup olive oil over medium-high heat. Remove from heat and add chicken, coating all over with oil. Distribute garlic around chicken and sprinkle herbs over all. Cover pan and bake 1 to $1\frac{1}{4}$ hours, until chicken is tender and juices run clear. Remove bay leaf.

4. To serve, cut chicken into serving pieces; season with salt and pepper to taste and spoon herbs and garlic over each portion. With a knife, split garlic cloves and squeeze out creamy inside to eat as a condiment with chicken.

Wine note: What a classic dish with which to serve a classic Bordeaux! You might want to get out your better reds for this: Margaux, St. Estephe, St. Emilion. But there are other choices, too. In virtually every wine-growing region of the world where kosher reds are produced, there is a fine red candidate for this marriage; where fine whites and rosés are grown, their bigger wines deserve equal consideration. The best choice may be to make this recipe often, pairing it with a different wine each time and enjoying the diversity.

Asparagus with Morels

Asperges et Morilles

MAKES 4 SERVINGS

Hunting for wild mushrooms in the French countryside is a popular pastime for many, a business venture for some. The woods of France yield a wide variety of mushrooms, including the prized and costly truffle and the slightly more prolific and earthy morel. I paired the latter with asparagus for a lovely side dish.

 5 ounces fresh morels, or $\frac{2}{3}$ cup dried
 2 tablespoons vinegar (optional)
   Salt
16 large asparagus (about 2 pounds)
 $\frac{1}{4}$ cup (4 tablespoons) margarine
   Freshly ground black pepper to taste
 6 shallots, peeled and finely chopped
 4 teaspoons freshly squeezed lemon juice

1 tablespoon chopped parsley
1 tablespoon chopped fresh chives
1 tablespoon chopped fresh chervil (optional)

1. Brush morels to remove sand and grit. If using fresh morels, cut off stems and soak 3 to 4 minutes in large bowl of cold water mixed with vinegar. Drain and pat dry. If using dried morels, soak in warm water. Drain on paper towels to extract moisture.

2. Break off bottom 2 to 3 inches of each asparagus spear. Peel each asparagus stalk, leaving tips intact. Tie asparagus into 2 to 3 bunches, grouping according to size.

3. In large saucepan, bring 8 cups salted water to a boil over high heat. Drop asparagus into boiling water; return to a boil. Cook asparagus 7 minutes. Remove thinner stalks, leaving thicker ones to cook 2 to 3 minutes longer. Drain well and dry on paper towels.

4. In large skillet, heat 1 tablespoon margarine over medium-high heat. Add asparagus; cook 4 minutes, shaking pan frequently. Season with salt and pepper to taste. Carefully remove asparagus to warm plate and keep warm.

5. In same skillet, melt another tablespoon margarine. Add morels and salt and pepper to taste. Cover and cook over medium heat 6 to 10 minutes, until tender. Remove morels from pan and pour them over asparagus; keep warm.

6. In same skillet, melt remaining 2 tablespoons margarine. Add shallots and sauté 2 to 3 minutes, until tender; remove from heat.

7. To serve, sprinkle asparagus with lemon juice; scatter shallots and chopped herbs on top.

NOTE: Morels are spongy, dark mushrooms often available in specialty shops or Korean greengrocers. If you can't get fresh ones, purchase dried morels or another dark, earthy type of mushroom.

Wine note: The morel is a wonderful foil for red wine but, paired with asparagus, the complexion changes. Asparagus is one of the most difficult of vegetables when it comes to wine—until you know the secret. Odd though true, Muscat is the *one and only* for asparagus. Try a dry Muscat from Alsace, if it's available.

Pears Poached in Wine Scented with Pepper and Bay Leaf

Les Poires au Vin de Poivre et de Laurier

MAKES 6 SERVINGS

These ruby-colored poached pears make a refreshing finale to a hearty Provençal dinner. Prepare this recipe at least 2 hours in advance, or longer, if possible, to give the fruit time to cool and steep.

1 tablespoon black peppercorns
2 cups strong red wine (Côtes du Rhône or Pinot Noir)
1 cup port or Madeira wine
  Grated peel of $\frac{1}{2}$ lemon
3 bay leaves
$2\frac{1}{2}$ tablespoons honey
6 ripe Bartlett pears

1. Place peppercorns in small square of cheesecloth and tie securely with string.
2. In large saucepan, combine wine, port, lemon peel, bay leaves, and wrapped peppercorns. Bring to a boil over high heat. Stir in honey; remove from heat.
3. Peel pears, leaving stems attached. Place pears in warm wine mixture in saucepan. Bring to a boil over medium-high heat. Reduce heat to medium-low and simmer 10 minutes, or until pears are fork-tender. Remove from heat; cover and let cool in liquid.
4. To serve, remove pears from liquid and arrange in large shallow bowl. Let stand at room temperature until serving time.

NOTE: This recipe can be prepared with peaches instead of pears. If using peaches, plunge them into boiling water for 1 to 2 minutes before peeling; add 1 vanilla bean to wine mixture before cooking.

Wine note: Now for a special treat—pair this dish with pear brandy or liqueur. There is a new brand on the market, Taam Pree, made by Shloime's Slivovitz of Monroe, New York, that is just out-and-out sensational. It is made from pears and plenty of them, as compared to flavored spirits that owe much to essences. The dessert should also be a smashing combo with med (mead), a fortified honey wine.

Cream of Carrot Soup—*Potage Lorraine*
Veal Chops with Mustard Sauce—*Veau au Moutarde*
Alsatian Noodles
Red Cabbage with Chestnuts and Wine—
Choux Rouge aux Marrons
Apple Tart—*Tarte aux Pommes*

Cream of Carrot Soup

Potage Lorraine

MAKES 4 TO 6 SERVINGS

Celery, carrots, and onions are sometimes called the aromatics when they are combined in cooking. Served hot, this creamy soup makes a bracing first course on a chilly night.

$\frac{3}{4}$ cup small dried white beans, soaked and drained
   (optional)
2 tablespoons margarine
2 pounds carrots, peeled and chopped (4 cups)
2 ribs celery, chopped
1 large onion, peeled and chopped
1 small potato, peeled and sliced
5 cups chicken broth, vegetable broth, or water
1 bay leaf
1 cup liquid nondairy creamer
   Salt and freshly ground black pepper

1. In medium saucepan, over high heat, bring beans and $2\frac{1}{4}$ cups water to a boil. Reduce heat to low; cover and simmer 45 minutes to 1 hour, until tender. Drain.

2. Meanwhile, in dutch oven or large saucepan over medium heat, melt margarine. Add carrots, celery, and onion; toss in hot margarine until well coated and softened, about 5 to 10 minutes, stirring often. Stir in drained white beans, if using.

3. Add potato, broth, and bay leaf; bring to a boil. Reduce heat to low; cover and simmer 20 minutes, or until carrots are tender.

4. Discard bay leaf. Transfer carrot mixture in batches to food processor or blender; purée each batch until almost smooth. Add creamer and salt and pepper to taste, and process until blended. Serve hot, or refrigerate to serve cold.

NOTE: If preparing this soup for a dairy meal, use butter instead of margarine, water or vegetable broth instead of chicken broth, and milk or cream instead of nondairy creamer.

Veal Chops with Mustard Sauce

Veau au Moutarde

MAKES 4 SERVINGS

Alsatian cooks are reputed to be able to prepare every part of the pig except the squeal. Pork chops would typically be used in this recipe, but veal chops work just as well, imparting a slightly less pronounced flavor of their own. Serve with Alsatian noodles.

$\frac{1}{4}$ cup dry bread crumbs
1 scallion, minced
1 tablespoon minced parsley
4 veal chops
   Salt and freshly ground black pepper to taste
1 egg, beaten
7 tablespoons margarine
3 tablespoons all-purpose flour
1 cup chicken broth or water
1 tablespoon Dijon or other French-style mustard

1. On waxed paper, combine bread crumbs, scallion, and parsley. Sprinkle chops with salt and pepper to taste. Dip chops in egg, then into crumb mixture, coating well.

2. In large skillet, melt 4 tablespoons margarine over medium-high heat. Add chops and brown 3 to 5 minutes on each side, until golden. Reduce heat to low and cook, uncovered, 15 to 20 minutes longer, or until chops are tender.

3. Meanwhile, in medium saucepan, melt remaining 3 tablespoons margarine over medium heat. Stir in flour and cook 1 minute. Gradually stir in broth or water; bring to a boil, stirring constantly. Reduce heat to low; simmer 5 to 6 minutes, or until sauce thickens. Whisk in mustard until blended. Pour sauce over chops and serve with Alsatian noodles.

NOTE: Plochman's mustard is a French-style kosher mustard that adds the right touch to this dish.

Wine note: Red wine is most often served with veal, and there is one imported kosher red from Alsace that would show imagination with this dish—a light Pinot Noir. Generally speaking, however, not to serve Riesling with veal in Alsace would be a crime—unless and only perhaps, a Pinot Blanc might be around. To many wine minds, Riesling is both king and queen of wine, with greater complexity, depth, fruit, and elegance than any other white wine and most reds.

Alsatian Noodles

MAKES 4 TO 6 SERVINGS

These noodles will absorb the delicious mustard sauce from the veal chops.

One 8-ounce package fine egg noodles
 $\frac{1}{4}$ cup (4 tablespoons) margarine
 2 tablespoons caraway seeds

1. Prepare noodles as package directs; drain. Set aside two-thirds of the cooked noodles; toss with 1 tablespoon margarine and keep warm.
2. In medium skillet, melt remaining 3 tablespoons margarine over medium heat. Add remaining one-third cooked noodles. Cook, stirring constantly, about 5 minutes, or until noodles turn crispy.
3. To serve, combine soft and crispy noodles; toss with caraway seeds.

Red Cabbage with Chestnuts and Wine

(Choux Rouge aux Marrons)

Chestnuts are a product indigenous to Alsace and appear in many Alsatian dishes. They go especially well with the onions, apples, and cabbage in this recipe.

$1\frac{1}{2}$ to 2 pounds chestnuts
$\frac{1}{4}$ cup vegetable oil
1 large onion, peeled and cut into crescents
2 apples, peeled, cored, and sliced
1 medium head red cabbage, cored and shredded
   (about 8 cups)
$\frac{1}{2}$ cup dry red wine
$\frac{1}{3}$ cup red wine vinegar
$\frac{1}{3}$ cup sugar (optional)
1 teaspoon salt
   Dash of freshly ground black pepper

1. Preheat oven to 400°F. With sharp knife, make an X in each chestnut shell. Place chestnuts on cookie sheet and bake 10 minutes. Remove from oven and cool just until easy to handle. Peel chestnuts.
2. In large skillet or dutch oven, heat oil over medium heat. Add onion and sauté in hot oil 5 minutes or until soft, stirring often.
3. Stir in apples, cabbage, chestnuts, wine, vinegar, sugar, salt, and pepper; reduce heat to low. Cover and simmer 40 to 50 minutes, until cabbage is tender but not mushy. Serve hot.

NOTE: The acid in the apples, wine, and vinegar helps the red cabbage retain its color.

Beverage note: Here is a no-no with wine—vinegar. Perhaps apple juice or cider would be a good choice. The vinegar would make any wine served with it taste like, well, vinegar!

Apple Tart

Tarte aux Pommes

MAKES 6 TO 8 SERVINGS

Open-faced tarts are the perfect way to show off the beautiful, luscious fruits from the orchards of Alsace and Lorraine. This pastry recipe is enough for 2 tart shells; the extra dough or baked shell may be wrapped and frozen for later use.

PASTRY

2 cups all-purpose flour
$\frac{1}{4}$ cup sugar
$\frac{1}{2}$ teaspoon salt
$\frac{1}{2}$ cup (1 stick) margarine
$\frac{1}{4}$ cup vegetable shortening
$\frac{1}{2}$ teaspoon vanilla extract or grated lemon peel
1 egg yolk
4 to 6 tablespoons cold water

FILLING

1 cup finely ground blanched almonds
2 tablespoons all-purpose flour
$\frac{1}{2}$ teaspoon salt
10 tablespoons margarine
$\frac{1}{2}$ cup plus 3 tablespoons sugar
1 egg
1 teaspoon almond extract
2 tablespoons dark rum or kirsch (optional)
3 to 4 apples, peeled, cored, and sliced
6 ounces apricot jam

1. Prepare pastry: In large bowl, combine flour, sugar, and salt. With pastry blender or 2 knives, cut in margarine and shortening to form coarse crumbs. Stir in vanilla or lemon peel, egg yolk, and enough water so dough holds together and comes away from the bowl. Form dough into 2 balls.

2. With floured rolling pin, roll out 1 ball of dough $\frac{1}{8}$ inch thick on lightly floured surface or between 2 sheets of waxed paper. Line an 8- or 9-inch tart pan with dough and trim edges. Refrigerate at least 30 minutes. (Either wrap and freeze remaining ball of dough or proceed as above and freeze the shell, raw or baked.)

3. Preheat oven to 400°F. Prepare filling: In food processor or with grinder, grind together the almonds, flour, and salt; set aside.

4. In medium bowl with electric mixer at medium speed, cream 8 tablespoons (1 stick) margarine and $\frac{1}{2}$ cup sugar until mixture is fluffy and sugar is dissolved. Add egg, almond extract, and rum or kirsch, if desired; beat until smooth. Beat in almond mixture; spread into chilled tart shell. (If using food processor, chop almonds, flour, and salt until fine. Add softened margarine, sugar, egg, almond extract, and rum or kirsch; process until smooth.)

5. Arrange apple slices in an overlapping pattern around edge of tart. Dot with remaining 2 tablespoons margarine and sprinkle with remaining 3 tablespoons sugar.

6. Bake tart 50 minutes to 1 hour, until golden. In small saucepan, melt jam. Brush warm jam over warm tart.

NOTE: Coat pastry blender with flour so dough doesn't stick to it. To remove excess dough from around tart pan, roll a rolling pin over top of metal rim and scraps will fall off.

Wine note: The wines of Alsace are exclusively dry, except great vintages when a small amount of sweeter wine is released for some very great prices. But such sweet, kosher Alsace wines are not in the United States, if indeed they are made. If dark rum or kirsch is used to flavor the tart, one or the other would be pleasant to sip alongside it; dry wine, of course, would be out of place in this dessert setting. A cream sherry or a sweet Muscat could also be appreciated.

Salmon with Olive Butter en Papillote—
Saumon au Beurre d' Olive en Papillote
Braised Artichokes with Beets and Beet Greens
Gratin of Fresh Peaches and Bananas—
Gratin de Pêches et Bananes

Salmon with Olive Butter en Papillote

Salmon au Beurre d'Olive en Papillote

MAKES 4 SERVINGS

The term en papillote *means in paper. The French often use parchment paper to wrap fish before cooking, but I find that aluminum foil does the job just as well. The idea is to enclose the fish and seasonings tightly in little packages to seal in the natural juices, which, in turn, lightly steam the fish.*

> 5 tablespoons unsalted butter
> 3 ounces pitted green olives
> 1 clove garlic, peeled
> 4 teaspoons olive oil
> 4 salmon fillets, about 6 ounces each
>   Salt
> 8 radishes, thinly sliced
> 4 scallions, thinly sliced on the diagonal
>   Minced fresh basil or dried basil leaves, to taste
>   Minced parsley, to taste
> $\frac{1}{2}$ cup white wine

1. Preheat oven to 475°F. Place baking sheet in oven to preheat.
2. Prepare olive butter: In food processor, combine butter, olives, and garlic; process until smooth.

3. Place 4 large rectangles of aluminum foil on countertop; spread 1 teaspoon olive oil over center of each. Place a salmon fillet on each rectangle; season with $\frac{1}{4}$ teaspoon salt.

4. Arrange radish slices neatly over salmon, entirely covering fillet. Sprinkle each with a quarter of the scallions, basil, parsley, and wine. Top each fillet with a quarter of the olive butter.

5. Fold foil over salmon, pinching seams together to tightly enclose each package. Bake packages on preheated baking sheet in hot oven about 10 minutes, or until salmon is pink in center.

6. To serve, place a package on each plate; carefully open foil to allow steam to escape.

Wine note: Salmon may be fish, but a light red wine is normally served with it. Olives also take red wine most of the time. Let's try a light red with this dish, even though white wine is used as an ingredient. A light Merlot would work well, as would a Chianti, Barbera, or Valpolicella, as well as some of the nonvarietal brand-name wines from Israel.

Braised Artichokes with Beets and Beet Greens

MAKES 4 SERVINGS

Although beets and artichokes are vegetables that have long been favored by French chefs, the preparation and presentation here are fairly novel. You may serve this dish either as an appetizer or a warm "salad" to accompany the salmon.

4 beets, trimmed (reserve green tops)
  Salt
1 tablespoon vinegar
4 artichokes
  Juice of 2 lemons, plus 1 tablespoon
  freshly squeezed lemon juice
2 teaspoons chopped fresh mint
2 teaspoons chopped fresh basil
2 teaspoons chopped parsley
1 teaspoon finely chopped garlic
  Freshly ground black pepper
10 ounces beet greens
1 tablespoon olive oil or vegetable oil
2 cloves garlic, peeled and sliced

1. In a medium saucepan, combine beets, 2 tablespoons salt, vinegar, and enough water to cover by 1 inch. Place over high heat and bring to a boil. Reduce heat to low; cover and simmer 40 minutes, or until beets are tender. Remove from heat; cool, peel, and cut into quarters.
2. Meanwhile, soak artichokes in water mixed with the juice of 2 lemons. When ready to cook, remove artichokes from soaking water; peel stems and remove fuzzy chokes.
3. In large bowl, combine remaining 1 tablespoon lemon juice, mint, basil, parsley, chopped garlic, 1 teaspoon salt, and $\frac{1}{4}$ teaspoon pepper. Add artichokes and toss to coat with marinade. Transfer artichokes and marinade to heavy-bottomed casserole or skillet; cover artichokes tightly with foil. Place over very low heat and cook about 25 minutes, or until artichokes are tender. Remove artichokes from casserole and cut into quarters; reserve cooking liquid.
4. In a medium saucepan over high heat, bring 6 cups salted water to a boil. Add beet greens and blanch about 5 minutes. Drain and refresh under cold running water. Drain again and squeeze dry.
5. In medium skillet, heat oil over medium-high heat. Add sliced garlic; sauté until lightly browned. Add beet greens; season with salt and pepper to taste and cook about 2 to 3 minutes, until thoroughly heated through.

6. To serve, alternate 4 quarters each of beets and artichokes on each of 4 plates. Mound a small amount of beet greens in center of each plate. Dress artichokes and beets with reserved cooking liquid, adjusting seasoning to taste.

NOTE: If fresh herbs are unavailable, substitute $\frac{1}{2}$ teaspoon each dried herbs for mint and basil.

Gratin of Fresh Peaches and Bananas

Gratin de Pêches et Bananes

MAKES 4 TO 6 SERVINGS

In this recipe, I used a classic pastry cream to make a contemporary fruit dessert. Prepare the pastry cream ahead of time and keep it refrigerated; then assemble the dessert just before serving.

PASTRY CREAM
- 2 cups milk
- 6 egg yolks
- $\frac{2}{3}$ cup sugar
- 1 teaspoon vanilla extract
- $\frac{1}{2}$ cup all-purpose flour

GRATIN
- Pastry cream (see above)
- $1\frac{1}{2}$ cups heavy cream
- 3 peaches, peeled and sliced $\frac{1}{4}$ inch thick
- 3 bananas, peeled and sliced $\frac{1}{4}$ inch thick
- $\frac{1}{4}$ cup sugar

1. Prepare pastry cream: In medium saucepan over high heat, bring milk to a boil; set aside.

2. In medium bowl with electric mixer at high speed, beat egg yolks, $\frac{2}{3}$ cup sugar, and vanilla about 8 minutes, or until mixture is pale in color and forms a ribbon when beaters are lifted. Add flour; mix until well combined.

3. Add half the hot milk to yolk mixture; mix well. Pour yolk mixture back into remaining hot milk, stirring constantly. Place over medium heat and bring to a boil. Reduce heat to low and cook, stirring constantly, 2 to 3 minutes.

4. Transfer pastry cream to medium bowl and cover with plastic wrap. Cool completely; refrigerate until ready to use.

5. Prepare gratin: In medium well-chilled bowl with electric mixer at high speed, whip heavy cream until stiff peaks form. (Do not over-beat the cream or the taste and texture will be too buttery.) Fold whipped cream into cooled pastry cream. (The mixture should hold firm but have a light texture.)

6. In lightly buttered gratin or baking dish, arrange peaches, slightly overlapping, in rows. Place banana slices between rows of peaches, overlapping slightly. Cover fruit with pastry cream mixture and sprinkle evenly with sugar.

7. Preheat broiler. Pass gratin under broiler until surface is evenly browned, turning dish from time to time to ensure even browning. Serve warm.

Beverage note: Although there are peach and banana brandies and liqueurs, this dessert would be a poor partner for them. There would be just too much cloying sweetness. Brewed decaffeinated coffee would seem the ideal accompaniment.

Japanese

apan's island locale in the Pacific Ocean has had a great effect on the development of its cuisine. The surrounding waters yield an ample supply of fresh fish and edible sea vegetables, and many of the country's most delicious dishes are based on this natural bounty. In the mountainous countryside, Japanese farmers grow the distinctive vegetables that add flavor, color, and crunch to the cooking. Some of the most widely used varieties include napa and mustard cabbage, mountain yams, daikon radish, and assorted mushrooms, sprouts, and root vegetables. Smaller, slenderer versions of some familiar American vegetables are also used as ingredients—eggplant and cucumber are two examples. In addition, citrus fruits flourish in the southern region of the nation. Of course, rice is the staple crop around which almost every Japanese meal revolves, although noodles play a supporting role.

Japan's small percentage of arable land has somewhat limited the size and types of crops that can be cultivated. However, Japanese creativity and the judicious use of seasonings and flavorings has helped develop native foods into a healthy and sophisticated diet. Among the ingredients that have added their own nuances of taste and texture are soy sauce, miso (fermented soybean paste), rice vinegar, pickled vegetables, tofu (bean curd), ginger, and wasabi (powdered horseradish).

But Japanese cooking is not about ingredients alone. Along with the emphasis on fresh and natural foods comes an equally important concern with presentation. No matter what is served, the food is always arranged in a simple yet elegant manner, offering harmonious contrasts of color, texture, and shape. The exquisite composition on the plate or lacquer tray can elevate a Japanese meal to a work of art. This focus on appearance reflects the strong Japanese reverence for nature and fertility.

Since Jews have never established a settlement in Japan, they have not had an influence on the country's food heritage. Nevertheless, some of the culinary customs of the two groups are alike, making it relatively easy to adapt Japanese cuisine to the laws of kashrut. For instance, very few dairy products make their way into the Japanese kitchen, and fish and meat are rarely used in the same recipe. In dishes that call for shellfish, it's usually fine to substitute any firm fin fish. In addition, most Japanese dishes are made with pure, fresh ingredients that are minimally processed. The foods that *are* processed (soy sauce, miso, and the like) are done so in factories that manufacture only that product. Nevertheless, here in the United States, kosher oriental-style products are widely available and should be the only ones used.

In my catering business and cooking school, I have not found it difficult to prepare sushi and other Japanese delicacies according to the dietary laws. By starting with the basics—crisp sheets of nori (toasted seaweed), vinegared rice, and strips of fish and/or vegetables—I have been able to create countless kosher variations on the sushi theme. My Jewish clients and students are always very pleased and surprised with the beautiful, tasty, and somewhat out-of-the-ordinary results.

Along with my chief assistant, Ursula Forem, I have developed detailed instructions for making sushi and other Japanese dishes. A sampling of those we taught at the 92nd Street Y follows, along with foolproof plans for duplicating them at home. When preparing Japanese cuisine, an eye to the visual is as important as a good palate, so we also demonstrate the art of presentation.

It does take years of practice and apprenticeship to become a master sushi chef, but it's still possible to learn quickly the knack for making the less complicated types of sushi, such as hand rolls, nigiri (fish-topped oblongs of vinegared rice), and even maki (rolled sushi). Although the results might not measure up to a sushi master's in appearance, they will resemble and taste like the national finger food of Japan.

—*Hidehiko Takada*

Hidehiko Takada and Ursula Forem

Hidehiko Takada has been wielding his sushi knife for more than thirty years now. Born and raised in Tokyo, the young Takada first learned his craft as an apprentice to a master sushi chef. After the five-year apprenticeship, he and his knife traveled all over Japan making sushi. Then in 1971, with many years of experience under his belt, Takada made the move to New York. His timing was perfect—this was the period when sushi was just beginning to catch on with Americans. With the sushi trend appearing to grow, Takada decided to open his own cooking school on East 23rd Street. He now includes classes in such Japanese specialties as tempura, noodle dishes, and dumplings, along with sushi. Currently, there's a waiting list for several of the sessions.

Through the cooking school and his work in several Manhattan restaurants, Takada started to build up a catering business on the side. One of his Jewish clients requested a selection of kosher sushi for a party, and Takada created a gorgeous spread. Since the fish came from a kosher fish store in Brooklyn and the nori, wasabi, and other ingredients were approved by the rabbi, it wasn't long before other kosher hosts and hostesses were ordering sushi for their events. These days, Chef Takada is hired by many kosher catering firms and synagogues in the New York metropolitan area to offer a change of pace from the usual knishes and pigs-in-the-blanket! His unique blend of skill, speed, and theatrics makes him one of the most entertaining caterers around.

Ursula Forem, Chef Takada's senior apprentice, has been studying with him for seven years. It is very unusual for an American, particularly a woman, to serve as apprentice to a sushi master, but it was this exclusivity that appealed to Ursula. And she proved she was able to meet the challenge by putting in countless hours learning the art of making sushi. The first year, for example, she spent four or five nights a week at the cooking school, practicing three to four hours at a stretch. Then she would go home and practice some more. "Everything that looked simple turned out to be difficult," said Ursula. "And just as I was beginning to get better, I would get worse."

Although she admits she still has a bit to learn, Ursula adeptly fashions maki and nigiri in no time flat. She also patiently assists the "all thumbs" sushi makers in her classes, both at Takada's Japanese Cooking School and the 92nd Street Y. In addition, she arranges most of Takada's catering engagements, has coauthored a chapter in a cookbook with him, and has appeared on TV and radio shows to promote Japanese cooking.

ALL ABOUT SUSHI

In Japanese, *su* means vinegar and *shi* is a word for rice. When you put the two together, they add up to *sushi* or vinegared rice—the starting point for all sushi. Once you master the preparation of vinegared rice, you can turn out an almost endless variety of sushi.

Basic Sushi Ingredients

Rice: Short-grain rice is the kind used for sushi. We recommend using the Nishiki or Kokuho Rose brands, sold in oriental and Korean groceries.

Rice Vinegar: Oriental rice vinegar is mixed with the hot cooked rice to give it the authentic sushi taste. The mixture (which also contains sugar and salt) then cools for 15 minutes.

Nori: Roasted or toasted seaweed is rolled around vinegared rice to create maki or sushi rolls. Sheets of nori come in sealed packages; the best quality is dark green in color.

Wasabi: A potent form of powdered green horseradish, wasabi is mixed with water to form a paste. This green paste gives sushi its characteristic fiery punch.

Pickled Ginger: Thin slices of ginger preserved in a pickling mixture always accompany sushi.

Fish: While not all sushi is prepared with raw fish, most Americans associate the dish with this ingredient. Before the start of any sushi lesson, we offer these guidelines for selecting fish:

- Buy only the freshest saltwater fish, choosing the kosher varieties with fins and scales. Freshwater fish or any fish that spawns in rivers or streams (such as salmon) should never be used *raw* for sushi. Smoked or cooked salmon, however, can be used with excellent results.
- If possible, choose whole fish—it's easier to judge freshness that way. The eyes of fresh fish should be clear, not cloudy; the flesh should spring back without making an identation when touched; the gills should be dark red, not pink; and the fish should have a pleasant ocean odor, not a fishy smell.
- Have the fish cut into fillets for ease in slicing into sushi-sized portions.
- Fresh fillets should be kept refrigerated no longer than two days before using.

Basic Sushi Equipment

- Knife: We cannot stress enough the importance of having a top-quality, sharp chef's knife before tackling sushi-making. I so value this tool that my own knife has never left my side since apprenticeship days. An 8- to 10-inch heavy stainless-steel knife with a smooth, sharp edge is the best choice.
- Sudare (bamboo mat): This rectangular mat is used for rolling the nori and vinegared rice into various forms of maki. Bamboo mats are not needed if you plan to stick to hand rolls or nigiri sushi.
- White cotton towel: Sushi rice is sticky stuff—a lot like instant glue! A dampened towel comes in handy for wiping hands and knife.
- Small bowl of water: Some extra water placed nearby is useful for dipping the knife before cutting sushi and moistening the fingers to form the rice.

With your ingredients and equipment in hand, you're now ready to start making sushi. The first step is to prepare the vinegared rice. We suggest preparing the mixture in a large quantity, tightly covering any extra and storing it in the refrigerator. The vinegared rice itself should be started about $1\frac{1}{2}$ hours before serving the sushi.

Vinegared Rice
Fish on Vinegared Rice—*Nigiri Sushi*
Basic Maki—*Rolled Sushi*
Big Roll
Hand-rolled Cone—*Temaki*
Bean Soup—*Miso*
Spinach with Sesame Dressing
Stir-fried Noodles and Vegetables—*Yaki Soba*
Broiled Skewered Chicken—*Chicken Yaki Tori*

VINEGARED RICE

MAKES 10 CUPS
ENOUGH FOR 6 SERVINGS

Rice for sushi is a little trickier to cook than ordinary rice. In fact, Japanese women usually use electric rice cookers or steamers to assure perfect results. However, if you follow these instructions exactly, you should manage well.

5 cups short-grain rice
$\frac{1}{2}$ cup rice vinegar
$\frac{1}{4}$ cup sugar
2 tablespoons salt

1. Measure rice into large heavy saucepan. Rinse rice several times with cold water until water runs clear. Drain off water and add 5 cups cold water.

2. Cover pot tightly and place over high heat; cook until rice starts to steam, about 3 minutes. Reduce heat to medium and cook 5 to 7 minutes. Reduce heat to low and cook 17 to 20 minutes longer.

3. Remove from heat and allow rice to rest, covered, for 15 minutes. *Do not uncover the pot at any time during cooking or resting.*

4. Meanwhile, prepare the vinegar mixture. In medium saucepan over medium heat, combine rice vinegar, sugar, and salt. Cook until sugar and salt dissolve, stirring constantly; do not boil. Cool to room temperature.

5. After rice has rested, stir in cooled vinegar mixture until completely absorbed. Cover rice with wet cloth and let cool about 15 minutes.

N O T E : Rice mixture should be slightly warm to provide a temperature contrast when combined with cold fish or vegetables for sushi.

SUGGESTED FISH AND VEGETABLES

To make enough sushi for about 6 servings, we suggest purchasing 1½ to 2 pounds of fish. This can then be sliced and formed into nigiri (fish on rice) and/or maki (sushi rolls made with nori). Choose from this list of fish:

Fresh raw tuna (bluefin or
  yellowtail)
Fresh raw red snapper
Fresh raw sea bass
Fresh raw fluke (flounder)

Smoked salmon
Smoked whitefish
Smoked herring
Sardines

If you prefer not to use raw or smoked fish, you can use any *broiled* kosher fish you desire; the texture will be different, but the presentation can be just as effective. We sometimes use tofu, cooked omelet, or smoked turkey for nigiri as well.

When preparing maki, you can also combine the fish with ¼- to ⅓-inch-wide strips of raw or steamed vegetables, or use vegetables alone. We have experimented with these types, but let your imagination soar!

Red, green, or yellow bell
  pepper
Cucumber
Carrots
Avocado

Watercress
Steamed asparagus
Zucchini
Spinach leaves
Scallions

Fish on Vinegared Rice

Nigiri Sushi

MAKES 6 SERVINGS

$1\frac{1}{2}$ to 2 pounds fish (see page 35)
  Vinegared Rice (see page 34)
  Prepared Wasabi (method below)
  Pickled ginger
  Soy sauce

1. With sharp knife, slice fish diagonally across the grain into pieces $2\frac{1}{2}$ to 3 inches long by $1\frac{1}{2}$ inches wide by $\frac{1}{4}$ inch thick (fig. A). On clean work surface, assemble fish slices and remaining ingredients and equipment (see illustration).
2. Wet hands. Scoop up a small handful of rice mixture and form it into a portion the size of a Ping-Pong ball (fig. B). Place on work surface.
3. Spread a dab of wasabi on a fish slice. Place fish, wasabi side down, on rice ball (fig. C). With fingers, push rice into an oblong or cylinder shape to meet ends of fish (fig. D).
4. Cupping the oblong in one hand, squeeze sides firmly while pressing fish into rice with fingers. Turn clockwise and repeat squeezing and pressing (fig. E).
5. Repeat Steps 2 through 4 until all fish slices are used. To serve, arrange on plate or lacquer tray. Accompany with additional wasabi, slices of pickled ginger, and soy sauce for dipping.

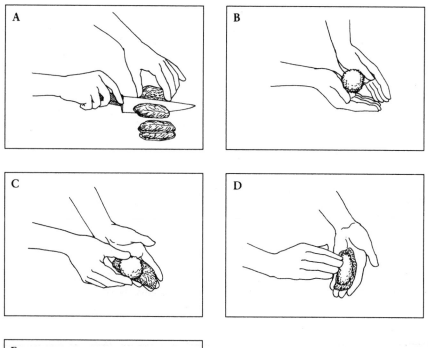

NIGIRI SUSHI

PREPARED WASABI

In cup, combine equal amounts of wasabi powder and cold water; mix to form a smooth paste. Start with 1 tablespoon each of wasabi and water, preparing more as needed. Let stand, covered, 10 to 15 minutes before using.

Rolled Sushi

Basic Maki

MAKES 6 SERVINGS

$1\frac{1}{2}$ to 2 pounds fish and/or vegetables (see page 35)
6 to 8 sheets packaged toasted nori (seaweed)
       Vinegared Rice (see page 34)
       Prepared Wasabi (see page 37)
       Pickled ginger
       Soy sauce

1. Cut fish or vegetables into strips $\frac{1}{4}$ to $\frac{1}{3}$ inch wide.
2. Divide each sheet of nori in half by folding down the center and breaking at crease. Place 1 piece of nori on bamboo mat, shiny side down.
3. Wet hands. Scoop out a handful of vinegared rice and form into a portion the size of a matzoh ball (fig. A). Wet hands again and press rice down on nori in an even layer all the way to three edges, but leaving a $\frac{1}{2}$-inch border or margin along the top (fig. B). (Use a few extra drops of water, if necessary, to spread evenly.)
4. With fingers, apply a streak of wasabi horizontally across center of rice. Place strips of fish and/or vegetables on top, laying pieces end to end to form a single row (fig. C).
5. Slowly roll up mat and nori jelly roll style, using mat and fingers to apply pressure as you roll (figs. D, E). When completely rolled, squeeze mat and maki together to seal edge and compress. Unroll mat. Repeat with remaining nori sheets and filling ingredients.
6. To cut maki, dip sharp knife in water. Cut roll in half down center. Slice each half roll into thirds to make 6 pieces in all (fig. F).
7. To serve, arrange on plate or tray with additional wasabi, slices of pickled ginger, and soy sauce for dipping.

NOTE: You may combine fish and vegetables in one roll, but it's best not to use more than 2 ingredients for each half piece of nori.

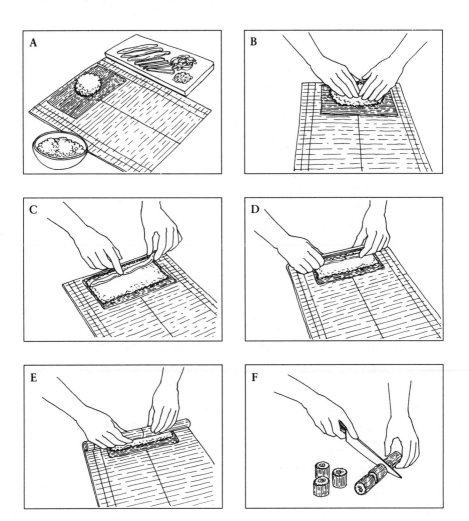

M A K I   S U S H I

Big Roll

MAKES 6 SERVINGS

For this jumbo maki, we use a whole sheet of nori and stuff it with up to 6 different ingredients. When sliced, each individual piece looks like a sparkling mosaic.

6 sheets packaged toasted nori (seaweed)
Vinegared Rice (see page 34)
Prepared Wasabi (see page 37)
Spinach leaves, well washed and patted dry
$\frac{3}{4}$ to 1 pound smoked salmon or raw tuna, cut into strips
1 cucumber, peeled and cut lengthwise into strips
1 red or yellow bell pepper, cut lengthwise into strips
1 small avocado, peeled and cut lengthwise into strips
Pickled ginger
Soy sauce

1. Place a sheet of nori on bamboo mat, shiny side down.
2. Wet hands. Scoop out a handful of rice and form into a portion the size of a softball. Wet hands again and press rice down in an even layer on nori, going to three edges but leaving a $\frac{1}{2}$-inch border along the top.
3. With fingers, apply a streak of wasabi horizontally across center of rice. Layer spinach leaves, fish, cucumber, bell pepper, avocado, and ginger on top of wasabi.
4. Slowly roll up mat and seaweed, jelly roll style, using fingers to apply pressure at right angles. (Roll is actually more a square shape than a cylinder.) When completely rolled, squeeze together mat and maki to seal edges and compress. Unroll mat (figs. A-D). Repeat with remaining sheets of nori and filling ingredients.
5. To cut, dip knife in water. Cut roll in half down center. Cut each half roll into thirds, holding knife at 45° angle (fig. E).
6. To serve, arrange on plate or lacquer tray with additional wasabi, pickled ginger, and soy sauce for dipping.

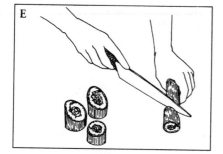

BIG ROLL SUSHI

Hand-rolled Cone

Temaki

MAKES 6 SERVINGS

A little less tricky than maki, the hand roll is made without a mat, free-form style. The popular California roll, made with avocado and crabmeat, is one version of this type of sushi. Another is our kosher smoked salmon hand roll, already a winner among those who have sampled it.

$\frac{1}{2}$ pound smoked salmon, diced
$\frac{1}{2}$ cup chopped scallions
6 sheets packaged toasted nori (seaweed)
   Vinegared Rice (see page 34)
   Prepared Wasabi (see page 37)

1. In small bowl, combine salmon and scallions.
2. Divide each sheet of nori in half by folding down the center and breaking at crease.
3. Wet hands. Scoop up a small handful of rice mixture and form into a portion the size of a squash ball.
4. Place nori, shiny side down, on one hand. Starting from the short side of nori, with wet fingers of opposite hand, spread rice over bottom quarter of seaweed (fig. A). Spread wasabi on top of rice.
5. Starting from rice-covered end, roll up nori into a cone shape (figs. B-D). Close seam with a few grains of sticky rice and a few drops of water. Repeat with remaining nori and filling.
6. Fill cones with equal portions of salmon mixture (fig. E).

VARIATION: For sushi cups, cut each sheet of nori into quarters to form 4 strips. Scoop out a portion of vinegared rice the size of a Ping-Pong ball and place on work surface. Wrap a strip of nori around rice, closing seam with a few grains of sticky rice and drops of water. Spread wasabi on rice mound and top with salmon mixture.

Wine note: Problems abound in matching wine to sushi, not so much because of the various fish but because of the strong-tasting ginger and wine-destroying vinegar involved. Perhaps such white wines as Sauvignon Blanc, Soave, Pinot Grigio, or Pinot Blanc could be tested for the individual palate's response. Japanese or Californian saki might be better choices. They certainly are more in keeping with the theme of the cuisine and, as each saki tastes different, it is a new category of drink to have fun investigating.

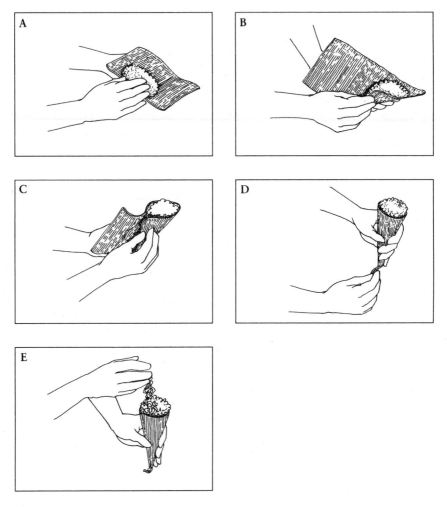

HAND ROLLED CONE

Bean Soup

Miso

This soup is often served before sushi. Both miso and tofu are available in oriental markets and many large supermarkets.

    5 cups water
$\frac{1}{3}$ to $\frac{1}{2}$ cup miso (soybean paste)
    1 cake tofu, cut into cubes
    2 scallions, thinly sliced

1. In large saucepan, bring water to a boil over high heat. Using a soup ladle, scoop up some boiling water and pour into small bowl. Add about $\frac{1}{3}$ cup miso, stirring to soften. Gradually stir back into pot of water. Taste soup and adjust flavor if necessary. For stronger flavor, add more miso; if too salty, add more boiling water.
2. Reduce heat to low; simmer, uncovered, 5 minutes. Add tofu and cook about 5 minutes longer, until heated through.
3. To serve, pour into bowls and sprinkle with scallions.

Spinach with Sesame Dressing

We serve this as a side dish with sushi or any hot Japanese dish. It's a popular item in Japanese restaurants as well.

$\frac{1}{2}$ cup toasted sesame seeds
$\frac{1}{2}$ cup sugar
$\frac{1}{2}$ cup water
$\frac{1}{4}$ cup soy sauce
1 pound fresh spinach, well washed

1. With rolling pin, mortar and pestle, or food processor, completely crush half the sesame seeds. Add remaining sesame seeds and partially crush. Transfer to small bowl. Stir in sugar, water, and soy sauce; blend well. Set dressing aside.

2. In large saucepan over high heat, combine spinach and enough water to cover; bring to a boil. Cook 3 to 4 minutes, or until just wilted.

3. Rinse spinach under cold running water until cool. Squeeze gently to remove excess water.

4. To serve, arrange spinach in a bowl and pour sesame dressing on top.

Stir-fried Noodles and Vegetables
Yaki Soba

MAKES 4 TO 6 SERVINGS

12 to 16 ounces Japanese-style noodles or thin spaghetti
    $\frac{1}{4}$ head napa cabbage
    1 large onion, peeled
    1 large red or green bell pepper
    2 medium carrots, peeled
    2 scallions
1 to $1\frac{1}{2}$ cups bottled steak sauce
    $\frac{1}{2}$ cup soy sauce
    $\frac{1}{2}$ cup honey
    $\frac{1}{4}$ cup vegetable oil
    2 tablespoons toasted sesame seeds

1. Cook noodles according to package directions, cutting cooking time in half so that noodles are substantially undercooked. Rinse noodles under cold running water to cool; drain well.

2. Chop cabbage, onion, and pepper into medium-sized pieces. Diag-

onally slice carrots into $\frac{1}{8}$-inch-thick slices. Cut scallions into $1\frac{1}{2}$-inch-long pieces.

3. In small bowl, combine steak sauce, soy sauce, and honey for sauce; mix well.

4. In wok or large skillet, heat oil over medium-high heat. Add carrots; stir-fry 1 minute. Add cabbage, onion, and bell pepper; stir-fry 2 minutes longer or until tender-crisp. Add noodles and scallions; stir-fry 4 to 5 minutes longer until noodles are well heated. Stir in sauce and cook 1 to 2 minutes longer, until heated through.

5. To serve, arrange on plates and sprinkle with sesame seeds.

NOTE: Lea & Perrins steak sauce is marked with a Ⓤ symbol.

Wine note: This is a red wine dish, despite the honey. The wine should be quite cool, though not as cold as soda pop. It should have hints of pepper and spice. That brings us to the Rhône and its adjacent areas. Some suggestions: Gigondas, Côtes du Rhône, and Minervois. Italy also has a couple of possibilities: Barbera and Valpolicella.

Broiled Skewered Chicken

Chicken Yaki Tori

MAKES 4 SERVINGS

Small chunks of chicken, meat, or fish are typically marinated and broiled by Japanese cooks, then served with hot cooked rice. If weather permits, cook the skewered chicken outdoors on a barbecue grill.

    4 boneless, skinless chicken breast halves
    $\frac{1}{2}$ cup orange juice
    1 bunch scallions, cut into $1\frac{1}{2}$-inch pieces

$\frac{1}{2}$ cup bottled steak sauce
$\frac{1}{4}$ cup soy sauce
$\frac{1}{4}$ cup honey

1. Trim chicken breasts if necessary, and cut into bite-sized pieces. In medium bowl, marinate chicken in orange juice 10 to 15 minutes; drain.
2. Alternately thread chicken pieces and scallions on bamboo or metal skewers.
3. In small saucepan, combine steak sauce, soy sauce, and honey. Over high heat, bring to a boil. Remove from heat.
4. Preheat broiler. Place skewers in a single layer on a foil-covered broiler pan or heatproof tray. Broil about 4 to 5 minutes on each side. Brush with warm sauce and broil 2 minutes longer on each side, or until chicken is thoroughly cooked. To serve, brush with additional sauce.

NOTE: If using bamboo skewers, they should be soaked in a bowl of cold water for at least 30 minutes before using to prevent burning.

Wine note: Just think of that juicy chicken sputtering on the grill and cooking up into a really sauce-rich dish. What a great recipe for a cold Riesling! If it comes from New York or California, it will have just a hint of sweetness to complement the richness of the chicken. A dry Riesling, with a cutting edge of acid, adds to the glass an elegance that would do almost any chicken proud.

Indian

I ndia is a land of sharp geographical and religious contrasts, and its cuisine is a reflection of these. In the north and central regions where the Mogul and Muslim influence is prevalent, the cooking centers on beef and lamb dishes. Wheat is the staple crop in this part of the country, so breads play a big role in the diet, too. The south of India is home to most of the nation's Hindus—a religion that forbids the eating of beef. The climate here is conducive to growing rice and a large variety of vegetables, making for a diverse and tasty vegetarian diet.

Although the strictly vegetarian Hindus now dominate the Indian population, there have been and still are some smaller religious enclaves scattered throughout the country, each practicing their own culinary traditions. These include the Catholics of Goa, the Syrian Christians of Kerala, and the Jews of the west coast. Today, the Jewish population in India is sparse, most of the Jews having dispersed to other parts of the world. But when I was growing up in pre–World War II Calcutta, we were part of a thriving Jewish community, carrying on the religious, social, and food customs that had been handed down through my family for generations.

Syrian Jews established this community when they came to India around 1757. About a hundred years later, Jews from Iraq joined the Syrian settlers. Most came as traders and merchants, and were able to act as liaisons between the British rulers and their Indian subjects. The families soon grew prosperous, acquired property and servants, and formed a large, well-organized, and lively Jewish neighborhood. Jews in Calcutta had their own hospital, school, burial board, and a number of synagogues. Since India has been respectful of different religions through the ages, the Jews were well accepted.

Coming from the Middle East, our Indian-Jewish families tended to cook in the Sephardic style of Turkey, Syria, Persia (Iran), and their neighbors. However, it wasn't long before the traditional dishes were spiced up with some of the more than a hundred Indian flavoring ingredients—chiles, ginger, turmeric, fennel, mustard seed, coriander, tamarind, cardamom, and lime among them. For example, a Mideastern-style fish and rice ball would be enlivened with green chiles and onion to give it an Indian accent.

Spices aside, Jewish cooks were able to expand and enhance their menus with other local food products as well. Fish were plentiful in the Arabian Sea and Indian Ocean, with a wide choice available from the kosher varieties. Fish was always purchased whole, then cut up in front of the shopper to guarantee it would conform to the dietary laws. Although their typical diet didn't include much meat, the Jews did occasionally take advantage of the domestically raised chickens, sheep, and goats. These could be easily kashered by the rabbi who always sat at the bustling market where live poultry and animals were sold.

The marketplace also overflowed with brightly hued and sometimes exotic fresh fruits, vegetables, and other cultivated crops. There were tropical papayas, bananas, mangoes, and coconuts; an assortment of nuts, including peanuts, cashews, and almonds; dried beans, peas, and lentils in every shape and color; and different types of gourds and squashes, to name just a handful. These would go into carefully spiced curries, pulaos, dals, chutneys, and other specialties that make Indian cuisine so distinctive. Of course, many of the market stalls were jammed with sacks of rice, India's most important agricultural product. The country produces countless varieties of rice, basmati being the type most frequently used in the recipes here.

Since the majority of the population were and still are Hindu, many Indian dishes are based on vegetables, rice, and lentils. The Indian Muslims, while not vegetarians, ban pork from their diets. This makes it relatively easy to adhere to the dietary laws when cooking Indian food. Another plus is that coconut milk—a nondairy ingredient—is often combined with chicken or lamb to make a curry dish, and is also used extensively for desserts. Occasionally, yogurt or ghee (clarified butter) is called for in meat-based Indian recipes, but it's not hard to work around this problem. I've experimented and found that coconut milk, soy milk, or tofu puréed with lemon juice makes a good substitute for the yogurt specified in the marinade for tandoori chicken or lamb. And vegetable oil or shortening make fine stand-ins when ghee is listed as a recipe ingredient.

To adapt my favorite dishes to Jewish-American tables, I've discovered a variety of produce that can be used instead of the unavailable Indian types. For instance, zucchini is closest to the ridged gourd used in India; regular orange carrots resemble the traditional red and brown carrots; and spinach, Swiss chard, or other leafy greens can substitute for the assortment of "green leaves" Indians use in their native land. Many of the tropical fruits that go into chutneys are stocked in Hispanic or oriental produce markets here. These include fresh lichees, mangoes, custard apples, and papayas.

Some American cooks may also want to tone down the spiciness of Indian fare. But I feel that most recipes have an undeserved reputation for being fiery. Usually only one dish in a menu will be very hot "to wake up the appetite"; others will be more subtly seasoned to balance the meal. It pays to experiment, increasing or decreasing the chiles to suit your palate.

The menus that follow represent three different Indian cooking styles. The Indian snacks are a national passion, eaten anywhere and everywhere people meet, from the stately drawing rooms of the upper class to street corners where vendors sell these savory deep-fried morsels from pushcarts. An assortment of chutneys (Indian relishes) makes the perfect accompaniment. The Burmese lunch includes un-no kauk swe, probably the most famous dish of Burma, a small seaside country between the Indian subcontinent and China. Un-no kauk swe was adapted by the Indian Jews, who substituted chicken for pork. The last menu is a complete Indian meal, highlighting the best and most typical dishes of the country.

—*Flower Silliman*

Flower Silliman

F*lower Silliman was born in Calcutta, India, to an Iraqi-Jewish family. As third-generation Indian Jews, Flower and her siblings* grew up in a wealthy, well-established Jewish community of five to six thousand people. The British rulers and local Indian population were quite tolerant of different religious beliefs, and it wasn't difficult for her family and others to preserve their Sephardic traditions.

The household's Muslim servants did the shopping and cooking, and since their own diets prohibited pork, they could be trusted to choose those foods that would fit the kosher guidelines. As a little girl, Flower sometimes accompanied the servants on their daily trips to the market. It was here that she first became enthralled with the incredible variety of Indian spices, fruits and vegetables, rice, and lentils. This interest, coupled with her desire to help alleviate hunger in her homeland, led her to pursue a degree in home economics.

After majoring in dietetics, Flower taught nutrition and food preparation in India. But her culinary skills were not all learned in school—she picked up many from the family's servants to pass on to her students. In fact, when Flower was first married, the servants traveled from her mother's house to the Sillimans' apartment to teach the young bride the family's cooking secrets! She was a quick study, and started building her reputation as the renowned cooking teacher she is today.

When India became independent in 1947, the majority of the British left the country and most of the Jews followed soon thereafter. According to Flower, Indian Jews were very British in their life-style at that time, and they felt the political and economic climate would not be as favorable as it had been. Some settled in Israel and America; others went to Australia, Canada, and England where they felt comfortable living as British citizens. From a once thriving Jewish community, there are now fewer than a hundred Jews left in India.

Flower brought up her children in Calcutta, but then the Silliman family relocated to other countries. Some went to Israel, and Flower followed, eventually opening an Indian restaurant in Jerusalem. After running the acclaimed eatery for several years, she came to the United States. Currently, Flower Silliman teaches cooking and consults on Indian food, shuttling back and forth between New York and Israel.

Vegetable Fritters—*Pakoras*
Potato Balls—*Bondas*
Meat Turnovers—*Samosas*
Lentil Cakes—*Vadas*
Vegetable Balls—*Vegetable Koftas*

Vegetable Fritters

Pakoras

MAKES 6 TO 8 SERVINGS

These tasty snacks are deep-fried in a spiced batter made from besan or gram flour. Besan, ground from chickpeas or lentils, is a good, highly nutritious source of protein. This flour doesn't absorb oil the way white flour does, and no eggs are used in the batter. The result is a light, crisp fritter that, when served with the other tidbits and chutneys in this chapter, makes tempting party fare. For best results, prepare the batter just before using.

BATTER
$1\frac{1}{3}$ cups besan or gram flour (lentil flour)
1 tablespoon freshly squeezed lemon juice
2 teaspoons melted margarine or oil
2 teaspoons ground coriander
$1\frac{1}{2}$ teaspoons salt
1 teaspoon Garam Masala (see page 63)
$\frac{1}{2}$ teaspoon baking powder
$\frac{1}{2}$ teaspoon ground turmeric
$\frac{1}{2}$ teaspoon cayenne pepper
Water
Choice of vegetables (below)
Vegetable oil for frying

1. In large bowl, combine first 9 ingredients with enough water to form a thick batter.

2. Prepare vegetables as directed below, and dip into batter, allowing excess to drip off.

3. In large saucepan or deep skillet, heat 2 inches oil over high heat until very hot. Add batter-coated vegetables, a few pieces at a time; fry until golden brown (cooking time varies from 3 to 10 minutes). If oil begins to spatter or smoke, reduce heat to medium.

4. Drain vegetables on paper towels. Serve hot.

Eggplant: Cut 1 medium unpeeled eggplant into wedges. Add 2 tablespoons khus-khus (white poppy seeds) to batter, if desired. Dip eggplant in batter, and fry 8 to 10 minutes, or until tender.

Potatoes: Cut 3 large peeled potatoes into thick slices. Dip in batter and fry 5 to 8 minutes, or until tender.

Green Peppers: Cut 2 seeded green bell peppers into wedges. Dip in batter, and fry 3 to 5 minutes, or until tender.

Cauliflower: Cut 1 small head cauliflower into florets. Dip in batter, and fry 5 to 10 minutes, or until tender.

Mushrooms: Dip ½ pound whole mushrooms into batter. Fry 3 to 5 minutes or until tender.

Onions: Cut 2 large peeled onions into thin slices; sprinkle with salt and allow to drain. Instead of using batter, coat onion slices with besan mixed with 4 chopped scallions, 1 tablespoon chopped cilantro, and 1 minced green chile (optional). (You may coat several slices at a time to form a fritter or pancake.) Fry 3 to 5 minutes until tender.

Potato Balls

Bondas

MAKES 15 PIECES

Bondas are eaten as either a brunch dish in South India or a snack in other parts of the country. These are the only deep-fried tidbits that I have successfully prepared ahead of time—they can then be reheated in the microwave just before serving.

2 tablespoons vegetable oil, plus additional for frying
1 medium onion, peeled and diced
1 teaspoon grated peeled fresh gingerroot
6 whole green curry leaves (optional, see Note)
3 large potatoes, parboiled, peeled, and broken into large chunks
$\frac{1}{2}$ cup frozen peas, thawed
2 tablespoons chopped toasted almonds or peanuts
3 tablespoons chopped cilantro
1 tablespoon freshly squeezed lemon juice
3 to 4 hot green chile peppers (optional)
  Salt, freshly ground black pepper, and cayenne pepper to taste
  Pakora Batter (see page 53)

1. In large skillet, heat 2 tablespoons oil over medium heat. Add onion; sauté 5 to 10 minutes until pale yellow and translucent, stirring often. Stir in gingerroot and curry leaves.
2. Remove from heat and stir in remaining ingredients except batter and oil for frying; mix well. Shape mixture into balls about 1 inch in diameter.
3. Prepare batter. Dip potato balls into batter, allowing excess to drip off.
4. Meanwhile, in large deep saucepan or large skillet over high heat, heat 2 inches oil until hot. Reduce heat to medium. Add potato balls, a few at a time; cook 5 minutes, or until golden brown. Drain on paper towels; serve hot.

NOTE: Curry leaves are an Indian herb in the basil family. You can buy them fresh at Indian groceries and store them for 2 weeks in the refrigerator, tightly closed in a glass jar. Use as needed, rinsing them just before using.

Meat Turnovers

Samosas

MAKES 6 TO 8 SERVINGS

Turmeric is one of the spices almost always used in Indian meat, poultry, or vegetable curries, as well as in fillings for turnovers like these. It imparts a characteristic yellow color to food, and in its root form was used extensively in India as a disinfectant.

    2 tablespoons vegetable oil
    1 medium onion, peeled and finely chopped
2 to 3 cloves garlic, peeled and minced
    1 teaspoon grated peeled fresh gingerroot
    1 teaspoon ground cumin
    $\frac{1}{2}$ teaspoon ground turmeric
    $\frac{1}{2}$ teaspoon ground cloves
    $\frac{1}{2}$ teaspoon ground cinnamon
    $\frac{1}{2}$ teaspoon ground cardamom
    Salt to taste
    1 cup ground beef
    $\frac{1}{4}$ cup chopped fresh mint leaves
    $\frac{1}{4}$ teaspoon crushed red pepper (cayenne) (optional)
    $\frac{1}{2}$ pound fresh or thawed frozen phyllo dough
    or strudel leaves
    Melted margarine

1. In medium skillet, heat oil over medium heat. Add onion and sauté 5 minutes, or until golden, stirring often. Add garlic, gingerroot, all ground spices, and salt to taste. Cook 5 minutes, stirring often.
2. Stir in ground beef; cook, stirring often, until meat loses its red color. Reduce heat to low; cover and simmer 10 to 15 minutes, until meat is tender. (Add a little water if mixture becomes too dry.) Stir in mint and cayenne, if desired; remove from heat.
3. Preheat oven to 400°F. Stack phyllo dough on oiled work surface. With sharp knife, cut lengthwise into strips $2\frac{1}{2}$ inches wide. Work with 1 or 2 strips at a time, keeping remaining phyllo covered with

towel. Spoon a small amount of beef filling on one end of phyllo strip. Fold phyllo over filling, then fold up diagonally three to four times to form a small triangle. Repeat with remaining phyllo and filling. (See illustrations.)

4. Place triangles on cookie sheet and brush with melted margarine. Bake 5 minutes. Reduce oven temperature to 375°F and bake 10 to 15 minutes longer, or until samosas are crisp and golden brown. Serve hot.

N O T E : You may also deep-fry samosas in hot oil for 5 to 10 minutes, until crisp and browned.

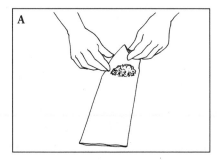

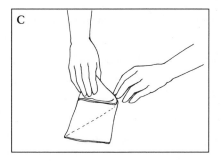

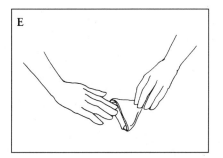

S A M O S A S

Lentil Cakes

Vadas

This savory deep-fried snack is made with lentils—collectively known as dal in India. Lentils come in a varied palette of colors, which can usually be interchanged in recipes.

- $\frac{2}{3}$ cup white lentils (urad dal) or red lentils
- 1 teaspoon freshly ground black pepper
- $\frac{1}{2}$ teaspoon cayenne pepper
- $\frac{1}{2}$ teaspoon ground cumin
- $\frac{1}{2}$ teaspoon salt
- $\frac{1}{2}$-inch piece peeled fresh gingerroot
  Vegetable oil for frying

1. Wash lentils several times in cold water. In medium bowl, combine lentils and enough water to cover. Let soak 4 to 6 hours or overnight.
2. In food processor or blender, purée lentils with remaining ingredients except oil.
3. In large saucepan or deep skillet over high heat, heat about 2 inches oil until hot. Drop lentil mixture by teaspoonfuls into hot oil. Fry until golden and crisp, about 5 to 8 minutes, turning once. (If oil begins to spatter, reduce heat to medium.)
4. Drain on paper towels. Repeat with remaining lentil mixture. Serve hot.

Vegetable Balls

Vegetable Koftas

MAKES 6 TO 8 SERVINGS

Koftas are an excellent way to use up odds and ends of fresh vegetables that may be collecting in your refrigerator.

$1\frac{1}{2}$ cups shredded raw vegetables, squeezed dry
(carrots, green beans, zucchini, and/or cabbage),
measured after squeezing out moisture
1 tablespoon ground coriander
$\frac{1}{2}$ tablespoon ground ginger
$\frac{1}{2}$ tablespoon ground cumin
1 clove garlic, peeled and minced
1 teaspoon dill weed (optional)
Salt and freshly ground black pepper to taste
$\frac{1}{2}$ to 1 cup besan or gram flour (lentil flour)
Vegetable oil for frying

1. In medium bowl, combine shredded vegetables, coriander, ginger, cumin, garlic, dill weed, if desired, and salt and pepper to taste; mix well.
2. Add enough flour to hold mixture together. With hands, shape mixture into 1-inch balls.
3. In large saucepan or deep skillet over high heat, heat 2 inches oil until hot. Add vegetable balls, a few at a time. Fry about 5 minutes, or until golden. (Reduce heat to medium if oil starts to spatter.)
4. Drain koftas on paper towels. Repeat until all are fried. Serve hot.

Chutneys are always available on the table at an Indian meal. Some are sweet and sour, others are hot; some are based on fruit, others on vegetables. The three recipes I've developed would nicely complement any of the deep-fried Indian snacks in this book, or one or more chutneys may be served along with a traditional Indian dinner.

Fresh Coconut and Mint Chutney
Cooked Tomato Chutney
Mixed Fruit Chutney
Garam Masala

Fresh Coconut and Mint Chutney

MAKES $\frac{3}{4}$ CUP

This condiment resembles thick mayonnaise in consistency.

- 1 to 2 hot green chile peppers, chopped
- $\frac{1}{2}$-inch piece peeled fresh gingerroot
- 15 blanched cashew nuts or almonds
- $\frac{1}{2}$ cup fresh mint leaves or cilantro leaves, or a combination of both
- 2 tablespoons freshly squeezed lemon juice
- 1 tablespoon sugar, honey, or maple syrup
- 1 teaspoon salt
- 1 cup grated fresh coconut

1. In food processor or blender, with machine running, place chiles, ginger, and nuts in that order. Process until smooth.
2. Add mint or cilantro, $\frac{1}{3}$ cup water, lemon juice, and sugar or other sweetener; process until well mixed.
3. Turn off machine and add coconut. Continue processing until creamy and smooth.

Cooked Tomato Chutney

MAKES 1½ CUPS

2 tablespoons vegetable oil
1 to 2 dried whole red chiles
1 teaspoon cumin seed
One 1-inch cinnamon stick
One 1-inch piece peeled fresh gingerroot
2 cups coarsely chopped fresh ripe tomatoes or drained canned plum tomatoes
2 tablespoons sugar or molasses
½ teaspoon salt

1. In medium saucepan, heat oil over medium heat. Add chiles, cumin, cinnamon, and gingerroot; stir-fry 2 to 3 minutes.

2. Add tomatoes and remaining ingredients. Cook 15 minutes, or until most of moisture evaporates, stirring often.

3. Cool to room temperature. Serve at once, or cover and refrigerate. This will keep 2 to 3 days in the refrigerator.

Mixed Fruit Chutney

MAKES 2 CUPS

3 tablespoons vegetable oil
1 tablespoon grated peeled fresh gingerroot
2 hot green chile peppers
1 teaspoon cumin seed
1 large tart apple, peeled, cored, and thinly sliced
2 peaches, peeled, pitted, and diced
4 apricots, peeled, pitted, and diced
2 tablespoons raisins
1 cup packed brown sugar
$\frac{1}{3}$ cup orange juice
$\frac{1}{4}$ cup unsweetened shredded coconut
2 teaspoons Garam Masala (recipe follows)
$\frac{1}{2}$ teaspoon salt

1. In large saucepan, heat oil over medium heat. Add gingerroot, chiles, and cumin; stir-fry 3 to 5 minutes until cumin starts to brown.
2. Stir in remaining ingredients; reduce heat to low and simmer 40 minutes, or until thickened and glazed. Cool to room temperature. Serve at once, or cover and refrigerate. This will keep 1 week to 10 days in the refrigerator.

GARAM MASALA

Masala is that blend of spices and/or herbs that gives each Indian dish its distinct character. In India, each cook custom-grinds his or her own seasonings on a flat stone. Here, they can be purchased already ground, then combined before being added to a recipe. Garam masala is either stirred into the cooking pot or sprinkled over cooked food before eating.

1 tablespoon ground coriander
1 tablespoon ground cumin
1 teaspoon ground cardamom
1 teaspoon ground cinnamon
1 teaspoon ground nutmeg
$\frac{1}{2}$ teaspoon ground cloves

1. In small skillet, combine coriander and cumin over medium-high heat. Cook 5 minutes, tossing and stirring constantly, until roasted.
2. In small bowl, combine roasted spices with remaining ingredients. Store in tightly covered jar or container.

Spiced Fish Cakes—*Arook Taheem*
Chicken and Coconut Stew—*Un-no Kauk Swe*
Stuffed Crêpes—*Alle Belle*

Spiced Fish Cakes

Arook Taheem

MAKES 6 TO 8 SERVINGS

The Burmese traditionally prepare this recipe with shrimp instead of fish, and use a dried shrimp powder to bind it. I've adapted it for the kosher cook by substituting cod for the shrimp and flour for some of the shrimp powder. The finished cakes resemble green-veined latkes in appearance, the green coming from the combination of scallions, cilantro, and dill favored by the Burmese.

1½ cups all-purpose flour
1 teaspoon salt
1 teaspoon peeled minced garlic
1 teaspoon ground ginger or peeled grated gingerroot
½ teaspoon ground turmeric
½ teaspoon cayenne pepper (optional)
½ pound cod or other mild white fish, chopped (see Note)
½ cup chopped scallions
2 tablespoons chopped fresh cilantro or dill
¼ teaspoon chopped fresh green chile
1 egg
Vegetable oil for frying

1. In small bowl, combine flour, salt, garlic, ginger, turmeric, and cayenne pepper. In medium bowl, combine fish, scallions, cilantro or dill, chile, and egg; mix well. Add flour mixture; stir to blend. Stir in enough water to hold batter together.

2. Heat about $\frac{1}{4}$ inch of vegetable oil in large skillet over medium-high heat. Drop fish batter by tablespoonfuls into hot oil; flatten slightly (do not crowd the pan). Fry 2 to 3 minutes on each side, until golden. Drain on paper towels and keep warm.

3. Repeat frying with remaining batter. Serve hot.

N O T E : Fish should be chopped by hand into small pieces; do not use the food processor or blender, or a fish paste will result.

Chicken and Coconut Stew

Un-no Kauk Swe

MAKES 6 TO 8 SERVINGS

Traditionally a festive meal, this dish has become a typical family dinner on holidays. The group gathers around the table, in the center of which stands the main chicken dish surrounded by its many accompaniments and garnishes. Each diner fills up a large, wide soup bowl with the stew, then adds one or more accompaniments, combining ingredients to suit personal taste. Diners often vie with each other as to who has concocted the best meal.

Salt
$\frac{1}{2}$ teaspoon ground tumeric
One 4-pound chicken, cut up
3 to 4 medium onions, peeled and cut up
6 cloves garlic, peeled
One 1$\frac{1}{2}$-inch piece peeled fresh gingerroot
2 tablespoons ground cumin
2 tablespoons ground coriander
2 teaspoons chili powder, or to taste
6 tablespoons vegetable oil
6 whole cloves
3 cardamom pods
One 3-inch cinnamon stick
6 black peppercorns
About 2 cups chicken stock (from cooking chicken)
About $\frac{1}{2}$ cup besan or gram flour (lentil flour)
2 cups fresh or canned coconut milk (not coconut cream)

1. Rub salt to taste and turmeric over chicken. Place chicken and water to cover in dutch oven or saucepot. Bring to a boil over high heat. Reduce heat to low; cover and simmer 45 minutes to 1 hour, or until chicken is tender but still firm, not falling apart.
2. Remove chicken from pot and remove meat from bones. Return bones to stock in pot and continue simmering. Shred chicken into large pieces and set aside; discard skin.
3. In food processor or by hand, coarsely chop onions, garlic, and ginger. Stir in cumin, coriander, and chili powder.
4. In wok or large skillet, heat oil over medium-high heat. Add onion mixture and cook, stirring constantly, 3 minutes. Add cloves, cardamom, cinnamon stick, and peppercorns and stir-fry 7 to 10 minutes, adding some chicken stock if spices stick to pan.
5. Add shredded chicken to wok; stir-fry 3 to 5 minutes longer.
6. Strain stock from dutch oven. In medium bowl, blend besan or gram flour with 1$\frac{1}{2}$ cups hot stock; stir until smooth. Stir in coconut milk until well blended.

7. Stir coconut milk mixture into chicken mixture in wok; bring to a boil. Boil 1 minute. (The mixture should have the consistency of thick pea soup. If necessary, add more stock or flour to reach proper consistency.) Adjust seasoning and remove from heat. Serve with choice of accompaniments listed below.

SERVING ACCOMPANIMENTS

- $1\frac{1}{2}$ to 2 pounds fresh or dried egg noodles or rice noodles, cooked and drained
- 12 cloves garlic, peeled, sliced thin, and lightly fried in oil to resemble fried almonds
- 3 hard-cooked eggs, peeled and chopped
- 2 onions, peeled and thinly sliced
- 6 to 8 scallions, chopped fine
- 6 to 8 hot green chile peppers, chopped fine
- Bunch of cilantro, chopped fine
- 3 bananas, peeled, sliced, and marinated in lemon juice
- Paprika or chili powder
- Toasted besan or gram flour or sesame seeds
- 3 lemons, cut into wedges

Stuffed Crêpes

Alle Belle

MAKES 6 TO 8 SERVINGS

CRÊPES

    1 cup all-purpose flour
    $\frac{1}{8}$ teaspoon baking powder
    Pinch of salt
    2 eggs
1 to $1\frac{1}{4}$ cups water, milk, or canned coconut milk

FILLING

    2 tablespoons margarine
    $1\frac{1}{2}$ cups unsweetened flaked dried coconut, or grated fresh coconut
    $\frac{1}{2}$ teaspoon ground fennel seed
    $\frac{1}{4}$ teaspoon ground ginger
    $\frac{1}{2}$ cup chopped almonds or cashews
    $\frac{1}{2}$ cup sugar
    $\frac{1}{4}$ cup water
    2 tablespoons raisins or chopped dates
    1 tablespoon molasses

1. In medium bowl or container of blender, combine flour, baking powder, and salt for crêpes. Add eggs and water or milk; whisk or blend until well mixed. Cover and refrigerate until ready to use.
2. Lightly grease nonstick 6- or 8-inch skillet and place over medium heat. When hot, add about 2 tablespoons crêpe batter. Tilt pan until batter covers bottom completely. Cook about 1 minute, or until lightly browned on bottom.
3. With spatula, turn crêpe over and cook 30 seconds on other side. Remove to waxed paper. Repeat with remaining batter, stacking crêpes between sheets of waxed paper until ready to fill.
4. Prepare filling: In medium skillet, melt margarine over medium

heat. Add coconut and spices; stir-fry 1 minute. Add remaining filling ingredients; cook about 10 minutes, or until thickened. Let mixture stand until cooled.

5. To serve, fill each crêpe with 2 to 4 tablespoons filling; roll up jelly roll style to enclose filling. Serve warm, at room temperature, or refrigerate to serve cold.

A complete Indian meal is customarily served in a *thal*—a round tray that holds several individual cups. The thal is designed in accordance with Indian eating habits; it's not polite to mix up food on one plate, so each cup holds a different course (rice, dal, salad, main dish, vegetable, chutney, and so on). No forks are used—diners eat with one hand only, savoring each taste separately. However, the center of the thal is sometimes used to combine rice with one of the other dishes.

Lentils with Ginger and Spinach—*Mung Dal*
Pulao with Vegetables—*Subzi-Ki-Chaval*
Salad—*Kachumber*
Okra with Mustard—*Bhindi-Subzi*
Chicken and Bamboo Curry with Coconut
Puffy and Flat Indian Breads—*Parathas and Pooris*
Indian Pareve Dessert—*Suji Halwa*

Lentils with Ginger and Spinach

Mung Dal

MAKES 6 TO 8 SERVINGS

Mung dal consists of mung beans without their skins. If you cannot find this type of lentil, you may substitute another (see list of variations, following). I often cook lentils or beans with garlic or fennel to counteract their gassy nature.

$\frac{2}{3}$ cup mung dal or yellow lentils
$\frac{1}{2}$ tablespoon ground coriander
$1\frac{1}{2}$ teaspoons grated or minced peeled gingerroot
1 teaspoon ground turmeric
1 tablespoon margarine

$\frac{1}{2}$ pound fresh spinach or Swiss chard, washed and
  chopped, or one 10-ounce package frozen chopped
  spinach
$1\frac{1}{4}$ teaspoons salt, or less to taste
2 tablespoons vegetable oil
1 teaspoon cumin seeds
$\frac{1}{4}$ to $\frac{1}{2}$ teaspoon freshly ground black pepper or paprika
$\frac{1}{2}$ tablespoon freshly squeezed lemon juice

1. Wash lentils. Place in 3-quart nonstick saucepan and cover with 5 cups water. Let soak about 1 hour; do not drain.
2. To saucepan with lentils and water add coriander, gingerroot, turmeric, and margarine. Bring to a boil over medium-high heat. Reduce heat to low; cover and simmer gently 1 hour, or until lentils are soft but still whole.
3. Stir in spinach and salt; cover and cook 5 to 10 minutes longer, or until spinach is cooked and dal is thick. (Thickness of dal is a matter of personal preference.)
4. Meanwhile, heat oil in small skillet over medium heat. Add cumin seeds; stir-fry 3 to 5 minutes until browned. Add black pepper or paprika; stir-fry 1 minute longer. Stir sizzling spices into dal; heat through for 1 to 2 minutes. Stir in lemon juice. Serve dal hot.

VARIATION: No two Indian women cook dal the same way. It's fun to mix and match the lentils with different types of bagar (whole spices fried in oil). Instead of mung dal and cumin, try your own combination:

LENTILS	BAGAR	
red lentils	onions	whole cardamom
yellow split peas	garlic	pods
green split peas	onion seed	gingerroot
mung dal	mustard seed	green chiles
urad dal (white lentils)	caraway seed	red chiles
orange lentils	cumin seed	fennel seed
or any of the 35 or	cinnamon stick	
more lentil varieties	whole cloves	

Pulao with Vegetables

Subzi-Ki-Chaval

MAKES 6 SERVINGS

The secret to cooking perfect rice is to use 2 cups water or liquid to every cup of rice, then cook until the water is absorbed, never uncovering the pot. The sign of success is that you can literally "count every grain" in the finished product.

- 3 tablespoons vegetable oil
- 8 black peppercorns
- 8 whole cloves
- One 3-inch cinnamon stick
- 2 to 4 cardamom pods
- 2 cups basmati rice, soaked and drained (see Note)
- 2 teaspoons grated peeled fresh gingerroot
- 2 teaspoons salt
- 1 teaspoon ground turmeric
- $1\frac{1}{2}$ cups diced fresh mixed vegetables (corn, peas, beans, zucchini, carrots, broccoli, or the like), or one 10-ounce package frozen diced mixed vegetables, thawed
- One $14\frac{1}{2}$-ounce can stewed tomatoes
- Lemon wedges or twists (optional)

1. In large saucepan, heat oil over medium heat. Stir in peppercorns, cloves, cinnamon, and cardamom; stir-fry 2 minutes.
2. Add drained rice; stir-fry 2 to 3 minutes longer. Stir in gingerroot, salt, and turmeric; add vegetables, tossing to combine.
3. Into 4-cup measure, pour tomatoes and their liquid plus enough boiling water to measure 4 cups. Add to saucepan and increase heat to high; bring to a rapid boil.
4. Reduce heat to very low. Cover pan and cook 10 to 15 minutes, or until liquid is absorbed; *do not stir.* (Rice should look as if it has holes in it.)
5. Remove from heat. Allow rice to stand in saucepan 5 to 10 minutes, or until rice grains look separate and fluffy.

NOTES: To soak rice, cover with cold water and let stand 5 minutes. Mix with hands, drain, and add clean water; let soak again for 5 minutes. Drain and proceed with recipe.

If using fresh vegetables, add to oil with whole spices and stir-fry first.

Salad

Kachumber

MAKES 6 SERVINGS

Indians don't eat salad as we know it in America. Fresh greens are thought to be too bug-infested to eat without cooking. A marinated mixture such as this is served instead.

 3 medium tomatoes
 3 medium cucumbers
 2 tablespoons chopped fresh cilantro, dill, or mint
 1 hot green chile pepper (optional)
 1 bunch scallions, chopped
    Juice of 1 lemon
    Salt to taste

1. Cut tomatoes and cucumbers into small cubes. Drain excess liquid and seeds and discard.
2. In medium bowl, combine tomatoes, cucumbers, and remaining ingredients; toss until well mixed. Let stand at room temperature or refrigerate until ready to serve.

Okra with Mustard

Bhindi-Subzi

MAKES 6 SERVINGS

In India, okra is called "lady's fingers," and it's much smaller than the okra we grow in the United States. To make the dish more authentic, cut frozen okra pods in half.

Two 10-ounce packages frozen whole okra, thawed, rinsed, and drained
$\frac{1}{4}$ cup vegetable oil
2 teaspoons onion seed (see Note)
3 tablespoons Dijon mustard
$\frac{1}{2}$ teaspoon ground turmeric
$\frac{1}{2}$ teaspoon chili powder, or to taste
2 to 3 hot green chile peppers, sliced (optional)
Salt to taste
$\frac{1}{2}$ teaspoon sugar

1. Cut a slit in each okra pod with a sharp knife.
2. In medium skillet, heat oil over medium-high heat. Add onion seed; stir-fry until it stops sputtering. Add okra; stir-fry 3 to 4 minutes.
3. When okra pods turn olive in color, stir in mustard, turmeric, and chili powder; blend well. Reduce heat to low; add green chiles and salt to taste. Cover and simmer gently about 10 minutes, or until okra is cooked through and sauce is thickened. Stir in sugar; serve hot.

NOTE: Onion seed is a typical Eastern spice available at Indian and Middle Eastern groceries. In recipes that call for hot green chiles, Mexican-style jalapeño peppers work well and are widely available.

Chicken and Bamboo Curry with Coconut

MAKES 6 TO 8 SERVINGS

I included this mild curry in this menu because it contrasts well with the flavors in the other dishes.

$\frac{1}{4}$ cup vegetable oil

6 whole cloves

6 black peppercorns

4 cardamom pods

2 bay leaves

One 3-inch stick cinnamon

4 medium onions, peeled and finely chopped

4 cloves garlic, peeled and minced

One 2-inch piece peeled fresh gingerroot, chopped

One 3- to 4-pound chicken, skinned and cut into pieces

1 teaspoon ground turmeric

1 teaspoon chili powder or paprika

Two 8-ounce cans bamboo shoots, drained, rinsed, and cut into julienne strips

2 cups canned coconut milk

1 teaspoon salt

1 teaspoon sugar

1. In large deep skillet or dutch oven, heat oil over medium-high heat. Add cloves, peppercorns, cardamom pods, bay leaves, and cinnamon; sauté 2 to 3 minutes, stirring often.

2. Stir in onions, garlic, and gingerroot; sauté 5 minutes longer, stirring often. (If ingredients start to stick, add a little hot water and continue cooking.)

3. Add chicken pieces, turmeric, and chili powder or paprika. Cook chicken 2 to 3 minutes on all sides, until golden. Stir in bamboo shoots and coconut milk; add $\frac{1}{2}$ cup hot water, salt, and sugar. Reduce heat to low; cover and cook about 45 minutes, or until chicken is tender.

4. Uncover; increase heat to medium-high. Cook about 5 minutes longer, or until liquid in pot evaporates slightly and mixture thickens. Continue cooking if mixture is too watery; it will thicken as liquid evaporates. To serve, remove bay leaves.

Puffy and Flat Indian Breads

Parathas and Pooris

MAKES 6 TO 8 PIECES

The basic dough for both of these traditional Indian breads is the same, but the rolling out and cooking of the dough makes the end products very different.

BASIC DOUGH
1½ cups whole wheat flour
1½ cups all-purpose flour
⅔ cup warm water
2 tablespoons melted margarine or oil
¾ teaspoon salt

In medium bowl, combine all ingredients. Mix with a wooden spoon or hands until dough forms. (Dough should be firm, not sticky, but soft enough to leave the impression of a finger when pressed.) Let dough stand 15 minutes.

PARATHAS

1. Grease wooden board or work surface with oil or margarine. With rolling pin, roll out dough into circles about 6 to 8 inches in diameter and ⅛ inch thick. Spread surface of each circle with ½ teaspoon oil or margarine.

2. Make a small diagonal slit in each circle and gather up dough into a spiral-shaped cone or roll into a jelly roll shape (figs. A-C). Reroll each piece of dough into a circle $\frac{1}{4}$ inch thick (fig. D).

3. Preheat griddle or heavy iron skillet over medium-high heat. Working with 1 dough circle at a time, place in pan and drizzle a little oil around the edges. Cook paratha 1 to 2 minutes, or until bottom browns lightly. Turn over and cook second side until brown (fig. E).

4. Repeat with remaining dough, keeping cooked parathas warm. Serve immediately.

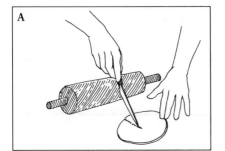

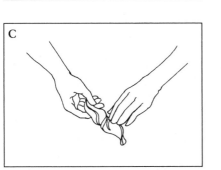

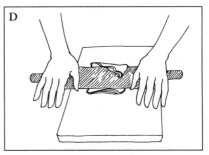

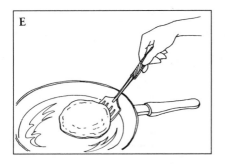

PARATHAS

NOTE: Each family shapes the dough for parathas in their own way. The most common shapes are a spiral or cone, a jelly roll, or a square. The idea is to form layers of dough similar to puff pastry, so after the shape is made, it's flattened into a circle again for cooking.

POORIS

1. Grease wooden board or work surface with oil or margarine. With rolling pin, roll out dough into circles about 3 inches in diameter (fig. A).

2. In wok over medium-high heat, heat 2 inches vegetable oil until hot. Add 1 dough circle; press down with spatula for a few seconds to immerse in hot oil (figs. B, C). This will cause the dough to puff up and become very light (fig. D).

3. Turn poori over and cook until golden. Drain on paper towels and keep warm while preparing remaining pooris. Serve immediately.

NOTE: A pancake turner or wide spatula will hold the poori down in the hot oil while the first side is cooking. Once the dough is turned over, there's no need to hold it down.

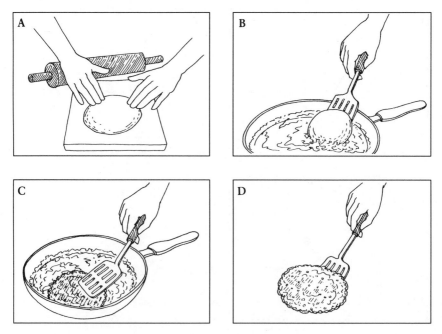

POORIS

Indian Pareve Dessert

Suji Halwa

MAKES 6 TO 8 SERVINGS

Halwa *is the word for "sweet" in the Hindu language. To make this dessert a little more festive, I sometimes garnish each serving with additional raisins and toasted almonds.*

2 cups water
¾ cup sugar, or ½ cup sugar plus ¼ cup honey
1 teaspoon grated orange peel or dried orange zest
¼ teaspoon ground cloves
¼ teaspoon ground cinnamon
¼ teaspoon ground nutmeg
¼ teaspoon ground cardamom
⅓ cup raisins
½ cup (1 stick) unsalted margarine
¼ cup sliced almonds
1 cup regular Cream of Wheat
⅛ teaspoon saffron threads

1. In small saucepan over low heat, combine water, sugar, orange peel or zest, and spices; cook 5 to 10 minutes, or until sugar dissolves, stirring often.
2. Stir in raisins and set aside.
3. In medium saucepan, melt margarine over medium-low heat. Add almonds and cook 5 to 10 minutes until golden, stirring often. Stir in Cream of Wheat and saffron; cook about 10 minutes, or until grains swell and darken to a golden color, stirring often.
4. Stir sugar syrup mixture into Cream of Wheat. Cook over very low heat until liquid is absorbed and mixture is fluffy, stirring constantly.
5. To serve, pour into cups. Serve warm.

Wine note: This is a cuisine that has historically been the bête noire of wine matchups. Of all the suggestions from professionals—Sauvignon Blanc for its grassiness, Gewürztraminer for its spiciness, Rhône reds for their pepperiness—still, nothing is so satisfying with dishes from India or Burma as coconut milk or beer. They tame the fire of curries and other foods without wiping out the palate memory. Diehard wine lovers will turn to lightly sweet sparkling wines, such as Asti Spumante or even a few from New York, which add a cleansing and cooling spritz to the mouth.

Moroccan

S ituated in the northwest corner of Africa, bordered by the
Mediterranean Sea and separated from Europe by a trickle of
water called the Straits of Gibraltar, Morocco has always
been more Mediterranean and Middle Eastern in feeling than
African. The original residents of Morocco were a mélange of several
races, descended from Phoenicians, Romans, Moors, and Berbers. In
A.D. 788, when invaders from Baghdad arrived in Morocco and other
North African lands, the natives were all practicing Christianity. But
the Arab conquerers came to spread the word of Allah, and it wasn't
long before the people were converted to the religious and cultural
beliefs of Islam.

Its close proximity to the Iberian Peninsula made Morocco one of
the chief refuges for Jews at the time of the Spanish Inquisition in
1492. The country was very hospitable to the expelled Jewish people,
who continued to adhere to the Sephardic heritage in their adopted
homeland. The Jews lived peacefully with the Arabs, neither group
posing a threat to the other, and each carrying on its special religious,
cultural, and culinary traditions.

During my childhood in Morocco, the exchange between the two
groups was tremendous. All of the Jews wore Arab garb, and a
number spoke a language we called Judeo-Arabic, which was written
in Arabic letters. While the Jews and Arabs retained many of their
individual food customs in this friendly atmosphere, others were
shared—resulting in a richly varied and colorful cuisine.

Since the dietary laws of Judaism and Islam do have a few points in common, sharing food customs wasn't as incongruous as it might seem. Both prohibit the eating of pork, and the Moroccan Arab diet features very few shellfish or creamed dishes that would mix milk products and meat. In fact, many meals revolve around starches, using vegetables and small amounts of meat or fish to stretch them and enhance their nutrition. In addition, oil is traditionally used for cooking rather than butter, and yogurt is never used in combination with chicken or lamb, as it is in Syria or India. Desserts center mostly on fruits, nuts, and other pareve ingredients.

When the French arrived in North Africa in the early 1900s, they pretty much left the Moroccan culinary heritage intact. The cuisine of Algeria, on the other hand, was given a more distinct French accent, but the Arabs of Morocco continued to cook and eat as they had for centuries, as did the Jews.

The cuisine of Morocco has been determined by its climate and geography as well as its civilizations. The balmy weather is conducive to the growing of olives, lemons, almonds, raisins, and several herbs and spices, including the cumin, coriander, anise, and mint that make the food so fragrant and unique. Located directly on the path to Europe from the Middle and Far East, Morocco and the other North African countries had access to all the spices en route to Europe, and we used them liberally.

Wheat has always been a plentiful crop, spurring the popularity of Morocco's national dish, couscous, a creation based on the fine semolina grain milled from wheat. The Mediterranean waters yield a steady supply of fish, and lambs and sheep graze on Moroccan fields, accounting for two other significant ingredients in the cooking of my homeland.

Many Moroccan dishes are one-pot meals, reflecting the widespread cooking technique of slowly simmering ingredients together in liquid. Meat or chicken might be combined with an assortment of vegetables, seasonings, and liquid, then braised until the liquid had almost evaporated and the flavors were melded. My mother would start cooking dishes such as these early in the morning, so the family could enjoy a hot meal every day at lunch. I remember anxiously waiting for the cooking vessel to be uncovered, as we all sat around the table—the aromatic steam escaping set my mouth watering.

At the Moroccan table, presentation and hospitality are almost as important as the food itself. The serving containers my mother used were so beautiful there was no need to garnish the contents. Today, I try to duplicate her style at the events I cater, using some of my family's heirloom platters and containers. And my staff carries out the Moroccan tradition of showing the diners the entire platter before serving, then dishing out the food on individual plates.

Both Arab and Jewish homes in Morocco are renowned for their gracious hospitality. In my house and others, there was always cooking going on, for guests often dropped by unexpectedly and they were never to leave hungry. Actually, they would leave quite full, after being treated to an array of foods that might include a hot dish such as couscous, tagine (an exotic stew), or a hearty soup; homemade relishes or preserves; freshly baked breads accompanied by olives; and mint tea. Regardless of their social standing, every family had at least one servant to help prepare and serve these dishes.

The two Moroccan menus presented here represent the Jewish and Arab influences respectively. As I mentioned, the cooking of the two groups did overlap. Nevertheless, there were some unique culinary contributions made by each. For example, the Jews were more adept at preparing fish, and the Arabs had a way with breads and other starchy foods. Both these multicourse menus are typical of festive or company meals; the Jewish one is an exemplary Shabbat dinner.

—*Levana Kirschenbaum*

Levana Levy Kirschenbaum

*L*evana Levy Kirschenbaum was born in Morocco to a family that had been there for many generations. The kitchen was the hub of her childhood home, and it was there and at her family's dinner table that she learned the pleasures of Moroccan cuisine and developed her innate sense of hospitality.

As a young girl, Levana studied in France, then spent a year in Israel. Although her studies focused on psychology, when she came to the United States in 1973 she preferred to take advantage of her rich cultural upbringing and travel experience. She eventually combined the two to branch out into the food business, where she can express her creativity and love for celebration to its fullest.

Her first venture was a small bakery on Manhattan's Upper West Side selling Moroccan-style pastries and cakes. Soon the bakery expanded into the space next door, eventually becoming an upscale kosher restaurant. Levana Kirschenbaum is still a co-owner in the popular restaurant, but she is concentrating on her one-of-a-kind catering venture, aptly named "Mostly Moroccan." Through this business, she prepares the specialties of her native country, introducing jaded palates to the likes of couscous, pastilla, and other trademark dishes. She frequently cooks up continental-style and vegetarian party fare as well. Through her diverse culinary skills and impeccable attention to detail, she has gained an excellent reputation, and her spirited kosher menus are requested by a large clientele for both religious and social events. One of Levana Kirschenbaum's more recent endeavors is a series of cooking workshops in which she shares her love of food and entertaining. She especially enjoys living and working in New York City, where the diverse cultural mix brings back memories of her childhood in Morocco.

Although Morocco still has a small Jewish community, most Jews began disbanding to other countries during and after World War II. Like Levana's family, many emigrated to the United States. Others went to Canada, France, and South America, establishing enclaves in Montreal, Cannes, São Paulo, and Buenos Aires. In these adopted cities, the Moroccan culinary heritage lives on.

Hot Cigars—*Garros*
Fish in Saffron Sauce—*Hout Metbuch*
Pumpkin Soup—*Mark del Gar'a*
Chicken Tagine with Potatoes, Olives, and Tomatoes—*Bel Btata*
Grated Carrot Salad—*Salada de Chizo*
Eggplant Salad
Shortbread—*Ghriba*

Hot Cigars

Garros

MAKES 3 DOZEN

These phyllo-wrapped appetizers are similar to Iraqi burags and Turkish boreks. I frequently make them for parties, where they get rave reviews.

1 pound chicken livers, thoroughly rinsed and broiled
¼ cup vegetable oil
2 tablespoons paprika
½ teaspoon cayenne pepper, or to taste
  Salt and freshly ground black pepper to taste
2 cloves garlic, peeled
1 egg
1 teaspoon ground cumin
1 pound fresh or defrosted frozen phyllo dough or strudel
  leaves

1. In medium saucepan, combine broiled chicken livers, oil, paprika, cayenne, salt and black pepper to taste, and garlic with enough water to cover. Cook, uncovered, over medium heat until all water has evaporated.

2. Transfer ingredients to food processor; add egg and cumin and process until smooth. Shape liver mixture into 36 logs or "cigars," each about 3 inches long. Set aside on a tray.

3. Preheat oven to 375°F. On oiled work surface, stack phyllo leaves; cut crosswise into thirds (fig. A). Work with one-third of the phyllo at a time, covering and refrigerating remaining two-thirds until ready to use. Working quickly, take 2 leaves and place them carefully on work surface; brush top leaf with oil (fig. B). Place 1 chicken liver log in the center of phyllo leaf (fig. C). With narrow end of phyllo facing you, roll phyllo over chicken liver log just to cover (fig. D). Fold sides of phyllo in toward center and continue to roll all the way up, jelly roll style (figs. E, F). Place on greased cookie sheet, seam side down.

4. Continue filling and rolling phyllo until all chicken liver mixture is used up. Brush tops of cigars with oil. Bake about 35 minutes, or until very crisp and very lightly browned. Serve piping hot.

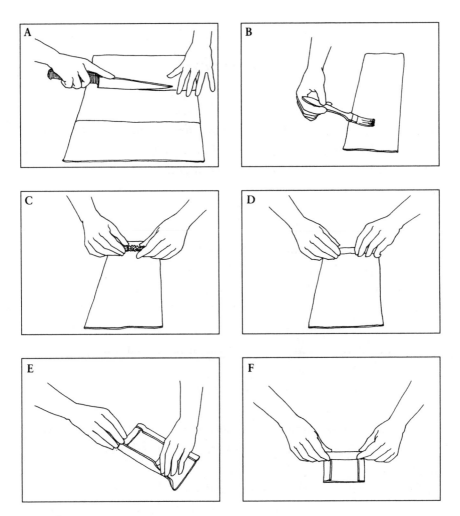

HOT CIGARS

Fish in Saffron Sauce

Hout Metbuch

MAKES 8 SERVINGS

The sea trout can be replaced with any firm white-fleshed fish, such as striped bass, cod, whitefish, or whiting. Saffron is widely used in Morocco, just as it is in neighboring Spain.

    8 sea trout steaks, rinsed
    ½ cup vegetable oil
    1 bunch parsley, coarsely chopped
    8 cloves garlic, peeled and left whole
       Generous pinch of saffron threads
    ½ teaspoon ground turmeric
       Pinch of cayenne pepper
    1 thick-skinned lemon, unpeeled, thinly sliced and seeded
    2 tablespoons capers
    2 tablespoons dry or prepared mustard

1. In dutch oven or large deep skillet, combine all ingredients except mustard with enough water to cover. Bring to a boil over medium-high heat.
2. Reduce heat to medium; cover and cook 30 minutes.
3. In cup, combine mustard with a little of the cooking liquid; stir mixture into pot. Continue cooking, uncovered, until liquid becomes thick and creamy, about 10 minutes.
4. To serve, carefully transfer fish to serving platter. Top each piece with a lemon slice, and pour remaining sauce evenly on top. Serve warm or at room temperature.

NOTE: Before using the lemon, taste a tiny piece of skin to make sure it's not bitter.

Pumpkin Soup

Mark Del Gar'a

MAKES 8 SERVINGS

The traditional Moroccan Rosh Hashanah soup, this dish is served to symbolize a sweet year ahead. I prefer to use butternut squash instead of pumpkin because it has a more consistent flavor and its flesh is always sweet and firm.

1 medium butternut squash, or ½ medium pumpkin, peeled, seeded, and cut into 2-inch squares
1 cup dried chickpeas, soaked overnight in cold water
3 medium onions, peeled and quartered
2 quarts beef broth or water
½ cup vegetable oil
Salt and freshly ground black pepper to taste
¼ cup honey or brown sugar
1 tablespoon ground cinnamon
Dash of ground cloves

1. In large saucepan or dutch oven, combine squash or pumpkin, chickpeas, onions, broth or water, oil, and salt and pepper to taste. Bring to a rolling boil over high heat. Reduce heat to low and simmer, covered, about 1 hour.

2. Stir in honey or brown sugar, cinnamon, and cloves; cook 15 minutes longer.

3. Transfer mixture in batches to food processor or blender and purée until smooth. Adjust seasonings and texture, adding more broth if necessary. (Soup should look light and creamy.) Serve hot.

NOTE: This soup holds its own very nicely without beef stock or meat, even though one of these must be added in Morocco, where soups made without meat are treated with contempt. Here in America, this soup can be made in a delicious vegetarian or pareve version, a kind of liquid takeoff on pumpkin pie!

Chicken Tagine with Potatoes, Olives, and Tomatoes

Bel Btata

MAKES 8 SERVINGS

Two 3-pound chickens, cut into pieces
24 small red-skinned new potatoes
6 plum tomatoes, peeled, seeded, and coarsely chopped, or 1½ cups canned tomatoes, chopped
1 small bunch parsley, coarsely chopped
24 pitted green olives
⅓ cup vegetable oil
About 12 saffron threads
½ teaspoon ground turmeric
Salt and freshly ground black pepper to taste

1. In dutch oven or large deep skillet over medium-high heat, place chicken and enough water to barely cover; bring to a boil. Reduce heat to medium; cover and simmer 30 minutes.
2. Add remaining ingredients. Cover and cook 45 minutes longer, stirring occasionally to prevent sticking. (Cooking liquid should form a nice thick gravy; if too thin, cook uncovered a few minutes longer over high heat. If too thick, stir in a little more water.)
3. To serve, arrange chicken in center of serving platter. Arrange potatoes all around and pour gravy evenly on top of both. Serve hot.

Grated Carrot Salad

Salada de Chizo

MAKES 8 SERVINGS

Delightful, and totally different from the usual grated carrot salad made with raisins and orange juice.

1 pound carrots, peeled and grated
4 parsley sprigs, chopped
3 cloves garlic, peeled and finely minced
$\frac{1}{3}$ cup vegetable oil
  Juice of 1 lemon
  Salt and freshly ground black pepper to taste

In medium bowl, combine all ingredients. Serve at room temperature.

Eggplant Salad

MAKES 8 SERVINGS

1 medium eggplant
2 cloves garlic, peeled and finely minced
2 tablespoons paprika
$\frac{1}{2}$ teaspoon cayenne pepper, or to taste
$\frac{1}{4}$ cup vegetable oil
  Juice of 1 lemon
1 teaspoon ground cumin
  Salt and freshly ground black pepper to taste

1. Preheat oven to 450°F. Place eggplant in nonmetal baking dish and bake about 1 hour, or until completely soft. Let cool until easy to handle.

2. Peel eggplant and place over colander to drain. In medium bowl, mash eggplant flesh. Stir in remaining ingredients and let stand for flavors to blend and until mixture reaches room temperature.

Shortbread

Ghriba

MAKES 4 DOZEN COOKIES

This little confection, served at virtually every celebratory event, has an intriguing texture and melt-in-the-mouth consistency. To me, it is reminiscent of the familiar shortbread and the French montecao, and is a great Moroccan favorite. Make sure the ingredients are measured accurately.

4 cups all-purpose flour
1 cup sugar
1 cup vegetable oil
   Ground cinnamon for sprinkling

1. Preheat oven to 325°F. Cover cookie sheet with aluminum foil.
2. In food processor, combine flour, sugar, and oil. Process until well mixed, letting the motor run for about 1 minute and scraping constantly to keep dough from sticking to the sides.
3. Form dough into little domes, each about $1\frac{1}{2}$ inches in diameter, slightly flattening the tops (figs. A, B). Place on prepared cookie sheet; sprinkle tops with cinnamon. Bake about 30 minutes, or until cookies are firm; they should not brown. (Tiny cracks will form on top.)
4. Cool cookies on wire rack. Store in tightly closed container.

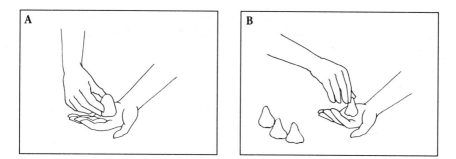

GHRIBA

Wine note: Yes, there is Moroccan wine and amazingly, not only is there kosher Moroccan wine but at least one is imported into the United States. So what would match Moroccan food so well as a wine from the same region? If your wine merchant doesn't want to be bothered trying to find this wine, call Steve Anchin at Yorkville Wine and Liquor, Third Avenue at 79th Street in Manhattan, at (212) 288-6671 and soon you might have the only table in the neighborhood with a bottle of kosher Moroccan wine on it! All else failing, turn yet again to the Rhône region of France, home to many Moroccan Jewish emigrés. A young Côtes du Rhône, Minervois, or Coteaux du Tricastin, white or red, depending on the choice of fish or fowl, would not be out of place. As for the cookies, a Vouvray Moelleux, a Sweet Chenin Blanc, a late-harvest Riesling from California, a Niagara from New York, a late-harvest Sauvignon Blanc from Israel, or Sauternes from France will provide sweet endings indeed.

"Pigeon" Pie—*Pastilla*
Fish in Red Sauce—*Hout Metbuch*
Moroccan Lentil Soup—*Harira*
Chicken Stew with Semolina—*Chicken Couscous*
Harissa
Raw Tomato Relish
Cooked Carrot Salad—*Salada de Chizo Metbucha*
Stuffed Dried Fruit—*Noix et Dates Fourées*

"Pigeon" Pie

Pastilla

MAKES 20 APPETIZERS

It takes just one bite to understand why pastilla has been placed among the world's greatest dishes. It epitomizes all that is Moroccan cuisine—sharp, sweet, delicate, intriguing. Traditionally, pastilla arrives at the table in a big round dish, then gets cut into wedges. But as an appetizer, this version of individual servings is ideal for a cocktail party or multicourse dinner. I substitute chicken for the pigeon originally used.

One 3½-pound chicken, cut up into pieces
4 medium onions, peeled and chopped
¼ cup vegetable oil
1 bunch parsley, chopped
4 cilantro sprigs, chopped
1 generous pinch saffron threads
1 teaspoon freshly ground black pepper
One 2-inch cinnamon stick
½ teaspoon ground cloves

$\frac{1}{2}$ teaspoon ground ginger

$\frac{1}{2}$ teaspoon ground turmeric

2 eggs, lightly beaten

1 cup blanched almonds, lightly toasted and coarsely chopped

2 tablespoons granulated sugar

1 pound fresh or frozen phyllo dough or strudel leaves, at room temperature
Confectioners' sugar for dusting

1 tablespoon ground cinnamon

1. In dutch oven or heavy saucepot, combine chicken, onions, oil, parsley, cilantro, saffron, pepper, cinnamon stick, cloves, ginger, and turmeric. Add 1 cup water; bring to a boil over high heat. Reduce heat to medium; cover and simmer 1 hour, or until chicken is tender.

2. Uncover; increase heat to high. Cook, stirring constantly, until all liquid evaporates, about 5 minutes.

3. Remove from heat; discard cinnamon stick. Remove chicken and set aside. Stir eggs into pot until they look set and mixture has thickened.

4. Remove skin from chicken; cut meat into very small pieces, discarding all skin, bones, and gristle. In large bowl, combine chicken and contents of pot. Add chopped almonds and granulated sugar; mix thoroughly for stuffing.

5. Preheat oven to 375°F. On oiled work surface, stack phyllo leaves flat. Cut crosswise into thirds. (Work with one-third of phyllo at a time, covering remaining two-thirds with damp towel.) Take out 3 phyllo leaves and stack on work surface, narrow ends facing you; brush top leaf with oil. Place 2 tablespoons stuffing in center, close to the end nearest you. Starting at narrow end, roll phyllo over stuffing, partway up, jelly roll style. Fold sides toward center and continue to roll up all the way.

6. Place seam side down on greased cookie sheet. Repeat with remaining phyllo and stuffing, always brushing top leaf with oil before filling. Brush tops of all the rolls with oil. Bake about 35 minutes, or until very lightly brown and very crisp. Sprinkle with confectioners' sugar and ground cinnamon; serve hot.

Fish in Red Sauce

Hout Metbuch

MAKES 8 SERVINGS

The Arabs prefer to cook their fish in a spicy red sauce.

- 8 small cod, bass, or salmon steaks
- 1 small bunch parsley, chopped
- 8 cloves garlic, peeled and left whole
- 2 tablespoons paprika
- $\frac{1}{2}$ teaspoon ground turmeric
- $\frac{1}{2}$ teaspoon cayenne pepper, or to taste
- Salt to taste
- $\frac{1}{2}$ cup vegetable oil
- 1 large red bell pepper, cut into thin strips
- 4 sprigs fresh cilantro (optional)
- $\frac{1}{4}$ pickled lemon (see Note), skin only, rinsed and finely chopped (optional)

1. In dutch oven or large deep skillet, combine fish, parsley, garlic, paprika, turmeric, cayenne, and salt to taste. Add oil and enough water to barely cover. Bring to a boil over high heat.
2. Reduce heat to medium. Cover and simmer about 30 minutes. Add red bell pepper, cilantro, and pickled lemon, if desired. Cover and cook 5 to 10 minutes longer, or until liquid in the pot thickens to the consistency of maple syrup.
3. Carefully remove fish steaks and arrange on platter. Pour sauce evenly on top. Serve warm or at room temperature.

NOTE: A pickled lemon is a lemon that has been cut, steeped in its own juice along with kosher salt, then kept in a dark, cool place until it swells and becomes very aromatic. Typically, the cut lemons are crammed in a wide-mouth jar, layered with the salt, and are available for purchase in Morocco. Since pickled lemons are rare in the States, you can use a very thinly sliced fresh lemon instead; add at the beginning of cooking time.

Wine note: Here is a strong fish dish indeed, and care must be taken in choosing its accompanying wine. Even without the pickled lemon, the cayenne, paprika, and cilantro give off aromas and tastes that might well overwhelm a Chardonnay, which would accompany the fish well if it had no sauce. One of the big, oaky California Chardonnays could work well, but a cold Gewürztraminer from Alsace or a big Riesling, also from Alsace or possibly from Israel, would be fine. A Sauvignon Blanc from Israel or California, or from the Touraine region of the Loire area of France, might also smooth out some of the sharp ingredients in the sauce.

Moroccan Lentil Soup

Harira

MAKES 8 SERVINGS

Harira is the traditional soup served at Ramadan, the month of atonement in the Arab calendar. During this time, Muslims do not eat or drink from sunrise until the bells start ringing at sunset. Then everyone hurries home to eat, and the streets are pervaded with the smells of mint tea, harira, and chebbakia. The latter is an incredibly rich fried-dough pastry made with quarts of honey and rolled in toasted sesame seeds. It's also incredibly heavenly! Being in a Moroccan street on a Ramadan day, watching all the bustle and savoring all the wonderful aromas, is a childhood memory of mine that I still cherish.

6 very meaty lamb bones

4 cups peeled and seeded coarsely chopped tomatoes, or 2 cups seeded canned tomatoes

$\frac{1}{2}$ cup vegetable oil

1 bunch parsley, chopped

1 small bunch fresh cilantro, chopped

3 ribs celery, cut up

6 saffron threads

$\frac{1}{2}$ teaspoon ground turmeric

Salt and freshly ground black pepper to taste

1 cup lentils, picked over, rinsed, and cooked

$\frac{1}{2}$ cup freshly squeezed lemon juice

$\frac{1}{2}$ cup all-purpose flour mixed smooth with 1 cup water

Dried dates (optional)

1. In dutch oven or large saucepot, bring lamb bones and 3 quarts water to a boil over high heat. Reduce heat to medium-low; cover and simmer 2 hours. Add remaining ingredients except lentils, lemon juice, flour mixture, and dates; cover and cook 1 hour.

2. Remove lamb bones; shred meat from bones and set aside. Discard bones. Add lentils, lemon juice, and flour mixture to pot. Cook, stirring constantly, just until heated through.

3. Stir in lamb meat. Serve soup hot, accompanied by dates if you like.

Chicken Stew with Semolina

Chicken Couscous

MAKES 8 SERVINGS

Couscous, the dish, was born in Morocco. Couscous, the grain, is really a type of pasta. In its original form, the semolina or durum wheat is mixed with water, then rubbed into tiny pellets, which are left out to dry in the sun. Traditionally, the vegetables and meat cook in the bottom part of the couscoussière (a special utensil) while the couscous grain steams on top. But I find it better to prepare the two separately so I have more control over the timing. Harissa is the fiery sauce typically served with couscous. Add as much as your taste buds will allow!

3 pounds onions, peeled and quartered
$\frac{1}{2}$ cup chickpeas, soaked overnight in cold water
Two 2$\frac{1}{2}$- to 3-pound chickens, cut into pieces
1 cup vegetable oil
$\frac{1}{2}$ teaspoon saffron threads
$\frac{1}{2}$ teaspoon ground turmeric
One 2-inch cinnamon stick
1 teaspoon freshly ground black pepper
  Salt to taste
1 medium butternut squash, unpeeled, cut into 2-inch squares, and seeded
2 to 2$\frac{1}{2}$ cups couscous (not instant; see Note)
1 cup dark seedless raisins
1 teaspoon ground cinnamon
1 teaspoon ground ginger
$\frac{1}{2}$ teaspoon ground cloves
$\frac{1}{2}$ cup toasted slivered almonds
  Harissa (recipe follows)

1. In dutch oven or saucepot, combine onions, chickpeas, chicken pieces, $\frac{1}{2}$ cup oil, saffron, turmeric, cinnamon, pepper and salt with enough water to barely cover. Bring to a boil over high heat. Reduce heat to medium-low; cover and cook 30 minutes.
2. Add squash; cook 15 minutes longer.
3. Place couscous in medium bowl. Gradually pour in 3 cups of the boiling cooking broth from pot. With 2 forks, mix very quickly.
4. Place couscous on top of couscoussière; fill bottom two-thirds full with boiling water. Cook, uncovered, 30 minutes. Transfer couscous back to medium bowl; fluff again with forks. Add 2 cups boiling water and remaining $\frac{1}{2}$ cup vegetable oil. Working quickly with 2

forks, fluff again. Return to top of couscoussière and cook, uncovered, 30 minutes longer.

5. Meanwhile, add all remaining ingredients except toasted almonds to chicken mixture; cook 30 minutes longer. (Total cooking time for chicken and vegetables is 1 hour 15 minutes; total for couscous, 1 hour.)

6. To serve, mound couscous in center of large serving platter. Pour some of the cooking liquid evenly on top of grain, using only as much as couscous can absorb. (It should not get wet or soupy.) Arrange chicken and vegetables decoratively on top and around couscous. Pass remaining broth separately and serve Harissa (recipe follows) on the side.

N O T E : Do not use instant or parboiled couscous in this recipe. The authentic couscous grain is sold loose and is available in most health-food stores. Although I *do* recommend using a couscoussière for this recipe, you may substitute a mesh sieve fitted over a saucepan of similar size.

HARISSA

1 cup dried red hot peppers, stems removed, soaked in boiling water for 1 hour and drained
$\frac{1}{2}$ cup vegetable oil
5 cloves garlic, peeled
2 tablespoons ground cumin
Salt and freshly ground black pepper to taste
1 bunch fresh cilantro (optional)

In food processor, purée all ingredients until smooth. Place in jar and cover tightly. Harissa will keep for several weeks in the refrigerator.

N O T E : Hot red peppers are available in Latin specialty stores. If unavailable in your area, substitute 1 cup chili powder mixed with 1 teaspoon cayenne pepper and 1 cup water.

Raw Tomato Relish

3 firm ripe tomatoes, peeled, seeded, and juiced
$\frac{1}{4}$ cup finely chopped parsley
2 tablespoons capers
1 gherkin, or $\frac{1}{4}$ pickle, finely chopped
12 pitted green olives, finely chopped
$\frac{1}{2}$ rib celery, finely chopped
$\frac{1}{2}$ cup vegetable oil
$\frac{1}{4}$ cup freshly squeezed lemon juice
Salt and freshly ground black pepper to taste
Small piece pickled lemon, skin only, finely chopped
(optional)

Cut tomato into small pieces and place in medium bowl. Add remaining ingredients and toss to combine. Serve at once.

NOTE: If you must make this recipe in advance, add the tomatoes at the last minute.

Wine note: Again, the red wine of Morocco would seem appropriate (see page 93), but watch out for all the sweet and spicy ingredients at the end of the couscous recipe. You might decide that they are too strong and/or sweet to take a dry red wine without loads of fruit to compensate. One of the Rhônes would perhaps be a better bet in red, while Riesling from Israel, California, or New York would complete the whites.

Cooked Carrot Salad

Salada de Chizo Metbucha

MAKES 8 SERVINGS

1 pound thin carrots, peeled and sliced ½ inch thick
¼ cup vegetable oil
Juice of 1 lemon
2 cloves garlic, peeled and minced (optional)
2 tablespoons paprika
1 teaspoon ground cumin
½ teaspoon cayenne pepper, or to taste
3 sprigs parsley, chopped
Salt and freshly ground black pepper to taste

1. In large saucepan, combine carrots and enough water to cover. Bring to a boil over high heat. Reduce heat to medium-high; boil 15 minutes, or until tender. Drain and rinse in cold water.
2. In medium bowl, combine carrots and remaining ingredients; mix gently. Serve at room temperature.

Stuffed Dried Fruit

Noix et Dates Fourées

MAKES 8 SERVINGS

Sun-dried apricots, dates, figs, and prunes are quite popular in Morocco. In this dessert, the fruit is stuffed with almond paste, which can be made quickly in the food processor.

1 pound blanched almonds
2 cups confectioners' sugar
2 egg whites

2 to 3 tablespoons orange-flower water, or 2 to 3 drops
orange extract
2 to 3 drops almond or vanilla extract (optional)
Assorted dried fruits (apricots, dates, prunes, figs, or
the like), pitted

1. In food processor, process almonds, sugar, egg whites, and flavorings until smooth dough forms. Shape almond paste into ball and wrap in plastic wrap. Refrigerate 1 hour before using.
2. With hands, shape almond paste into 1½-inch-long logs. Place logs snugly in the center of pitted dried fruit.
3. To serve, arrange stuffed fruit on platter.

NOTE: Almond paste freezes well; recipe can be doubled and half can be wrapped and frozen for future use.

VARIATION: Stuffed Nuts: Shape almond paste into little balls about 1¼ inches in diameter. Sandwich each ball between 2 perfect toasted walnut or pecan halves.

Wine note: Muscat without a doubt! Try an Asti Spumante, one of the sparkling, fruity wines of New York, or a sipping still wine, such as a real sherry from Spain, one of the sweet whites from Israel, or a white port from Israel. Beware of overwhelming the taste of the dessert with a wine that's too sweet.

Turkish

t urkey has been inhabited and ruled by a number of different civilizations through the ages, each making its own contribution to the tasty stew that is Turkish cooking. Before the rise to power of the Ottoman Empire in the mid-fifteenth century, Turkey had been home to its original central Asian nomadic settlers, Romans, Greeks, Armenians, and Persian Islams—all of whom freely exchanged food customs. During the reign of the Ottomans, the territory expanded to include the Balkans and Anatolia, enriching the cuisine with fish from the Mediterranean and Black Sea, olives and olive oil, and a wealth of fruits and vegetables grown in new, very fertile soil.

The Ottomans were broad-minded rulers, and when the Jews were expelled from Spain in 1492, large numbers emigrated to Turkey, the Middle East, and the small islands in the Mediterranean. Gradually, Turkish cuisine became permeated with some of the Iberian flavor as well.

My own ancestors fled Spain during the Inquisition and settled in Rhodes. Through the years, my family continued some of the Spanish food traditions they originally brought with them, but Turkish culinary style and ingredients eventually dominated their cooking. As a young girl, I learned to create the Turkish and Sephardic specialties that I now cook in my classes and catering business.

The Ottomans actually developed and elevated Turkish cuisine to the esteemed position it holds today. The kitchen staff in the sultan's palace numbered in the hundreds, with each group responsible for a specific category of food. These included soups, kebobs, boreks, pilafs, vegetable dishes, fish, breads, pastries, candies, syrups, jams, and beverages. Food was so important to the Ottomans that one sultan issued a set of regulations standardizing recipes for such traditional fare as boreks and baklava! These rulers also helped spread Turkish culinary practices to the neighboring Balkan and Arab lands. In Syria and Iraq, for example, the pilafs and phyllo pastries bear a close resemblance to those of Turkey, as do the boreks and lamb dishes of Yugoslavia and Bulgaria.

Since Turkey was a Muslim country when the Jews arrived, the eating of pork was forbidden and there were no pork dishes to adapt to the dietary laws. Lamb was and still is the primary meat used, and many families, including mine, raised their own animals. On special occasions, such as Passover, a delectable roast leg of lamb was the main attraction—a cut permitted by Turkish Sephardic households because the sinew was removed under rabbinical supervision. However, meat was not plentiful most of the time, and inventive cooks learned to make a little go a long way. A small portion of lamb or a meat bone might be cooked with lots of vegetables, dried beans, and/or rice to provide some substance and flavor. And like other Mediterranean cooks, the Turkish Jews took full advantage of the many species of fish available in the waters surrounding their country. Mullet, herring, snapper, and other varieties were typically grilled over an open fire or stuffed and jellied for the Shabbat meal.

The Turkish enthusiasm for fruits and vegetables is obvious at every meal. In my childhood home, fresh produce was eaten or prepared when it was at its peak season, with large quantities preserved, canned, or dried for future enjoyment. Eggplant, okra, celery, beans (both fresh and dried), tomatoes, and zucchini were the most common vegetables. When they weren't being cooked in meat-stretching casseroles or stews, eggplant, artichokes, peppers, and onions might be stuffed with bulgur (cracked wheat—Turkey's prevalent grain), rice, or meat mixtures. The stuffings were usually spiced with oregano, cumin, garlic, parsley, and/or lemon juice, then baked inside the hollowed-out vegetables.

Many fruits grew in abundance too, including cherries, pears, quince, oranges, lemons, melons, apricots, and figs. These sun-ripened fruits were eaten fresh or in a simple compote, or they were turned into intensely flavored preserves and jams. I remember my family's servants preparing quince paste, tiny preserved pears, and other sweet delicacies to have on hand when visitors dropped by. It was customary in my household and others in Rhodes and Turkey to offer guests something sweet to accompany a cup of strong Turkish coffee or tea and good conversation.

Dairy foods make up a good part of the Turkish diet, and the country produces a number of its own cheeses. In Jewish homes, the Saturday afternoon meal was typically dairy. My family made their own yogurt and some cheeses, including a Parmesan, feta, and dry ricotta-type product. Friday was spent preparing the boreks and other cheese pastries that would just need a brief heating for Shabbat lunch. These were made in the kitchen's wood-burning stove, while the homemade breads were usually taken to the village bakery to be finished in a brick oven. Sephardic families enjoyed other make-ahead Shabbat dishes, too. One example was *huevos hamimodas* ("hot eggs"), which baked all Friday night to be savored on Saturday.

Holidays called for special dishes, their recipes frequently passed down from generation to generation. The major attraction on Rosh Hashanah was a cooked whole fish with its head attached, a symbol for the beginning of the new year. Leeks and pomegranates were other Rosh Hashanah foods, the former also representing a new beginning, and the latter, with its multitude of seeds, symbolizing abundance. On Passover, we always had fresh beans and peas. While these are prohibited for Ashkenazic Jews, the Sephardim allowed them, and a typical Passover dish was baby lamb with fava beans.

Although many years of marriage and life in New York City have Americanized me a bit, I have carefully preserved my Sephardic food heritage. Through hours of testing, retesting, and demonstration, I have found ways to simplify and modernize the cooking methods for my favorite childhood dishes. In the menus that follow, you will discover that none of the ingredients is extraordinary or difficult to find, and the results are delightfully different.

—*Esther Shear*

Esther Shear

E sther Shear was born into a Sephardic family in Rhodes, a small island located between Greece and Turkey. Until 1912, Rhodes belonged to Turkey; then it fell into Italian hands. The island boasted a large Jewish settlement prior to World War II, started by Jews who fled Spain at the time of the Inquisition. These Jews brought with them the culture and customs of the Iberian area, where they had lived for several centuries. Soon their cooking became spiced with Greek, Turkish, and, eventually, Italian influences, along with the Spanish and Portuguese flavors in which it was rooted.

Esther has an intimate and extensive knowledge of the foods of the Sephardic Jews. As the youngest in her family, she spent her formative years amid the sights and smells of the Sephardic kitchen, learning to cook from her mother and several aunts and sisters. In 1939, when Esther was forced to leave Rhodes for America, she carried her Sephardic and Turkish cooking legacy with her. Today, she passes this legacy on to Jewish students who have known only the typical Ashkenazic or Eastern European dishes (potato pancakes, stuffed cabbage, and the like).

The "exotic" recipes she teaches include such Sephardic favorites as stuffed grape leaves, sautéed artichokes, stuffed onions, and korabies, a rich, buttery cookie. For entrées, small amounts of fish, lamb, beef, or chicken are combined with fresh vegetables for healthy, hearty eating. This cuisine is especially adaptable to contemporary life-styles, since many dishes can be prepared ahead of time and completed or reheated at the last minute—a boon for the busy.

Esther Shear now lives with her husband on Manhattan's Upper West Side and is very active in that neighborhood's Spanish-Portuguese synagogue. She has taught cooking classes at this famous Sephardic institution, catered parties and affairs there, and helped organize various social, cultural, and religious events for the congregation. Her summers are spent in Cannes, France, visiting with her brother and renewing her acquaintance with authentic Mediterranean food.

Chicken Turkish Style—*Gayina à la Turka*
Cracked Wheat with Chickpeas—*Bulgur*
Rice with Pine Nuts—*Pilaf Piñones*
Celery with Carrots—*Apio con Zanahorias*
Leek Pancakes—*Keftes de Prasa*
Nut Cookies—*Korabies*

Chicken Turkish Style

Gayina à la Turca

MAKES 4 TO 6 SERVINGS

Chicken was often featured at our Friday evening Shabbat dinner in Rhodes. This recipe blends traditional Turkish ingredients into a hearty main dish. I usually serve the dish with rice or bulgur to absorb the flavorful cooking liquid.

   3 tablespoons olive oil or vegetable oil
One 4-pound chicken, cut into 8 to 10 pieces
   2 large onions, peeled and chopped
   2 cloves garlic, peeled and chopped
   $\frac{1}{2}$ cup chopped parsley
   1 green or red bell pepper, seeded and diced
One 28-ounce can peeled plum tomatoes
   $\frac{1}{2}$ cup pitted green olives
   1 teaspoon ground coriander
   1 teaspoon ground cumin
     Salt and freshly ground black pepper to taste
     Hot cooked rice or bulgur (optional)

1. In dutch oven or large deep skillet, heat oil over medium-high heat. Add chicken; fry 10 minutes, or until browned on all sides, turning frequently.

2. Remove chicken from pot and set aside. To drippings, add onions, garlic, and parsley. Sauté about 5 minutes, or until onions are lightly browned, stirring often.

3. Stir in diced bell pepper, tomatoes with their liquid, olives, and seasonings; bring to a boil. Add chicken; reduce heat to low. Cover and simmer 30 to 45 minutes, or until chicken is tender.

4. Serve hot, over rice or bulgur, if desired.

Wine note: As Turkey is not noted for producing wine and certainly not kosher wine, we look elsewhere. The tomatoes, olives, and in fact, just about all the ingredients, call for red wine, bespeaking Chianti first. But a fine Bordeaux would also be in keeping, as would a Cabernet from Israel or California, or a good burgundy.

Cracked Wheat with Chickpeas

Bulgur

MAKES 4 SERVINGS

Bulgur is a popular grain in Turkish cuisine. Here it's combined with tomato sauce and chickpeas, but its versatility makes it compatible with many other ingredients. Rich in nutrients and fiber, bulgur also fits in with the trend toward healthy eating.

3 tablespoons olive or vegetable oil
1 medium onion, peeled and chopped
1 cup cooked chickpeas
$\frac{1}{4}$ cup tomato sauce
  Salt and freshly ground black pepper to taste
1 cup bulgur, washed and soaked for 1 hour

1. In medium saucepan, heat oil over medium heat. Add onion; cook 5 minutes, or until golden brown, stirring often.
2. Add 2 cups water, chickpeas, tomato sauce, and salt and pepper to taste; bring to a boil. Stir in bulgur and cook 10 minutes, or until water has been absorbed and bulgur is soft.

Rice with Pine Nuts

Pilaf Piñones

MAKES 4 SERVINGS

1 cup converted rice
2 tablespoons olive oil or vegetable oil
1 teaspoon salt
$\frac{1}{4}$ cup toasted pine nuts

1. Wash rice in cold water and drain well; set aside.
2. In medium saucepan over medium-high heat, combine 2 cups water, oil, and salt; bring to a boil.
3. Stir rice into boiling liquid. Cover pot; reduce heat to low and simmer 20 minutes.
4. Uncover rice and stir in pine nuts. To serve, fluff with a fork.

Celery with Carrots

Apio con Zanahorias

MAKES 4 TO 6 SERVINGS

Braising vegetables in oil, lemon juice, and water is a typical Turkish preparation. I particularly like the combination of celery and carrots, although vegetables such as eggplant, fennel, and zucchini are often braised as well.

1 large bunch celery
4 carrots, peeled
¼ cup olive oil or vegetable oil
1 teaspoon sugar
Juice of 1 lemon
Salt

1. Wash celery ribs and remove all tough threads. Cut celery into thin strips. Cut carrots into strips the same size as celery.
2. In large heavy saucepan, combine 2 cups water, oil, sugar, a few drops of lemon juice, and salt to taste. Bring to a boil over high heat.
3. Add celery; reduce heat to medium-low. Cover and simmer about 10 minutes.
4. Add carrots and remaining lemon juice; adjust seasonings to taste. Cover and cook 10 minutes longer, or until celery and carrots are tender.

Leek Pancakes

Keftes de Prasa

MAKES 4 TO 6 SERVINGS

Although the Turkish Sephardim serve these at any time of the year, they make an especially welcome treat for Passover and Rosh Hashanah.

4 or 5 leeks
1 cup mashed potatoes
3 eggs, beaten
$\frac{1}{4}$ cup matzoh meal
Salt and freshly ground black pepper to taste
Vegetable oil for frying

1. Clean leeks thoroughly, washing out all sand and grit. Cut white *and* green parts into small pieces, discarding the tough outer leaves.
2. In large saucepan, combine leeks with enough water to cover. Bring to a boil over high heat. Reduce heat to medium; cover and cook 30 minutes until tender. Drain and cool.
3. With hands, squeeze out all excess water from leeks. In medium bowl, combine cooked leeks with potatoes, eggs, matzoh meal, and salt and pepper to taste; mix well.
4. Heat about $\frac{1}{2}$ inch oil in medium skillet, over medium-high heat. With spoon, form leek-potato mixture into small patties. Drop into hot oil and fry 3 minutes on each side, or until golden. Drain on paper towels. Serve hot.

Nut Cookies

Korabies

MAKES 3 DOZEN

Accompanied by fruit, these rich confections not only make a sweet ending to dinner, they also go exceptionally well with an afternoon cup of tea or coffee. If the cookies are not to follow a meat meal, I prefer making them with sweet butter instead of margarine.

1 cup (2 sticks) unsalted margarine
$\frac{1}{2}$ cup confectioners' sugar
1 teaspoon vanilla extract
$2\frac{1}{4}$ cups all-purpose flour
$\frac{1}{2}$ cup ground walnuts
    Confectioners' sugar for dusting

1. Preheat oven to 350°F. In large bowl with electric mixer at low speed, or with wooden spoon, combine margarine, sugar, and vanilla; blend thoroughly until creamy.
2. Add flour; beat until well incorporated. Stir in nuts; knead with hands until a soft dough forms.
3. Shape dough into walnut-size balls. Place on ungreased cookie sheet. Bake 15 to 20 minutes, or until cookies are very lightly browned on bottoms and firm to the touch. Remove to wire racks to cool.
4. Dust cookies with confectioners' sugar. Store in tightly covered container.

Wine note: Walnuts call for port, but that need not be the end of possibilities for these cookies. Cream sherry would sip well, as would a still or sparkling Muscat or one of the sweeter Israeli wines that usually have the word *golden* as part of their name.

Fish Roe Dip—*Tarama*
Fish Turkish Style—*Kapama*
Okra—*Bamias*
Stuffed Onions—*Cebollas Rellenas*
Spinach with Chickpeas—*Spinaca con Garbanzos*
Stuffed Zucchini—*Calabasas Rellenas*
Fried Vermicelli—*Fideos*
Pastry Horns—*Travados*

Fish Roe Dip

Tarama

MAKES 1 CUP

*Several Mediterranean countries have a version of this piquant dip.
Serve it with cut-up raw vegetables or triangles of pita bread.*

2 heaping tablespoons tarama (carp roe)
4 slices white sandwich bread, crusts removed, torn into
  small pieces
1 cup olive oil or vegetable oil
  Juice of 2 large lemons
  Pita bread, French bread, raw vegetables, or crackers

1. In small bowl, combine carp roe, bread, and oil. Beat 5 minutes
with electric mixer at medium speed.
2. Gradually add $\frac{1}{2}$ cup ice water and lemon juice; continue beating
at high speed until mixture becomes smooth.
3. Cover dip and refrigerate several hours, or up to 3 days, to blend
flavors. Serve with pita bread, French bread, raw vegetables, or
crackers for dipping.

NOTE: Kosher carp roe is available fresh or in jars at specialty food stores, delicatessens, and Middle Eastern groceries. Be sure to use very cold ice water in this recipe.

Wine note: A perfect opportunity to bring out Sancerre, the white wine that partners fish so well. Other French wines for this dish would include Pinot Blanc, white Bordeaux, or Chablis.

Fish Turkish Style

Kapama

MAKES 6 SERVINGS

1 whole 3- to 4-pound striped bass or snapper
  Salt and freshly ground black pepper to taste
5 tablespoons olive oil or vegetable oil
2 onions, peeled and thinly sliced
2 large potatoes, parboiled, peeled, and thinly sliced
1 green bell pepper, seeded and thinly sliced
2 fresh tomatoes, peeled and chopped
$\frac{1}{2}$ cup tomato sauce
  Juice of 2 lemons
$\frac{1}{2}$ cup chopped parsley

1. Remove head and tail from fish and discard. Cut fish into 3-inch slices and season with salt and pepper to taste; set aside.
2. In large skillet, heat oil over medium-high heat. Add onions and sauté about 5 minutes, or until translucent but not brown, stirring often. Remove from heat. Add potatoes, green pepper, and tomatoes to skillet; arrange in even layer in bottom of pan. Lay fish pieces on top of onion mixture.

3. Dilute tomato sauce with ¾ cup water and lemon juice; pour over fish. Bring to a boil over high heat. Reduce heat to low; cover and simmer 10 minutes.

4. Sprinkle fish with parsley; cover and simmer 5 to 10 minutes longer, or until fish is opaque. (Cooking time depends on thickness of fish; do not overcook.) Serve immediately.

Wine note: The tomatoes call for red wine, even though the fish by itself would require white. A light Chianti, Valpolicella, Minervois, or proprietary Israeli red would do. If white wine is a must, a weighty Chardonnay from California or Burgundy might fit the bill of fare.

Okra

Bamias

MAKES 4 TO 6 SERVINGS

When this dish is served in Turkish homes, its appearance is very striking. I have a very clear picture of the okra being arranged in concentric circles like the spokes of a wheel, with the tomato placed in the center to form the hub.

1	pound small fresh okra or two 10-ounce packages frozen okra, thawed, rinsed, and drained
3 to 4	cloves garlic, peeled and chopped
2 to 3	fresh tomatoes, peeled and chopped
	Salt and freshly ground black pepper to taste
3	tablespoons olive oil
	Juice of 2 lemons

1. Cut tips off okra and discard. Set okra aside.
2. In large skillet, combine garlic and tomatoes. Arrange okra on top; sprinkle with salt and pepper to taste. Add 1 cup water; dribble oil evenly over all ingredients.
3. Place skillet over medium heat; cover and cook 15 minutes. Add lemon juice; uncover and cook until most of liquid evaporates.
4. To serve, arrange okra in concentric circles on round platter; place chopped tomato in center. Serve warm.

Stuffed Onions

Cebollas Rellenas

MAKES 6 SERVINGS

This is one of the most requested Sephardic dishes at my catering functions, and a great favorite in my cooking classes. The recipe has been handed down through my relatives for several generations.

     10 medium onions
      1 pound ground beef
      3 slices white bread, soaked in water
1 to 2 pinches ground cumin (optional)
         Salt and freshly ground black pepper to taste
      1 egg
         All-purpose flour
         Vegetable oil for frying
      1 teaspoon sugar
      1 cup canned plum tomatoes, undrained

1. Peel onions and cut crosswise in half. With small knife, scoop out center from each onion, leaving shells intact. Chop centers and set shells and chopped onions aside.

2. In medium bowl, combine ground beef, bread, cumin, and salt and pepper to taste. Fill onion shells with meat filling.

3. In shallow bowl, beat egg. Dip stuffed onions in flour and then in beaten egg, coating all sides; set aside.

4. In large skillet, heat about $\frac{1}{2}$ inch oil until hot over medium heat. Fry stuffed onions in hot oil, meat side first, until lightly golden on both sides. Remove from skillet and set aside.

5. Drain most of oil from skillet, leaving about 2 tablespoons. Add reserved chopped onion and sugar; stir to combine. Stir in tomatoes and their liquid and salt to taste. Simmer over medium-low heat 10 to 15 minutes, or until chopped onions are tender, stirring often.

6. Meanwhile, preheat oven to 350°F. Transfer tomato-onion mixture to large rectangular baking dish; arrange stuffed onions on top. Cover with aluminum foil and bake about $1\frac{1}{2}$ hours, or until stuffed onions are tender and most of liquid has been absorbed. Serve with cooked rice or bulgur.

Wine note: A good red wine, just about any one with lots of fruit, a little tannin, and some peppery quality would match up nicely. Bordeaux, Burgundy, the Rhônes, Rioja, and Cabernets from around the world all love beef and onions for their own reasons.

Spinach with Chickpeas

Spinaca con Garbanzos

MAKES 6 SERVINGS

3 tablespoons olive oil or vegetable oil
1 medium onion, peeled and chopped
1½ pounds fresh spinach, washed and drained,
    or two 10-ounce packages frozen leaf spinach,
    thawed and drained
1 cup cooked or canned chickpeas, drained
¼ cup tomato sauce
    Salt and freshly ground black pepper to taste
    Pinch of sugar
    Juice of ½ lemon

1. In large saucepan or dutch oven, heat oil over medium heat. Add onion; sauté about 5 minutes until tender, stirring often.
2. Stir in spinach, chickpeas, tomato sauce, salt and pepper to taste, and sugar. Reduce heat to low; cover and simmer 15 minutes.
3. Stir in lemon juice; cover and cook 10 minutes longer. Serve hot.

Stuffed Zucchini

Calabasas Rellenas

MAKES 6 SERVINGS

These are an alternative to the stuffed onions on this menu. I sometimes serve the zucchini with fideos (recipe follows) for a light supper or side dish.

5 to 6 zucchini, about 5 to 6 inches long and $1\frac{1}{2}$ inches in diameter
3 to 4 scallions, cut into pieces
    2 medium tomatoes, peeled and seeded
    2 large cloves garlic, peeled and chopped
    3 tablespoons plus 1 teaspoon vegetable oil or olive oil
   $\frac{1}{2}$ pound ground beef
    2 tablespoons uncooked rice
    1 tablespoon chopped fresh parsley or dill
     Salt and freshly ground black pepper
   $\frac{1}{2}$ cup tomato sauce

1. Cut each zucchini crosswise in half. Trim ends and scoop out centers, leaving shell intact; reserve zucchini centers. (Trimmed zucchini should resemble hollow tubes.)
2. Chop zucchini centers with scallions, 1 tomato, and 1 garlic clove; mix well. In dutch oven, heat 3 tablespoons oil over medium-high heat. Add chopped zucchini mixture and cook 10 minutes, stirring often. Remove from heat; spread into an even layer on bottom of pot.
3. In medium bowl, combine ground beef, rice, 1 teaspoon oil, 1 chopped garlic clove, 1 chopped tomato, parsley or dill, 1 tablespoon water, and salt and pepper to taste; mix well. Fill zucchini tubes with meat mixture and place on zucchini mixture in pot.
4. Pour in about $\frac{1}{2}$ cup water and the tomato sauce. Sprinkle zucchini with salt and pepper to taste. Place over medium heat and bring to a boil. Reduce heat to low; cover and simmer about $1\frac{1}{2}$ hours, or until zucchini are tender and meat is cooked through. Serve hot.

Wine note: Just about the same wines as for Cebollas Rellenas (see page 119), except a notch less good, as the zucchini isn't as fine a match for wine as is onion.

Fried Vermicelli

Fideos

MAKES 4 TO 6 SERVINGS

This type of pasta is also referred to as Sephardic vermicelli. I usually buy a brand in which the thin strands are coiled in the package.

　　　　Vegetable oil for frying
　One　6-ounce package fideos (long thin coiled pasta)
　One　8-ounce can tomato sauce
　　1　teaspoon salt
　　　　Freshly ground black pepper to taste

1. In medium skillet, heat oil over medium-high heat. Add fideos and fry until golden brown on both sides. Remove from heat.
2. In large saucepan over medium-high heat, combine $1\frac{1}{2}$ cups water, tomato sauce, salt, and pepper to taste; bring to a boil. Add fideos; reduce heat to low. Cover and cook 10 to 15 minutes, or until liquid is absorbed and fideos are tender, stirring occasionally. To serve, sprinkle with additional pepper.

Pastry Horns

Travados

An authentic Turkish-style dessert made with a nut-and-honey filling.

FILLING

  2 cups ground walnuts
  2 tablespoons honey
  $\frac{1}{2}$ teaspoon ground cinnamon
    Pinch of ground cloves

DOUGH

    About 3 cups all-purpose flour
    Pinch of baking soda
  1 cup vegetable oil
  $\frac{3}{4}$ cup orange juice
  $\frac{1}{4}$ cup sugar

SYRUP

  $1\frac{1}{2}$ cups sugar
  $\frac{3}{4}$ cup water
  $\frac{3}{4}$ cup honey
  1 teaspoon freshly squeezed lemon juice

1. Preheat oven to 350°F. Grease cookie sheets.
2. In small bowl, combine nuts, 2 tablespoons honey, 1 teaspoon water, cinnamon, and cloves. Mix well, using a bit more water if necessary to hold mixture together, and set aside.
3. In large bowl, combine flour and baking soda. Stir in oil, orange juice, and sugar to form a soft dough. With hands, roll dough into small balls and flatten into 2-inch circles. Place about $\frac{1}{2}$ teaspoon nut filling in center of each; fold dough over filling and press edges together to seal, forming turnovers.

4. Place on cookie sheets and bake 20 to 25 minutes, or until lightly browned. Remove to wire racks to cool.

5. Meanwhile, prepare syrup: In medium saucepan over medium-high heat, combine sugar and water; bring to a boil. Add $\frac{3}{4}$ cup honey and lemon juice; continue boiling gently 10 to 15 minutes, until mixture spins a thread when a little is pulled out with a spoon. Drop cooled travados, a few at a time, into syrup, coating all sides. Remove and place on plate to cool again.

Iraqi-Syrian

*P*ositioned as they are in the crossroads of the Middle East, Iraq and Syria have been occupied by several different racial and religious groups through the years. Babylonians, Greeks, Assyrians, conquerers from Arabia, Jews, Muslims, and Christians are among those who have left their mark, forever affecting the culture and cuisine of these lands.

Iraq has also been known as Mesopotamia, that part of the world considered the cradle of civilization. Flowing through the center of the country and out to the Persian Gulf, the Tigris and Euphrates rivers embrace a lush growing area. This very arable piece of land was often referred to as "the fertile crescent." On the shores of the Tigris River stands the legendary city of Baghdad, well situated for its role as a major center of trade in the Middle East.

Jews have lived in this part of the world since Biblical times, the Jewish community dating back to the days following the destruction of the first temple. The Babylonian conquerers exiled the Jews from Israel (Canaan), and many fled to the fertile crescent, then part of Babylonia. Although some Jews soon returned to their homeland, others stayed on and prospered. Jewish life flourished for many centuries in Iraq and Syria, until the political climate grew unfriendly in the early 1970s.

My own family is descended from a long line of Talmudic scholars. In fact, my great-grandfather was the chief rabbi in Baghdad and the author of several books on Judaism. Other Jews became merchants, bankers, and doctors—education was always of top importance in our families.

Iraqi and Syrian Jews ran their lives and households according to the Sephardic tradition. Therefore, the food customs that evolved were similar to those of the Jews in Turkey, Iran, Morocco, and other Middle Eastern and North African countries. But there were some notable differences, based on the unique ethnic mix of the population, the available natural resources, and the ingenuity of Iraqi and Syrian cooks.

The mild climate and rich soil in both these countries have been hospitable to the cultivation of lemons, mangoes, oranges, dates, and quince. Among vegetables, tomatoes, eggplant, squash, beets, and peppers proliferate. These are often filled with rice and/or meat stuffings enhanced with spices, almonds, and/or dried fruits. Nuts and dried beans are other native crops that have made their way into a number of dishes. And, as in other Middle Eastern countries, rice is the grain eaten at most meals.

Main dishes focus on lamb, chicken, and sometimes, fish. As my mother remembers it, the lamb raised in her birthplace is much leaner than American lamb, because all the fat is bred into the tail. This makes the meat perfect for barbecuing, baking, skewering on kebobs, stewing, or grinding for meatballs. Beef is usually cooked by the same methods. Shesta kebob—meatballs made from ground beef, parsley, and other seasonings, then cooked on a skewer—is the national dish of Iraq. In fact, meatballs of many kinds are prevalent in Syrian and Iraqi cuisine.

Since these have long been Muslim nations, pork is not part of the diet. This prohibition has made it relatively easy for Sephardic Jews to prepare a variety of Arab-style dishes without changing the ingredients. The meat they used, however, was kashered according to Jewish dietary laws, as the Muslims used different slaughtering techniques. The fish eaten are mostly the freshwater species, and may be barbecued or smoked over charcoal—typical Middle Eastern cooking styles used on a number of foods. Shellfish, on the other hand, are not readily available and have never gained importance in these cuisines, a plus for the Sephardic cook.

Spices and herbs have achieved great status in Iraqi and Syrian cooking. They're still sold loose in the bazaars of Baghdad and Damascus as they have been for centuries, an affirmation of their value to the countries' culinary heritages. My family's recipe file includes beef marinated in saffron, grated onion, and lemon juice, and barbecued lamb topped with an edible form of sumac. Other spices used extensively include cinnamon, cumin, coriander, and allspice. Desserts are typically flavored with orange-flower water or rosewater.

Although rice is the main starch in the Middle Eastern diet, breads and bulgur are not too distant seconds. Afghan-style bread or lavash (thin Middle Eastern bread) is often eaten for breakfast along with feta cheese and eggs with dates. Aside from this morning meal and an occasional dairy supper or Shabbat lunch, perishable milk products were not used a great deal, making it all the more simple for the Sephardic Jews to adapt Arab dishes.

My mother and I have worked together to develop the menus offered here. The first is for a traditional Shabbat meal, featuring tabeet—a dish that cooks in the oven all Friday night to be served as a hot meal on Saturday. The other menu highlights two recipes that use delicate phyllo dough—one a savory appetizer, the second a sweet dessert. Along with the other festive dishes included here, this menu could make an interesting company meal. Iraqis and Syrians love entertaining, and our parties usually revolve around three to four main dishes, a few different kinds of rice, and several salads, as well as an assortment of desserts. Our scaled-down, mostly do-ahead meal is more in line with today's busy life-styles.

Although Syrian and Iraqi foods may sound exotic, the ingredients used to prepare them are fairly easy to find in most large supermarkets. With the influx to the States of Syrians, Iranians, Iraqis, and Lebanese in recent years, Middle Eastern grocery stores are springing up in a number of American cities. These specialty shops stock a variety of ingredients, including the more unusual ones needed to make authentic Middle Eastern dishes.

—*Carole Basri*

Carole Basri and Annette Basri

Although both Carole Basri and her mother, Annette, are of Iraqi descent, Carole was born in England and Annette in Belgium. When Annette was eleven, she returned with her parents to her homeland, taking up residence in Baghdad. In the first half of the twentieth century, Jews were well respected in Iraq, living in harmony with the Arabs, who were taught by Mohammed to treat the Jews as brothers. Both men and women received excellent educations, often going abroad for their studies. The result was a significant number of Jewish professionals who, along with their families, led comfortable, fulfilling lives.

In 1949, Annette moved to the United States, but two years later she returned to England to marry an Iraqi-Jewish doctor. In the postwar years, London had a fairly large and active Iraqi-Jewish community. Soon after Carole was born, the Basris left England for America, settling in New Jersey.

In her kitchen in the States, Annette Basri was able to duplicate the Sephardic specialties she picked up as a child from her family's servants. Carole was often by her side, learning the recipes and traditions she would later pass on to her own family. Today, Carole Basri carries on this food heritage in her own home in New York City. She divides her time between being a lawyer for an apparel company, a mother to twin boys, and an occasional cooking teacher. She and Annette have taught several classes in Iraqi cuisine at the 92nd Street Y, each personalizing the dishes presented with their own experiences and expertise.

Annette Basri now lives in Lakewood, New Jersey, about twenty miles from a large and very cohesive Sephardic community in Deale. Deale boasts several Middle Eastern-style kosher restaurants, groceries, and bakeries, as well as a formidable Sephardic synagogue—all catering to the Syrian, Iranian, and Iraqi Jews who live in and around this vital community.

Sweet and Sour Meatballs—*Kubba Bamish*
Stuffed Grape Leaves—*Dolmahs*
Chicken Baked in a Pot—*Tabeet*
Beef Phyllo Rolls—*Burag*
Nut Pastries—*Malfuf*

Sweet and Sour Meatballs

Kubba Bamish

MAKES 4 SERVINGS

Kubba actually means "meatball" in Iraqi. The Sephardim are very fond of meatballs, and this recipe is just one of many in our repertoire. These can be prepared ahead and frozen, then cooked when needed.

        1 pound lean ground beef
    $\frac{1}{2}$ cup finely chopped parsley
    $\frac{1}{4}$ cup dry bread crumbs
        Salt and freshly ground black pepper to taste
    $\frac{1}{8}$ teaspoon ground turmeric or cumin
        1 small onion, peeled and chopped
        2 medium-sized fresh tomatoes, peeled, seeded, and
           chopped
      One 10-ounce package frozen baby okra, thawed,
           or 1 pound fresh okra
           Juice of 3 lemons
        2 tablespoons brown sugar (optional)
           Cooked white rice

1. In medium bowl, combine ground beef, parsley, bread crumbs, $\frac{1}{4}$ cup water, salt and pepper to taste, and turmeric or cumin; blend well.

2. With palms of hands, form mixture into meatballs 1 inch in diameter; set aside. (At this point, meatballs can be frozen.)

3. In large saucepan, bring 3 cups water to a boil over medium-high heat. Add onion, tomatoes, and okra; return to a boil.

4. Add meatballs, lemon juice, and salt and pepper to taste. Reduce heat to low; cover and simmer 20 minutes. If you prefer a sweet-sour taste, stir in brown sugar; cook 5 minutes longer. Serve with rice.

Wine note: A rosé or light red wine is best for this dish; a sparkling rosé if the sugar is included in the ingredients. Choose from Chianti, Valpolicella, Barbera, the Rhônes, or Beaujolais among the reds; white Zinfandel, white Gamay, or Cabernet Blanc in the rosé or blush category. Italy and Spain produce good kosher sparkling rosés. In addition, there are a few semidry red wines produced in Israel that might match this dish when it's sweet and sour.

Stuffed Grape Leaves

Dolmahs

MAKES 6 SERVINGS

Serve these nibbles before or with the meal. We can usually find Orlando grape leaves—a kosher brand that's readily available in supermarkets and Middle Eastern delis.

    25 to 30 grape leaves in brine
    1 to 1½ cups instant rice
        1½ tablespoons dried dill weed
         1 tablespoon chopped onion

$\frac{1}{4}$ medium tomato, peeled, seeded, and chopped
Salt and freshly ground black pepper to taste
3 tablespoons olive oil
2 tablespoons freshly squeezed lemon juice

1. Preheat oven to 350°F. Drain grape leaves and soak for 5 minutes in enough water to cover. Drain; remove and discard stems.
2. In small bowl, mix well rice, dill weed, onion, tomato, salt and pepper to taste, and 1 tablespoon olive oil for stuffing.
3. Place each grape leaf, shiny side down, on work surface. Place 1 tablespoon stuffing on each leaf. Fold three sides of leaf over stuffing; roll up leaf, jelly roll style, and tuck in end.
4. In 12- by 8-inch baking dish, place stuffed grape leaves, seam side down. In small bowl, combine $\frac{1}{2}$ cup water, lemon juice, and remaining 2 tablespoons oil; pour on top of stuffed leaves. Cover and bake 15 minutes, or until heated through.

N O T E : If you have extra grape leaves, lay them flat on top of stuffed ones for protection during baking.

Wine note: A dry sparkling wine is just right when serving these as an appetizer; there are good bottles produced in Italy, France, and Israel.

Chicken Baked in a Pot

Tabeet

MAKES 4 SERVINGS

Tabeet makes an excellent Shabbat meal; it starts cooking on Friday before sundown and is then kept over a low flame or in a 200°F oven overnight to be eaten on Saturday. If you prefer, you can cook the dish by a faster method we've developed—directions for both techniques are provided.

One $2\frac{1}{2}$-pound chicken
1 cup uncooked instant rice
$\frac{1}{4}$ cup diced cube steak
2 medium tomatoes, peeled, seeded, and chopped
$\frac{1}{8}$ teaspoon crushed cardamom pods or ground cardamom
1 tablespoon olive oil
1 medium onion, peeled and chopped
Salt and freshly ground black pepper to taste
$1\frac{1}{2}$ cups uncooked long-grain rice, rinsed

1. Rinse chicken and pat dry. In small bowl, combine instant rice, steak, half of 1 chopped tomato, and cardamom; mix well. Stuff chicken with rice mixture and close cavity with skewers or thread.
2. In dutch oven, heat oil over medium heat. Sauté onion in hot oil 5 minutes, stirring often. Add remaining $1\frac{1}{2}$ chopped tomatoes, 3 cups water, and salt and pepper to taste; bring to a boil. Add the stuffed chicken; boil 15 minutes over medium heat.
3. Stir in long-grain rice; cook until most of water is absorbed. Reduce heat to very low. For quick results, cover and cook 1 hour 15 minutes, or bake in 350°F oven for 2 hours, or until chicken is tender and water is all absorbed. Or bake in a 200°F oven overnight to use for a Shabbat meal.

Wine note: Bring out a red Bordeaux for this dish, especially one from the Medoc or St. Emilion. From the States, a Cabernet from California should never be turned down, except for the nonmevushal Cabernets, which have a bit too much tannin for this dish.

Beef Phyllo Rolls

Burag

MAKES 4 TO 6 SERVINGS

Made with phyllo dough, this meat-filled pastry is similar to the Turkish borek and the Moroccan garro.

$\frac{1}{4}$ cup light vegetable oil, preferably safflower
1 small onion, peeled and chopped
1 pound lean ground beef
$\frac{1}{4}$ cup chopped parsley
$\frac{1}{2}$ cup fresh or thawed frozen peas
1 teaspoon ground cinnamon
 Salt and freshly ground black pepper to taste
1 pound fresh or defrosted frozen phyllo dough
 or strudel leaves

1. Preheat oven to 375°F. In medium skillet, heat 1 tablespoon oil over medium-high heat. Sauté onion in hot oil 5 minutes, stirring often. Add ground beef and parsley; cook until meat loses its red color, stirring often. Gently stir in peas, cinnamon, and salt and pepper to taste; cook 3 to 5 minutes longer. Remove from heat and let cool.
2. Stack phyllo sheets on oiled work surface; cut crosswise in half. Work with 1 or 2 pieces of phyllo at a time; cover unused sheets with towel.

3. On each half sheet of phyllo, place 1 heaping tablespoon meat mixture across narrow end closest to you (fig. A). Roll dough over to cover meat (fig. B), then fold sides of phyllo in to meet at center (fig. C). Continue rolling phyllo over meat, jelly roll style, to form a cylinder (fig. D).

4. Brush burags all over with oil, using about $\frac{1}{2}$ teaspoon per side. Arrange on cookie sheet and bake 15 minutes, or until golden. Serve warm.

NOTE: If meat mixture is too stiff, stir in a little water to break it up.

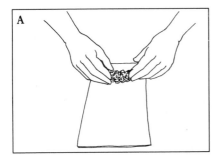
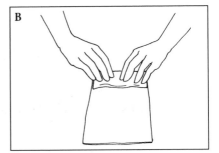
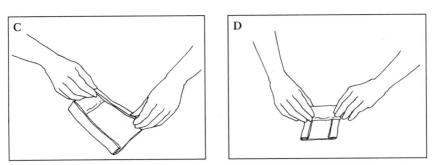

BURAG

Nut Pastries

Malfuf

MAKES 6 SERVINGS

With just a hint of sweetness, these delicate treats make a light but satisfying dessert. We would typically serve these or similar pastries on a dessert plate accompanied by dried fruits, fresh fruits, nuts, and kaah, a type of halvah.

    2 cups shelled whole almonds, pistachios, or walnuts,
      blanched and finely ground
    ½ cup sugar
    1 tablespoon orange-flower water or rosewater
    ½ pound fresh or defrosted frozen phyllo dough or strudel
      leaves

1. Preheat oven to 350°F. In medium bowl, blend well ground nuts, sugar, and orange-flower water or rosewater.
2. On oiled work surface, stack phyllo leaves; cut in half crosswise. Remove 1 sheet at a time; cover remaining sheets with a damp towel.
3. On each half sheet, spread 1 to 2 teaspoons nut mixture along narrow end closest to you (fig. A). Fold dough about 1½ inches over nut mixture (fig. B).
4. Insert a clean new pencil or a narrow wooden stick below fold-over (fig. C). Roll dough around pencil to make a narrow cigar shape (fig. D). Press dough in from both ends to pleat (fig. E); gently remove pencil (fig. F).
5. Place pastries in ungreased 13- by 9-inch baking pan or cookie sheet. Bake about 10 minutes, or until golden. Cool slightly before serving.

Wine note: Light dessert wines are a good accompaniment for these lightly sweet pastries: sparkling or still Muscat, one of the golden sweet or semidry (which means semisweet) wines from Israel, or perhaps one of the New York State sparklers.

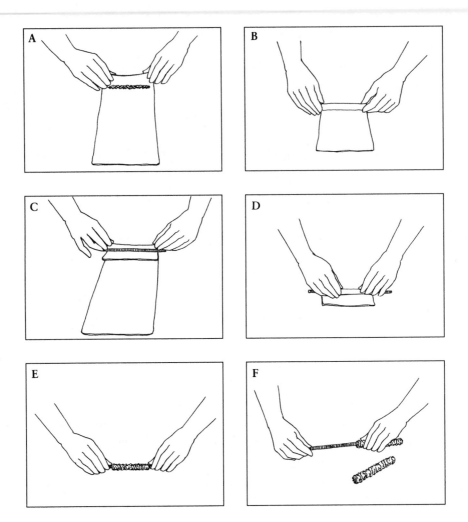

MALFUF

Sesame Paste Dip—*Tahini Dip*
Beef and Eggplant Casserole—*Engreyee*
Iraqi-style Rice
Chicken Phyllo Rolls—*Burag Bejag*
Stuffed Vegetables—*Mahasha*
Baklava (Syrup-soaked Pastry)—*Baklowa*

Sesame Paste Dip

Tahini Dip

MAKES 4 SERVINGS

Accompanied with pita bread and raw vegetables, this dip is a good way to curb hunger while waiting for dinner.

$\frac{1}{2}$ cup tahini (sesame paste)
$\frac{1}{4}$ to $\frac{1}{3}$ cup freshly squeezed lemon juice
About $\frac{1}{4}$ cup water
2 or 3 cloves garlic, peeled and minced
Pita bread and assorted cut-up raw vegetables

1. Place tahini in small bowl. Stir in enough lemon juice and water to form a creamy consistency. Stir in garlic.
2. Serve with pita bread and raw vegetables for dipping.

Wine note: Sipping wine also helps to while away the predinner period. A dry sparkling wine from the Loire or Champagne would not be amiss; don't overlook the dry Italian or Israeli sparklers, either.

Beef and Eggplant Casserole

Engreyee

We find Syrian and Iraqi cooking to be very flexible. As a rule, recipes need not be followed exactly as far as ingredient amounts go. For example, adding a little more onion or lemon juice won't hurt this dish a bit, and might even enhance its flavors.

2 medium eggplants, peeled
¼ cup vegetable oil, preferably safflower
1 pound cube steak, cut into bite-sized pieces
1 large onion, peeled and chopped
½ cup freshly squeezed lemon juice
2 tablespoons tomato paste
2 large tomatoes, peeled (if desired), and sliced
Hot cooked rice

1. Preheat broiler. Cut eggplant into 1-inch-thick slices; brush on both sides with oil. Place eggplant on broiler pan in single layer. Broil 2 minutes on each side until lightly browned.

2. Preheat oven to 400°F. In 12- by 8-inch nonmetal baking dish, combine steak, onion, 2 cups water, lemon juice, and tomato paste; mix well. Arrange tomatoes and eggplant slices on top of meat mixture.

3. Cover with foil and bake 35 minutes. Remove foil and bake 5 minutes longer, or until meat and vegetables are tender. Serve with rice.

Wine note: Try a red wine of medium body and intensity for this entrée: the lesser Bordeaux, Italian, Spanish, and proprietary Israeli wines would match.

Iraqi-style Rice

MAKES 6 SERVINGS

The Iraqis always rinse rice before cooking to remove excess starch. We recommend using basmati rice or a good brand of long-grain rice.

2 tablespoons margarine
2 cups rice, rinsed and drained

1. In medium saucepan, melt margarine over high heat. Add 2 cups water and bring to a boil.
2. Stir in rice and cook, stirring, until most of water is absorbed.
3. Reduce heat to low; cover and simmer about 10 minutes longer, or until water is completely absorbed.

Chicken Phyllo Rolls

Burag Bejag

MAKES 4 SERVINGS

We created this chicken phyllo roll as a variation to the beef-filled burag in the preceding menu (see illustration on page 134). It's a lighter, more delicate version of a Middle Eastern classic.

$\frac{1}{4}$ cup vegetable oil, preferably safflower
1 medium onion, peeled and chopped
2 cups diced cooked chicken
1 cup fresh or defrosted frozen peas
$\frac{1}{2}$ cup chopped parsley
   Salt and freshly ground black pepper to taste
$\frac{1}{2}$ pound fresh or defrosted frozen phyllo dough or
   strudel leaves

1. Preheat oven to 375°F. In medium skillet, heat 1 tablespoon oil over medium heat. Add onion; sauté 5 minutes, stirring often. Stir in chicken, peas, parsley, and salt and pepper to taste; cook 3 minutes longer. Remove from heat.

2. Stack phyllo sheets on oiled work surface; cut crosswise in half. Remove 1 piece of phyllo at a time; cover unused sheets with damp towel.

3. On each half sheet of phyllo, spread 1 tablespoon chicken mixture across narrow end closest to you. Roll phyllo over to cover chicken, then fold sides of phyllo in to meet at center. Continue rolling phyllo up over chicken, jelly roll style, to form a cylinder.

4. Brush burags all over with oil, using about $\frac{1}{2}$ teaspoon per side. Arrange on cookie sheet and bake 15 minutes, until golden. Serve warm.

NOTE: To fry burags, heat remaining 3 tablespoons oil in large skillet over medium-high heat. Add burags and fry about 3 minutes, or until golden, turning several times during cooking.

Wine note: A rosé is probably your best choice.

Stuffed Vegetables

Mahasha

MAKES 6 SERVINGS

Mahasha—*an assortment of whole vegetables stuffed with a meat and rice mixture—are very popular in Iraq and Syria. In the fall, we often stuff a whole, hollowed-out pumpkin with a similar filling, enhanced with almonds, raisins, and cinnamon.*

4 fresh beets, or one 16-ounce can whole beets, drained
1 large onion
2 large green bell peppers
2 large tomatoes
2 medium zucchini
1 pound lean ground beef or ground lamb
1 cup regular long-grain rice
$\frac{1}{2}$ cup freshly squeezed lemon juice
2 tablespoons olive oil
   Salt and freshly ground black pepper to taste
2 tablespoons brown sugar (optional)

1. Prepare vegetables for stuffing: Peel and core beets, reserving centers. Peel and carefully scoop out center of onion, leaving several outer layers for shell; reserve center. Cut tops off peppers; remove and discard seeds and core. Cut tomatoes in half; scoop out seeds and pulp, leaving outer shell; reserve pulp. Cut zucchini lengthwise in half; scoop out pulp and reserve.

2. Chop reserved centers and pulp from all vegetables and place in medium bowl. Add ground beef, rice, 2 tablespoons lemon juice, olive oil, and salt and pepper to taste. Stuff meat mixture into vegetable shells.

3. Arrange vegetables in a single layer in large deep skillet or dutch oven. (You may need to use two pots.) Sprinkle remaining lemon juice on top and add salt and pepper to taste.

4. Place over medium-high heat and bring to a boil. Reduce heat to low; cover and simmer 1 hour, or until vegetables are tender. If you like a sweet-sour taste, stir in brown sugar and cook 5 minutes longer. Serve hot.

NOTE: Mahasha may also be cooked in the oven. Preheat oven to 350°F. Arrange vegetables in 1 or 2 baking dishes and sprinkle with lemon juice. Cover with foil and bake about 1 hour, or until tender.

Wine note: The stuffing's the thing, here, and a hearty red wine is needed. Think Merlot, Bordeaux, the Rhônes, and even some mevushal Cabernet from California or the proprietary reds from Israel.

Baklava (Syrup-soaked Pastry)

Baklowa

Our baklava is perfumed with rosewater, a characteristic Middle Eastern flavor. It's less sweet than the similar Turkish rendition that's soaked in honey or syrup, but should please the most discriminating dessert lover.

2 cups whole shelled almonds, blanched and finely ground
1 cup sugar
$\frac{1}{4}$ cup rosewater or orange-flower water
1 pound fresh or defrosted frozen phyllo dough or strudel leaves
1 cup (2 sticks) margarine, melted

1. Preheat oven to 350°F. In medium bowl, combine almonds, sugar, and rosewater.
2. In 15- by 10-inch jelly roll pan, layer 3 or 4 sheets phyllo; brush with melted margarine. Repeat with 3 or 4 additional sheets phyllo, brushing with margarine once more. Spread half the almond mixture evenly over the phyllo. Repeat layering phyllo sheets and brushing with margarine twice more; spread with remaining almond mixture. Layer remaining phyllo sheets on top, brushing with margarine as before.
3. With sharp knife, make diagonal cuts in phyllo in both directions, about $1\frac{1}{2}$ inches apart, almost to the bottom. Brush remaining margarine on top.
4. Bake about 20 minutes, or until golden brown. Let cool on wire rack before serving.
5. To serve, cut all the way through phyllo into diamond-shaped portions.

Thai

*t*he food habits of Thailand have largely been molded by its neighbors—Burma and India to the west, China to the north, and the Indochinese countries of Cambodia, Laos, and Vietnam to the east. The result is a cuisine that is a delicious amalgamation of Indian, Chinese, and Southeast Asian cooking styles. What sets Thai cooking apart, however, is its unique blend of sweet, spicy, and salty flavors, and its exciting contrast of textures and temperatures.

The people who currently call themselves Thai came to their country from southwestern China in the thirteenth century. Then part of the Cambodian Empire, Thailand was already inhabited by Indian and Chinese settlers. After many years of battle with the Cambodians and other hostile neighbors, Thailand established its present borders and became an independent land. In fact, it's the only country in Southeast Asia that has never been occupied by a foreign power. Nevertheless, much of the culture and many customs of the nation's Indian and Chinese forebears have been retained, particularly in the culinary realm. Thailand's population is now composed of about 85 percent of the original Thais, 12 percent Chinese, and a 3 percent mix of Malaysian, Cambodian, and Vietnamese, and its cooking reflects this composition.

My collaborator and friend Pojanee Vatanapan, nicknamed Penny by her American family, grew up in a small village in south-central Thailand. Her family is part Chinese, and many of the dishes she ate as a child were her mother's versions of Chinese favorites. The Chinese introduced stir-frying to Thailand, and a number of typical Thai recipes are based on this quick-cooking method. India is represented in the Thai dishes known as kaengs, which are quite similar to Indian curries. And several of the ingredients used in Thai cuisine—peanuts and fish sauce, for example—show up repeatedly in Vietnamese cooking.

The food products that grow in Thailand have also affected its culinary style. Peanuts, coconuts, palm trees (the sap of which is made into palm sugar), citrus fruits, and rice thrive in Thai soil, as do an assortment of plants used for seasoning. Many Thai dishes are perfumed with the distinct flavors of tamarind (a pod that imparts a sour taste), lemon grass (a fragrant tall grass), galanga root (similar in appearance to fresh ginger but with a special flavor of its own), cilantro, and chile peppers. Chinese-style vegetables such as bok choy and bean sprouts are cultivated too, as are beautiful and luscious papayas, melons, and other tropical fruits.

Thai cooks in the cities and villages have access to the freshest ingredients. Penny tells many stories about her shopping trips to the floating market that traveled down the canal near her house. Vendors piled fruits, vegetables, condiments, meats, poultry, fish, and other items on long rafts and sold their wares from the water. At the shore, Penny's mother stood and bartered with the vendors each morning, trying to get the best products at the best price. Then she would take her groceries home and start the day's meal preparations.

Dinner usually consisted of a large bowl of rice, one or two soups, a nonspicy stir-fried vegetable dish, a curry dish (kaeng), a pad (a spicy meat or fish dish), and sometimes, a salad on the side. Small amounts of seafood, pork, beef, chicken, or duck are the main sources of protein in the Thai diet. For lunch, noodles are popular, served either in a soup or a stir-fried dish. Most meals in Thailand are eaten with Western-style silverware, but chopsticks are always used with noodle dishes. Thai noodles are most commonly made of rice flour or mung bean flour. Like most other Thai ingredients, they are available in oriental groceries located in most larger American cities.

There is no record of a Jewish community existing in Thailand, but Thai recipes can be converted to kosher ones without much difficulty. Dairy products are rare in Thailand, and coconut milk, a pareve ingredient, is used extensively instead of regular milk. Therefore, the possibility of combining dairy and meat in the same dish is almost nonexistent. Since Thai cuisine does have its share of shellfish and pork recipes, however, these have to be adapted to the dietary laws or eliminated. I have found that boneless chicken or turkey can substitute nicely for pork, and a firm, white-fleshed fin fish can replace shrimp or crab. The diverse tastes and textures mingling in Thai cooking more than make up for the absence of seafood and pork.

Through constant testing and tasting, I have also developed a credible replacement for fish sauce (nam pla), one of the main flavorings in many Thai dishes. Although the fish sauce produced in Thailand and other Southeast Asian countries usually does not contain shellfish, it cannot be certified as kosher because it might be processed in the same plant as shrimp paste, another widely used Thai ingredient. In the dishes Penny and I created for the 92nd Street Y cooking classes, we have substituted black soy sauce for fish sauce —an easy recipe for this substitution is provided. I have also worked out recipes for homemade versions of black bean sauce and curry paste.

Americans are probably best acquainted with the classical dishes served in restaurants here and in Bangkok, the capital of Thailand. This is high-style Thai cooking, as opposed to the provincial or peasant cooking done in the villages. Although the techniques are similar, the presentation is much fancier in the former—classical dishes are always served with elaborate, decorative garnishes.

Through years of experience in her mother's kitchen and in restaurants in both Bangkok and New York City, Penny has more or less integrated these two cooking styles, and I have helped adapt them to the Jewish dietary laws. If you wish to serve these meals authentically, do as the Thais do and put everything on the table at once. Each diner gets a large plate of rice, then takes small portions from each dish to combine with the rice. The soup is traditionally placed in a communal bowl in the center of the table to be sipped as a beverage throughout the meal. It's a real family dining experience!
—Linda Alexander

Linda Alexander and Pojanee Vatanapan

Linda Alexander and Pojanee (Penny) Vatanapan met through mutual friends on Manhattan's Upper West Side. At the time, Linda was a songwriter giving guitar lessons on the side, and Penny was cooking Thai food in a nearby restaurant, yearning to play the guitar. Linda agreed to give her guitar lessons in exchange for Thai cooking instruction; thus the two struck a deal and became fast friends.

Linda began to eat many of her meals at Penny's restaurant, becoming enthralled with Thai food in the process. To learn more and earn more, she eventually landed a job waitressing. After serving Thai cuisine every night and eating native dishes with Thai people, Linda became totally ensconced in the Thai community. Friends of hers and Penny's encouraged the two to write a cookbook together; they agreed and sold the idea to a publisher. The result is Pojanee Vatanapan's Thai Cookbook with Linda Alexander (Harmony Books, 1986).

To this joint venture, Penny brought years of cooking experience and a fabulous reputation as a cook, but not much knowledge of recipe writing. She grew up as one of ten children in a small village called Damnoen Saduak in Thailand. As the youngest daughter, it was Penny's responsibility to help her mother shop and cook. She was an eager assistant, and soon mastered the basics of Thai provincial cooking. But like many mothers, Mrs. Vatanapan's idea of cooking was "a little of this and a little of that." Exact recipes weren't written down or followed.

Penny refined her techniques a bit while she was a math student in Bangkok, where she lived with one of her sisters. Several of her sister's friends worked in the large international hotels in this capital city, and would occasionally drop by and cook classical Thai cuisine. Penny watched, tasted, and experimented in the kitchen.

In 1978, Penny moved with her American husband to New York City. Here she opened and operated two very successful Thai restaurants, integrating dishes from both the peasant and classical styles of cooking.

Linda brought her expertise in both writing and food to the book project and the cooking classes the pair gave at the 92nd Street Y. Brought up in the Chicago area and Florida, she has worked as a copywriter for an ad agency, a songwriter and performer, a caterer, a waitress, a cook, and a restaurant promoter.

Linda's mother was a great hostess who gave many parties. As a child, Linda liked to hang out in the kitchen with the caterers and the housekeeper, an accomplished cook from the South. Linda's next kitchen experience, in her teens, found her working at a Jewish summer camp preparing kosher meals. Through the years, Linda has worked in lots of other kitchens, getting involved with all kinds of food. She is now self-employed as a publicist and food stylist, but loves to spend her free time teaching and cooking Thai cuisine.

Marinated Chicken on Skewers with
Peanut–Coconut Milk Dipping Sauce—
Saté Gai Leh Nam Jim Saté
Red Curry Paste—*Nam Prik Kaeng Dang*
Coconut Milk—*Ka-Ti*
Spicy Cucumber Salad—*Thangua Dong*
Spicy Coconut Milk and Chicken Soup—*Tom Kha Gai*
Sautéed Rice Noodles with Beef and Broccoli—*Pad See-um*
Black Soy Sauce
Sweet Rice Pudding with Apricots—*Khow Neeow Sum*

Marinated Chicken on Skewers with Peanut–Coconut Milk Dipping Sauce

Saté Gai Leh Nam Jim Saté

MAKES 4 TO 6 SERVINGS

Although this recipe is typically served as a first course, it can easily be doubled to serve as a main dish. When weather permits, we like to grill the skewered chicken outdoors on the barbecue.

  1½ cups unsweetened Coconut Milk (see page 151)
  1 tablespoon Red Curry Paste (see page 150)
  1 tablespoon soy sauce
  2 teaspoons yellow curry powder
  4 skinless, boneless chicken breast halves (about 1 pound)
    Peanut–Coconut Milk Dipping Sauce (recipe follows)

1. In 12- by 8-inch baking dish, combine coconut milk, red curry paste, soy sauce, and curry powder.
2. Place chicken breasts between 2 sheets of waxed paper. With wooden mallet or heavy skillet, pound chicken to flatten. Cut chicken

into long, narrow strips, about 3 inches long and 1 inch wide. Add chicken to baking dish, coating well with marinade. Cover and marinate in refrigerator at least 5 hours or overnight.

3. Preheat broiler. Drain chicken from marinade. Thread 2 strips of chicken on each 6- to 8-inch bamboo skewer, weaving the strips back and forth (figs. A–D). Place skewers on broiler pan in one layer.

4. Broil chicken 3 to 5 minutes on each side, or until cooked through. Serve hot, with dipping sauce.

N O T E : The bamboo skewers should be soaked in a bowl of cold water for at least 30 minutes before using to prevent them from burning under the broiler. Curry powder is a dried spice blend sold with most kosher dried herbs and spices.

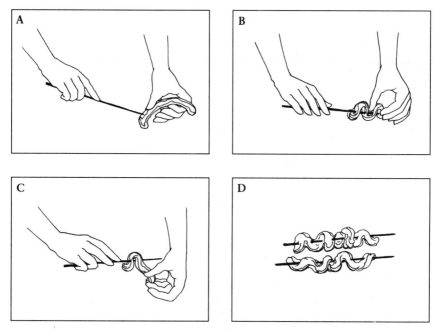

S A T É

$1\frac{1}{2}$ cups Coconut Milk (see page 151)
 1 tablespoon Red Curry Paste (recipe follows)
 $\frac{1}{2}$ cup unsalted chunky-style peanut butter
 2 tablespoons sugar
$1\frac{1}{2}$ tablespoons white vinegar
 1 tablespoon soy sauce

1. In medium saucepan over medium heat, combine $\frac{3}{4}$ cup coconut milk with curry paste. Cook until well blended and pale amber in color, stirring constantly.

2. Add remaining $\frac{3}{4}$ cup coconut milk and all other ingredients. Continue simmering over low heat 8 to 10 minutes longer, until slightly thickened, stirring constantly. Let cool slightly before using.

Red Curry Paste

Nam Prik Kaeng Dang

MAKES $\frac{1}{2}$ CUP

6 to 8 dried red chile peppers
 1 stem fresh lemon grass (white part only), or 1
      teaspoon dried lemon grass (see Note)
 5 cloves garlic, peeled and chopped
 3 medium shallots, peeled and chopped
 1 teaspoon grated lemon peel
 1 teaspoon (about 2 pieces) minced galanga root (kha),
      fresh or dried (see Note)

1. Cut chile peppers into small pieces and soak in 1 cup cold water 15 minutes to soften. Remove seeds from chiles and discard; reserve 2 to 3 tablespoons soaking liquid.

2. Place chile pepper pieces in food processor, blender, or mortar with pestle. Add remaining ingredients; process or pound until thick paste forms. (Texture should be similar to peanut butter; if too thick or dry, add a few drops water or reserved soaking liquid to reach proper consistency.)

3. Store red curry paste in tightly covered container and refrigerate until ready to use. It will keep up to 1 month.

NOTES: Galanga root is available in oriental groceries, either frozen or dried. If frozen, thaw before using. If dried, soak in cold water 15 minutes to soften before using.

Fresh lemon grass is available in Thai groceries and oriental produce markets in larger cities. Dried lemon grass is more accessible—sold wherever oriental ingredients are found.

COCONUT MILK

Ka-Ti

MAKES ABOUT 4½ CUPS

5 cups fresh or dried shredded unsweetened coconut meat
(also known as desiccated coconut)
5 cups boiling water

1. In large bowl, combine coconut meat with boiling water. Let stand at least 2 hours.

2. Strain mixture through 2 layers of fine cheesecloth. Discard coconut; reserve liquid. Liquid may be stored in refrigerator up to 1 week.

NOTE: Shiloh Farms desiccated coconut is widely available at health-food stores.

Spicy Cucumber Salad

Thangua Dong

MAKES 4 TO 6 SERVINGS

*Thais usually serve this as an appetizer along with the chicken saté.
The different textures and temperatures of the two provide an intriguing contrast.*

1 cup white vinegar
$\frac{1}{4}$ cup sugar
$\frac{1}{2}$ teaspoon soy sauce
1 large cucumber, halved lengthwise, peeled, seeded, and thinly sliced
1 small red onion, peeled, halved, and thinly sliced
1 large carrot, peeled and thinly sliced
1 small green or red bell pepper, seeded and cut into julienne strips
$\frac{1}{4}$ teaspoon crushed red pepper or red pepper flakes

1. In small saucepan over low heat, combine vinegar, sugar, and soy sauce. Simmer about 5 minutes, or until sugar dissolves, stirring occasionally. Remove from heat and let cool completely.
2. In serving bowl, combine cucumber, onion, carrot, bell pepper, and crushed pepper or flakes; add vinegar mixture. Gently stir a few times to coat vegetables well.
3. Let stand at room temperature 2 hours or longer for flavors to blend. Serve immediately, or refrigerate up to 1 week.

Spicy Coconut Milk and Chicken Soup

Tom Kha Gai

MAKES 4 TO 6 SERVINGS

If you're not yet acquainted with Thai cooking, you'll be surprised at how quick and easy it can be. This soup is a good example—its intriguing flavor would lead one to believe it had simmered all day long, but it actually cooks in less than 30 minutes!

  5 cups homemade or canned chicken broth
  2 cups unsweetened Coconut Milk (see page 151)
  ½ cup freshly squeezed lemon juice
  ½ cup soy sauce
3 to 4 medium-sized pieces frozen or dried galanga root (kha)
3 to 4 lemon leaves, or 1 teaspoon grated lemon peel
  2 stalks fresh lemon grass, or 2 teaspoons dried lemon grass
  1 cup dried shiitake mushrooms, soaked
  4 skinless, boneless chicken breast halves (about 1 pound), cut into 1-inch pieces
  2 hot green chile peppers, seeded and thinly sliced (optional)
  ½ teaspoon sugar

1. In large saucepan or dutch oven, bring chicken broth to a boil over high heat. Stir in coconut milk until well blended. Add lemon juice and soy sauce; continue stirring until blended. Stir in galanga root, lemon leaves or peel, lemon grass, drained mushrooms, and chicken pieces; bring to a boil.
2. Reduce heat to low; simmer, uncovered, 15 to 20 minutes or until chicken is cooked through.
3. Discard galanga root, lemon leaves, and lemon grass. Stir in chile peppers and sugar. Serve hot.

NOTE: Jalapeño peppers work well in this recipe. If dried shiitake mushrooms are unavailable, you may substitute tree ears or other dried Chinese mushrooms.

Sautéed Rice Noodles with Beef and Broccoli

Pad See-um

MAKES 4 TO 6 SERVINGS

We prefer this dish on the hot side, but you can make it spicy or not by regulating the amount of red pepper. In Thailand, sautéed rice noodles are often prepared with shrimp or pork; here we've substituted beef with excellent results.

One 16-ounce package rice noodles (fettuccine-width rice sticks)

¼ cup vegetable oil or peanut oil

6 to 7 cloves garlic, peeled and coarsely chopped

1 pound round steak (London broil), sliced against the grain into very thin strips

1 cilantro stem, chopped

1 medium bunch broccoli, stems peeled and cut into 1½-inch pieces and florets separated

1½ tablespoons white vinegar

¼ cup Black Soy Sauce (recipe follows)

1 to 2 tablespoons regular soy sauce

2 to 3 eggs, beaten

2 tablespoons sugar

½ teaspoon crushed red pepper or red pepper flakes (optional)

Cilantro leaves for garnish (optional)

1. In large bowl, soak noodles in 10 to 12 cups cold water for 1 hour. Drain and cover with wet towel to retain moisture.
2. In wok or large nonstick skillet, heat oil over medium-high heat. Stir-fry garlic in hot oil about 3 minutes, until light brown.
3. Add sliced steak and cilantro stem; stir-fry 5 minutes, tossing to coat well.
4. Add broccoli stems and vinegar; stir-fry 2 to 3 minutes. Reduce heat to medium; add broccoli florets, noodles, black soy sauce, and regular soy sauce. Continue cooking 5 minutes longer, stirring constantly.
5. With large spoon, push ingredients to the side of the pan, creating a space in the middle. Add eggs to space and quickly stir, folding them into noodle-beef mixture. Continue stirring vigorously to combine the ingredients well. Add sugar and red pepper; stir-fry 3 to 5 minutes longer.
6. To serve, transfer to large platter and garnish with cilantro leaves, if desired.

NOTE: Rice noodles resemble long, white fettuccine. They're available in 16-ounce packages in oriental markets.

BLACK SOY SAUCE

MAKES ½ CUP

½ cup soy sauce
1 to 1½ tablespoons molasses

In small bowl, mix soy sauce and molasses well. Store in tightly covered container in refrigerator.

NOTE: Prepare this mixture ahead of time to have on hand. It can be kept in the refrigerator almost indefinitely. Use it instead of black bean sauce in oriental-style recipes.

Sweet Rice Pudding with Apricots

Khow Neeow Sum

MAKES 4 TO 6 SERVINGS

Like several Thai dishes, this dessert can be prepared mostly ahead of time to avoid any last-minute crunch. Instead of apricots, you may use your favorite canned fruit—mandarin oranges, fruit cocktail, pears, peaches, lichees, or the traditional Thai longan fruit all work well.

> 1 cup short-grain glutinous rice (Kohuko Rose or Nishiki brand)
> $\frac{1}{2}$ cup sugar
> One 16-ounce can apricot halves in syrup
> $\frac{1}{2}$ cup unsweetened Coconut Milk (see page 151)
> $\frac{1}{2}$ teaspoon salt

1. Rinse rice under cold running water. In large saucepan, soak rice in 2 cups cold water for 20 minutes. Drain; add 3 cups fresh cold water.
2. Place over medium-high heat and bring to a boil. Cook, uncovered, 30 minutes, stirring every 5 minutes to prevent sticking.
3. Stir in sugar; cook 5 minutes longer, stirring occasionally.
4. Gently fold apricots and their syrup into rice mixture. Reduce heat to low; cook 3 minutes. Cover and remove from heat.
5. In small saucepan over high heat, bring coconut milk and salt to a boil. Remove from heat and let cool 10 minutes.
6. Serve rice pudding in large bowl or individual serving dishes topped with coconut milk mixture.

NOTE: Pudding may be prepared up to Step 4 and set aside while you prepare the rest of the meal. The rice will stay warm if placed on top of the stove but off the burner; cover tightly to retain moisture. Complete Step 5 just before serving.

Corn Fritters—*Khao Pud Tod*
Ground Beef Salad—*Lap Nuea*
Chile Steak with Mint—*Nuea Pad Prik*
Stir-fried Bean Threads—*Pad Woon Sen*
Marinated Chicken in Coconut Milk—*Gai Yang*
Gai Yang Dipping Sauce—*Nam Jim Gai Yang*
Curried Rice—*Khow Phat Pong Kali*
Bananas in Coconut Milk—*Khrow Buad Chi*

Corn Fritters

Khao Pud Tod

MAKES 12 FRITTERS

In Thailand, chopped string beans are often used instead of corn, which has to be imported. You can try these with small pieces of any vegetable; we like to serve them as an appetizer, side dish, or snack.

One 16-ounce can corn niblets, drained if necessary (2 cups corn)
$\frac{1}{2}$ cup all-purpose flour
1 teaspoon baking powder
1 teaspoon baking soda
1 teaspoon sugar
2 eggs
1 tablespoon Red Curry Paste (see page 150)
4 cloves garlic, peeled and finely chopped
1 teaspoon soy sauce
1 lemon leaf, crushed, or $\frac{1}{2}$ teaspoon grated lemon peel
$\frac{1}{4}$ teaspoon coarsely ground black pepper
$1\frac{1}{2}$ to 2 cups vegetable oil or peanut oil

1. Place corn in medium bowl. With back of wooden spoon, lightly press kernels to crush slightly and extract some liquid; set aside.

2. Sift flour, baking powder, baking soda, and sugar into large bowl.

3. In small bowl, beat together eggs, curry paste, garlic, soy sauce, lemon leaf or peel, and pepper. Add mixture to dry ingredients and blend well. Fold in corn kernels and their liquid; mix to form a thick, pancakelike batter.

4. In wok or large skillet, heat oil over medium-high heat until almost smoking. Drop batter by heaping tablespoonfuls into hot oil. Fry about 3 minutes on each side, or until golden brown. Drain on paper towels. Serve hot.

N O T E : When fresh corn is in season, cook 4 large ears until tender and scrape off enough kernels to measure 2 cups.

Ground Beef Salad

Lap Nuea

MAKES 4 TO 6 SERVINGS

Ground beef salad may be served hot or cold, and is usually combined with crisp raw vegetables to offer textural interest. The toasted rice powder adds an unexpected crunch and flavor that's not unlike popcorn.

> 1 tablespoon uncooked rice
> 2 tablespoons vegetable oil or peanut oil
> 4 to 5 cloves garlic, peeled and finely chopped
> 2 pounds lean ground beef
> 1 cup freshly squeezed lemon juice
> $\frac{1}{4}$ to $\frac{1}{2}$ cup soy sauce

1 medium onion, peeled and coarsely chopped
3 scallions, chopped
1 tablespoon crushed red pepper or red pepper flakes,
  or to taste
1 small head crisp iceberg or romaine lettuce
1 large tomato, cut into wedges
1 cucumber, peeled, seeded, and thinly sliced
  Lemon wedges (optional)

1. In small dry skillet over high heat, toast uncooked rice 3 to 5 minutes, or until grains turn light brown. Remove rice to mortar with pestle or place in food processor or blender. Crush or process rice to a coarse powderlike consistency; set aside.

2. In wok or large skillet, heat oil over medium-high heat. Add garlic and stir-fry 3 minutes until light brown in color. Add ground beef; stir-fry 7 to 10 minutes until meat loses its red color.

3. Stir in lemon juice, soy sauce, and onion. Reduce heat to low; simmer 2 to 3 minutes to blend flavors. Remove wok from heat; stir in crushed rice, scallions, and red pepper.

4. To serve, arrange lettuce on large platter; top with ground beef mixture and surround with tomato wedges, cucumber slices, and lemon wedges, if you like.

N O T E : We borrowed this trick from Penny's mother: To get all the juice out of a fresh lemon, halve the fruit, squeeze it, and use a wooden spoon to ream each half.

Chile Steak with Mint

Nuea Pad Prik

MAKES 4 TO 6 SERVINGS

$\frac{1}{3}$ cup vegetable oil or peanut oil
5 to 6 cloves garlic, peeled and finely chopped
2 pounds round steak (London broil), sliced against the grain into very thin strips
2 fresh red chile peppers, seeded and thinly sliced
2 fresh green chile peppers, seeded and thinly sliced
1 medium onion, peeled and coarsely chopped
$\frac{1}{4}$ cup soy sauce
1 tablespoon sugar
$\frac{1}{4}$ cup coarsely chopped fresh mint leaves
Hot cooked rice

1. In wok or large skillet, heat oil over medium-high heat. Add garlic and stir-fry 3 to 5 minutes until light brown.
2. Add steak strips; stir-fry 5 minutes, or until meat is browned.
3. Add chile peppers, onion, soy sauce, and sugar. Continue stir-frying 8 to 10 minutes longer, or until beef is cooked through. Toss in mint leaves. Serve at once with rice.

Stir-fried Bean Threads

Pad Woon Sen

MAKES 4 SERVINGS

Almost transparent in appearance, bean thread noodles or woon sen are also known as cellophane noodles. They're made from mung bean starch, which gives the noodles a chewy texture that complements soups and stir-fries.

One 12-ounce package, or three 4-ounce packages, bean
thread noodles
$\frac{1}{2}$ cup peanut oil or vegetable oil
6 to 7 cloves garlic, peeled and finely chopped
1 cup coarsely chopped napa (celery) cabbage or savoy
(green leaf) cabbage
2 tablespoons soy sauce
2 tablespoons sugar
2 large tomatoes, peeled and coarsely chopped
3 eggs, beaten
3 scallions, chopped
2 hot green chile peppers, seeded and thinly sliced
diagonally, or to taste

1. In large bowl, soak bean thread noodles for 30 minutes in enough
cold water to cover. Drain and set aside.
2. In wok or large skillet, heat oil over medium heat. Add garlic;
stir-fry in hot oil 3 to 5 minutes until toasted light brown. Add
cabbage; stir-fry 1 minute longer until well coated with garlic and oil.
3. Add soy sauce, sugar, tomatoes, and soaked, drained bean thread
noodles. Raise heat to high; stir-fry 3 to 5 minutes.
4. With spoon, push ingredients around sides of pan to make a well
in center; add eggs to well. As eggs begin to set, quickly fold in
noodles and vegetables, stirring to mix well with cooked eggs.
5. Quickly stir in scallions and chile peppers. Transfer to large platter to serve.

N O T E : Bean thread noodles are available in most large supermarkets
in the oriental or Chinese grocery section.

Marinated Chicken in Coconut Milk
Gai Yang

Thai restaurants in America almost always feature gai yang on their menus, but in Thailand, this dish is served at everyday family meals. We often leave the chicken in its marinade for 1 to 2 days, so the recipe is an ideal choice for a do-ahead dinner. It can be cooked either under the broiler or on an outdoor grill.

    1 cup unsweetened Coconut Milk (see page 151)
    ¼ cup soy sauce
    1 tablespoon Red Curry Paste (see page 150)
    1 tablespoon yellow curry powder
    2 tablespoons sugar
 3 to 4 cilantro stems, finely chopped
    2 chickens, about 2½ to 3 pounds each, halved
      lengthwise
    2 tablespoons cracked black peppercorns
      Gai Yang Dipping Sauce (recipe follows)
      Curried Rice (see page 164)

1. In small bowl, thoroughly mix coconut milk, soy sauce, red curry paste, and curry powder. Add sugar and cilantro stems; mix well.

2. On work surface, sprinkle chicken halves all over with peppercorns. With back of large spoon, press pepper into chicken. Place chicken, skin side down, in shallow baking dish. Pour coconut milk mixture over chicken. Cover and refrigerate in marinade at least 7 hours, or overnight.

3. Preheat oven to 350°F. Uncover chicken and bake in marinade 40 minutes to 1 hour, or until thoroughly cooked.

4. Just before serving, preheat broiler. Place chicken on broiler pan and broil 5 minutes to crisp the skin.

5. To serve, cut chicken halves into 4 pieces. Serve with individual side dishes of dipping sauce and rice.

GAI YANG DIPPING SAUCE
Nam Jim Gai Yang

$3\frac{1}{2}$ cups cold water
$1\frac{1}{2}$ cups sugar
$\frac{1}{2}$ cup chopped preserved or pickled garlic
$\frac{1}{4}$ cup white vinegar
1 small onion, quartered
2 fresh red chile peppers, seeded and chopped
$1\frac{1}{2}$ teaspoons salt

1. Combine all ingredients in large saucepan. Place over high heat and bring to a boil. Reduce heat to low; simmer, uncovered, 40 minutes.
2. Strain sauce, reserving liquid. Mash or blend solids into a thick pastelike consistency.
3. Return paste to saucepan. Place over low heat and slowly stir in reserved liquid. Continue cooking until sauce thickens, stirring constantly.

N O T E : Preserved or pickled garlic is available in oriental groceries. You may substitute 1 to 2 cloves fresh garlic, peeled and minced, if the preserved garlic is difficult to find. Dipping sauce can be stored in the refrigerator for 2 weeks, or may be frozen for several months.

Curried Rice

Khow Phat Pong Kali

MAKES 4 TO 6 SERVINGS

½ cup unsweetened Coconut Milk (see page 151)
1 medium onion, peeled, halved, and thinly sliced
1 tablespoon soy sauce
2 teaspoons yellow curry powder
3 cups cooked rice
½ cup fresh or defrosted frozen peas

1. In medium saucepan, bring coconut milk to a boil over medium heat. Add onion; reduce heat to low and simmer 5 minutes, or until onion turns translucent and soft.
2. Stir in soy sauce and curry powder; stir until thoroughly mixed and curry powder has dissolved. Fold in rice and peas; cover and cook 5 minutes longer. Serve steaming hot.

Bananas in Coconut Milk

Khrow Buad Chi

MAKES 4 TO 6 SERVINGS

This fast-to-fix dessert is well loved by children and adults alike.

$2\frac{1}{2}$ cups unsweetened Coconut Milk (see page 151)
$\frac{1}{4}$ cup sugar
$\frac{1}{2}$ teaspoon salt
4 large ripe bananas, peeled and sliced diagonally into
   $1\frac{1}{2}$-inch pieces

1. In large saucepan, bring coconut milk to a boil over high heat. Stir in sugar and salt.
2. Reduce heat to low; add bananas. Cover and simmer 5 minutes; *do not stir* or bananas will become mushy. Serve hot or cold.

Beverage note: Wine is not a natural complement of this style of cooking. Thai beer is much better and provides that authentic touch.

Tunisian

*t*he tiny country of Tunisia shares the northern coast of Africa with Algeria and Morocco. Although the cuisines of these three lands collectively called the Maghreb have threads in common, Tunisia's geography and history have left a unique mark on its culinary customs.

Despite its small size, Tunisia's climate is quite diverse. To the north and east is the Mediterranean Sea, bringing with it warm breezes and sunny skies. To the south is the dry, hot Sahara desert, and toward the center are snowy mountain peaks. These climatic variations are responsible for the wide range of food products featured in Tunisian cooking.

The proximity of the Mediterranean allows the fresh morning catch to be cooked and served that same afternoon or evening. Such fish as rouge, tuna, porgy, and sole go into a number of enticing dishes, including the famous couscous au poisson, a Tunisian seafood rendition of that legendary North African specialty. The colder weather in the central part of the country helps produce abundant wheat crops, the staple grain of Tunisia from which couscous is actually milled. And the sun-drenched fields yield a bounty of fruits, vegetables, and nuts, all of which find their way into the cooking pot. Among the most prevalent are okra, spinach, turnips, kohlrabi, eggplant, squash, fennel, many types of beans, oranges, lemons, peaches, apricots, dates, figs, cactus pears, nefle (a tiny pear-shaped fruit), pistachios, pignoli (pine nuts), and almonds. Native spices and herbs enliven these basic ingredients with a definite Tunisian twist that shows Turkish and Egyptian influences. Caraway, cumin, cinnamon, and pepper are used extensively in savory dishes, while rosewater and orange-flower water are favored for desserts. Tunisian cooks can purchase fresh fruits, vegetables, fish, and spices daily in the colorful open-air markets located both in the larger cities and smaller villages.

History has also played an important role in the development of Tunisian cuisine. Throughout the ages, invaders and settlers from many different parts of the world have lived within its boundaries. The Phoenicians were the first to arrive, establishing Carthage as a rich center of culture and trade. Today, the ruins at Carthage are a major tourist attraction. On the heels of the Phoenicians came the Romans, Byzantines, Berbers, Turks, Spaniards, Italians, and French.

Jews lived peacefully in Tunisia for centuries. In fact, a temple thousands of years old still stands on the island of Djerba off the east coast. Other Jewish families, mine included, were of Sephardic heritage and emigrated from Spain, Italy, and Turkey later on. Although there are still some Jews left in Tunis, the capital city, the vibrant Jewish community that flourished for so long is gone. Once the country gained its independence from France in 1956, most Tunisian Jews left for Israel, Canada, France, and Italy, with a few going to the United States. The new government was and still is friendly to the Jews, but most of the European community has departed.

The Tunisian-Jewish food I grew up with shows a pronounced Berber or Arab flavor. In my home, the cooking reflected my family's Italian and Sephardic background as well, and paid strict attention to the dietary laws. However, traditional Tunisian fare can be prepared kosher without much difficulty. Very few dairy products are used, and combinations of milk and meat are therefore rare. In addition, the Arab-Muslim prohibition against pork has always been widespread throughout Tunisia; instead, the cooking centers around lamb, chicken, and beans as sources of protein. While the Arabs do eat camel and boar meat, the Jews make up for these nonkosher ingredients by eating more beef and veal. For the Sabbath, inventive Jewish cooks have created their own version of couscous made with beef and *boulettes* (meatballs). Leftovers from Friday night's dinner are often served for Saturday lunch, revitalized with a topping of cooked beans and other vegetables.

During my childhood in Tunisia, the calendar in my home was filled with wonderful celebration days, some observed in the customary way, others with a special ethnic bent. These occasions called for homemade sweets and fancy cakes instead of the usual fruit desserts. On Chanukah, for instance, pastries made of semolina were fried and dipped in honey in the Sephardic tradition. In one rendition of this treat called *debla,* the dough is rolled around a fork, then quickly cooked in hot oil and coated with a lemon-flavored syrup. *Makroud,* another Chanukah sweet, is a deep-fried date confection dipped in honey.

I fondly remember celebrating some thoroughly Tunisian days as well. One example was Children's Holiday, a festival geared especially to youngsters. On this occasion, an assortment of homemade cakes was served, each baked in a miniature size appropriate for a small child. Honey-dipped macaroons were also among the treats. There were also special feasts for long-dead rabbis, called Saint Days. On these holidays, a large selection of hot and cold dishes would be set out buffet style, and families hosted large parties. The one-pot meals and make-ahead recipes that characterize Tunisian cuisine adapted well to this setup.

To Americans, Tunisian cuisine may seem a bit exotic. However, the dishes are relatively simple to prepare in Western kitchens in accordance with the dietary laws. I frequently make full-fledged kosher Tunisian meals in my rather tiny New York City apartment kitchen. Ingredients are easy to find in most supermarkets and produce stores. Couscous, for example, is available in bulk form at health-food stores or in packages on supermarket shelves. Although most Mediterranean species of fish are not obtainable here, I usually substitute whiting or cod for similar results.

The two menus that follow include one for a typical Shabbat dinner and one for a popular summer meal. Both are truly representative of Tunisian-Jewish cooking.

—Jacqueline Friedman

Jacqueline Friedman

When Jacqueline Friedman was growing up in Tunisia during the forties and fifties, the country was imbued with a strong international spirit. The population was predominantly French, Italian, and Arab, with a sprinkling of other nationalities forming smaller communities. This diversity made for a rich and varied cultural mix. In Jacqueline's family alone, French was spoken, the household help was Italian, the laws of kashrut were observed, and the cooking was eclectic.

The meals in Jacqueline's home were prepared by her mother, Ninette Lucido, a woman well-known for her expertise in the kitchen. As a teenager, Mrs. Lucido carefully watched the professional cooks at her uncle's house and memorized their techniques and recipes. She was then able to duplicate the results for her own family later on, creating meals that were strictly kosher with Tunisian, Sephardic, French, and Italian nuances.

Jacqueline, in turn, learned her culinary skills at her mother's side. When she came to the United States twenty-five years ago, she brought along a great treasury of Tunisian dishes and an intense affection for cooking. Although there were no Tunisian open-air markets selling Arab spices, fresh fish, and exotic produce in New York City, Jacqueline was able to cook up her favorite family recipes in the apartment she shared with her American husband and son.

These days, much of Jacqueline's time is taken up by her job as a French teacher at the Horace Mann School in New York City, but she still finds the opportunity to prepare such Tunisian specialties as couscous complet and tagine ganaouia au poulet for relatives and friends. Recently, Jacqueline shared her enthusiasm and skill, cooking these traditional dishes with the students in her classes at the 92nd St. Y Cooking School. Right before their eyes, she demystified Tunisian cuisine, showing how much fun it could be to prepare this North African fare with easily obtainable ingredients, basic culinary know-how, and no fancy equipment.

Complete Couscous with Meat and Meatballs—
Couscous Complet avec Viande et Boulettes
Marinated Vegetable Salad—*Torchi*
Vegetable Ragout—*Marmouma*
Stuffed Dates—*Dattes Farcies*

Complete Couscous with Meat and Meatballs

Couscous Complet avec Viande et Boulettes

MAKES 6 SERVINGS

Tunisian-Jewish families like mine eat this hearty meal every Friday night. The couscous is cooked over the bubbling stew to absorb its flavor, and the meatballs are prepared separately. At the table, each diner piles some couscous grain on a plate and moistens it with a little cooking liquid from the stew. The meat, vegetables, and meatballs are then served along with the couscous.

COUSCOUS (SEMOLINA GRAIN)

1 pound couscous, or two 8- to 10-ounce packages
2 tablespoons vegetable oil
1 teaspoon salt

1. Place couscous in a wide, shallow bowl. Add a few drops of water to moisten the grain. With your fingers, rapidly blend in $\frac{1}{2}$ to $\frac{2}{3}$ cup more water. Add oil and salt; continue mixing, rolling the couscous between your fingers to separate the grains.

2. Place the couscous mixture in the top portion of a couscoussière or in a mesh sieve steamer basket with small holes; insert over simmering stew or 1 cup boiling water. Cover and let steam 30 minutes, or until couscous is tender.

3. Remove couscous and transfer to shallow bowl; let cool. When cool enough to handle, spread out couscous and separate grains with fingers.

4. To serve, spoon liquid from stew over couscous.

NOTE: The Near East brand of couscous is kosher and widely available.

MEAT SOUP OR STEW
Bouillon

The vegetables should be cut into large, distinct chunks for this dish.

- ⅓ cup vegetable oil
- 2 large onions, peeled and quartered
- 2 large tomatoes, peeled, seeded, and quartered
- 1½ pounds beef chuck stew meat, cut into chunks
- 4 ribs celery, cut into 2-inch pieces
- 4 small to medium potatoes, peeled and cut into large chunks
- 3 carrots, peeled and cut into 2-inch pieces
- 3 turnips, peeled and halved
- 2 small zucchini, cut into 2-inch pieces
- 2 heads kohlrabi, cut into large chunks
- ½ small head green cabbage, cut into 3 wedges
  Salt and freshly ground black pepper to taste
- 3 sprigs fresh dill
- 3 sprigs cilantro

1. In dutch oven or bottom section of couscoussière, place oil over medium-low heat. Layer onions, tomatoes, and beef on top. Cover and cook 15 minutes.

2. Add celery, potatoes, carrots, turnips, zucchini, kohlrabi, cabbage, and salt and pepper to taste. Cover and cook 15 minutes.

3. Raise heat to medium-high; add 4 cups water and bring to a boil. Reduce heat to low; cover and simmer 1¼ hours longer, or until meat is tender. Stir in dill and cilantro; cook 5 minutes longer.

4. To serve, arrange meat and vegetables on large platter. Pour cooking liquid into gravy boat or pitcher.

LITTLE MEATBALLS
Boulettes à la Viande

My mother would prepare and cook this dish on Thursday night or Friday morning for the Shabbat meal. Since the meatballs were done ahead of the other couscous components, they were available for Friday's lunch. It wasn't uncommon for my father to come home at noon and sneak a boulette or two, accompanied by a squeeze of fresh lemon juice. Extras were always prepared just for this purpose! The rest of these light meatballs were reserved for dinner. In other Tunisian families, some of the ground beef mixture was set aside and stuffed into hollowed-out zucchini, bell peppers, or potatoes. These stuffed vegetables would cook along with the boulettes.

½ pound stale Italian bread (3 days old), cut into cubes
¾ pound lean ground beef
2 large onions, peeled and finely chopped
½ cup chopped parsley
5 cloves garlic, peeled and minced
1 teaspoon dried mint leaves, or 4 fresh mint leaves, chopped
3 eggs
 Salt and freshly ground black pepper to taste
½ cup all-purpose flour
⅓ cup vegetable oil
2 large tomatoes, peeled, seeded, and chopped
1 tablespoon chopped fresh dill (optional)
1 tablespoon chopped fresh cilantro (optional)

1. Place bread in shallow container or bowl. Pour in enough water to cover bread by 1 inch. Let soak 30 minutes.

2. Squeeze out water from bread and discard; shred bread into small pieces. In large bowl, combine bread, ground beef, onions, parsley, 3 minced garlic cloves, mint, 1 egg, and salt and pepper to taste; mix until well blended. Roll meat mixture into $1\frac{1}{2}$-inch balls.

3. In shallow bowl, beat remaining 2 eggs. Measure flour onto waxed paper. Roll each meatball in flour, coating all sides, then roll in beaten egg.

4. In large deep skillet, heat oil over medium-high heat. Add meatballs in one layer and fry 10 minutes, or until browned on all sides, turning once or twice. Remove from skillet to large saucepan; brown remaining meatballs, adding to saucepan when done.

5. To saucepan with meatballs, add tomatoes, remaining 2 minced garlic cloves, oil from skillet and 1 cup water. Cover and cook over low heat 1 hour. Stir in dill and cilantro, if desired.

6. Serve boulettes in a large dish, along with couscous and bouillon.

Wine note: A wide variety of red wines would complement this dish. The one imported kosher Moroccan red would be fine (see page 93), as would any of the petites chateaux of Bordeaux; a young Rioja from Spain or one of the light red generics from Israel.

Marinated Vegetable Salad

Torchi

MAKES 6 SERVINGS

2 carrots
2 turnips
1 rib celery
2 tablespoons salt
$\frac{1}{2}$ cup white vinegar

1. Wash and scrape the vegetables; do not peel. Cut vegetables into 1-inch-long sticks. In medium bowl, combine vegetables and salt. Let stand at room temperature for 1 hour.
2. Stir vinegar into vegetable mixture. Let stand 1 hour longer.
3. To serve, drain vegetables of all liquid.

NOTE: The flavor of this salad improves if it is made 2 days ahead, refrigerated in vinegar mixture, and drained just before serving.

Vegetable Ragout

Marmouma

MAKES 6 SERVINGS

I usually serve this vegetable dish as an accompaniment to couscous complet, but some Tunisians make a main dish out of marmouma by adding raw eggs.

$\frac{1}{4}$ cup vegetable oil
3 large tomatoes, peeled, seeded, and cubed
2 green bell peppers, seeded and cubed
4 cloves garlic, peeled and minced
  Salt and freshly ground black pepper to taste
$\frac{1}{2}$ teaspoon ground caraway or caraway seeds

1. In medium saucepan, combine oil, tomatoes, peppers, and garlic. Place over high heat and cook 2 minutes.
2. Add salt and pepper to taste and caraway; reduce heat to low. Cover and cook 30 minutes, stirring occasionally. Serve hot or cold.

Stuffed Dates

Dattes Farcies

MAKES 6 SERVINGS

Similar to the Moroccan recipe for Stuffed Dried Fruit (see page 102), this version is simpler to prepare for a quick addition to a fresh fruit platter. I use the largest dates I can find for this confection.

One 10-ounce container pitted deglas (dates)
4 ounces walnuts (about 1 cup), broken
1 teaspoon orange-flower water, or $\frac{1}{2}$ teaspoon grated orange peel
$\frac{1}{2}$ to 1 cup granulated sugar

1. With sharp knife, split dates lengthwise in half almost to bottoms.
2. In small bowl, combine walnuts and orange-flower water or orange peel. Stuff each date with some of walnut mixture.
3. Place sugar on waxed paper. Roll each stuffed date in sugar, coating well.

Wine note: A tangy, sweet wine partnered with dates ends a meal in unbeatable fashion. The trick is to get those two attributes in the same bottle. Port wouldn't do at all. Traditional sweet Concords and their ilk wouldn't either. Try a cold, late-harvest Riesling or a sweet Gewürztraminer.

Puffy Tunisian Omelet—*Maakoude de Poisson*
Chicken and Okra Casserole—*Ganaouia au Poulet*
Pine Nut Confections—*Bouchées aux Pignons*

Puffy Tunisian Omelet

Maakoude de Poisson

MAKES 6 SERVINGS

This unusual appetizer, which resembles a crustless quiche or frit-tata, really has no counterpart in American cuisine. I make it often for Tunisian friends, preparing the dish ahead and serving it at room temperature. Sometimes I serve the maakoude as a main dish for a light, warm-weather lunch or picnic.

  3 slices dry Italian bread
  $\frac{1}{2}$ pound fish fillets (flounder, sole, or cod), diced
  2 hard-cooked eggs, chopped
  4 parsley sprigs, minced
  1 clove garlic, peeled and minced
  1 teaspoon salt
$\frac{1}{2}$ to 1 teaspoon freshly ground black pepper
  8 eggs, lightly beaten
    Juice of $\frac{1}{2}$ lemon
  2 tablespoons vegetable oil
    Lemon wedges for garnish

1. In shallow container, combine bread and enough water to cover. Let stand 15 minutes. Squeeze out water and discard; shred bread into small pieces.

2. In medium bowl, combine bread, fish, hard-cooked eggs, parsley, garlic, salt, and pepper; mix well. Add raw eggs and juice of $\frac{1}{2}$ lemon. Blend with fork until well combined.

3. In large skillet, heat oil over low heat. Add egg mixture; cover and cook 8 minutes. With fork, lift egg mixture up from sides and bottom of skillet to loosen. Cover and cook 20 minutes longer.

4. With spatula, lift maakoude and turn over; cook 10 minutes longer, or until completely set. To serve, transfer to large platter; cut into wedges. Serve warm, at room temperature, or cold, garnished with lemon wedges.

Wine note: The fish, garlic, oil, and bread blending in this egg dish could make for an elegant and different brunch, as well as lunch or a picnic. A dry or barely sweet sparkling wine would go well with brunch or lunch; for a picnic, the charm of a New York blush Chablis or white Gamay from California might match the setting.

Chicken and Okra Casserole

Ganaouia au Poulet

MAKES 4 SERVINGS

This one-dish dinner, often referred to as a tagine, brims with the aromas and flavors of Tunisia. In my family, this recipe was reserved for relaxed summer dining.

$\frac{1}{2}$ cup vegetable oil

2 large onions, peeled and very thinly sliced

2 medium tomatoes, peeled, seeded, and diced

One 3-pound chicken, cut into pieces

1 pound fresh okra, washed, or one 10-ounce package
   frozen okra, defrosted
1 teaspoon ground coriander
   Salt and freshly ground black pepper to taste

1. Heat oil in heatproof casserole or large skillet over medium-high heat. Add onions; sauté in hot oil 5 minutes, or until slightly browned, stirring often. Stir in tomatoes; reduce heat to low and simmer 10 minutes. Add chicken pieces; cook 10 minutes, turning once.

2. Meanwhile, trim ends from okra and cut each piece into 2 or 3 slices. Add okra and coriander to chicken mixture; cover and cook 10 minutes.

3. Add 4 cups water and salt and pepper to taste; raise heat to high and bring to a boil. Reduce heat to low; cover and simmer 1 hour, or until chicken is tender.

4. Serve warm, accompanied by crusty bread.

Wine note: Chicken is easy to match, but chicken with okra? The wine-food experts have yet to catch up to this one. Okra, however, comes closest to asparagus toward the end of the list of matchups and there is only one partner of any merit to asparagus—Muscat, odd as it sounds. Try for a dry Alsace Muscat or a slightly sweeter Muscat from California.

Pine Nut Confections

Bouchées aux Pignons

MAKES 1½ DOZEN

The true translation of this dessert is "mouthfuls of pine nuts." Each bite-sized confection is as big as a mouthful and utterly delicious.

2¼ cups sugar
2 teaspoons freshly squeezed lemon juice
One 8-ounce can almond paste or marzipan
1 egg yolk
½ cup pine nuts (pignoli)

1. In large saucepan, combine sugar, 1 cup water, and lemon juice; bring to a boil over high heat. Reduce heat to medium and cook 15 minutes, stirring occasionally, or until mixture forms a syrup. Remove from heat.
2. In medium bowl, combine almond paste, egg yolk, and 2 teaspoons sugar syrup. With hands, form mixture into walnut-sized balls. Quickly drop balls into syrup in saucepan, coating all sides. Place pine nuts on waxed paper or in a shallow bowl. Roll each syrup-coated ball in pine nuts.
3. Arrange pine nut confections on platter in one layer. Let stand several hours or overnight at room temperature to dry.

Hungarian

t he cuisine of Hungary has been shaped by the countries that share its borders and the different cultures that have mingled therein. Magyar tribes first settled the land in the ninth century, and are credited with introducing the technique of slowly simmering cubes of meat in large cauldrons. This cooking method, in turn, has produced such renowned Hungarian dishes as *gulyas* (goulash). Later came the Romans and Turks, the latter bringing paprika, tomatoes, coffee, and the paper-thin dough known as *retes* (strudel) to Hungarian kitchens.

In the following centuries, and then for over three hundred years, the country was part of the vast Austro-Hungarian Empire ruled by the Hapsburgs. Vienna was the political, artistic, and culinary capital of this great empire, exerting tremendous influence on the customs that evolved throughout its domain. In larger cities like Budapest, for example, traditional peasant cooking became a bit more refined and continental. The result is a Hungarian cuisine that is highly original and worldly.

The first Jews are thought to have come to Hungary during Roman times, with greater numbers arriving after the Crusades in the Middle Ages. In the capital city of Budapest, ruins of a medieval synagogue dating back to the fourteenth century have been excavated, and another building houses the second largest synagogue in the world. The Jewish community in my native land is one of the oldest continuing communities of Jews in Europe. Even during

World War II, when Jews were deported from the countryside of Hungary, the Jews of Budapest were detained mostly in local ghettos. There, some hundred thousand survived, and continued to maintain a lively Jewish enclave in Budapest—a presence in Eastern Europe.

Throughout history, Jews have been able to make significant contributions to Hungarian culture. These began as far back as the Ottoman Empire, when they acted as liaisons between the Turks and other ethnic groups in Hungary. And they continue to the present, in an atmosphere that is still rather hospitable to over 125,000 Jewish people and supportive of Talmudic scholarship. In fact, Hungary boasts a theological seminary for rabbis and a Jewish Institute filled with rare books.

Jews have had little trouble adapting Hungarian cooking to the dietary laws, and in the process have affected the development of the country's food patterns. With the exception of pork, Jewish cooks have always been able to enjoy the mainstays of Hungarian cuisine—beef, chicken, duck, goose, fish, dumplings, noodles, sauerkraut, potatoes and other hardy vegetables, and fruits. When gentile cooks cured countless cuts of pork and put away large quantities of lard in anticipation of the long, cold Hungarian winters, resourceful Jews substituted the goose for the pig. Every part of this bird was used in an inventive way—from the neck, stuffed with rice in lieu of making pork sausages, to the fat, rendered for cooking and baking. When it came to the popular Hungarian meat dishes prepared with sour cream, like chicken paprikas, the Jews made another adaptation. They simply eliminated the dairy ingredient from the recipe, turning out a different but somewhat similar version of the dish.

The changes made by Jewish cooks throughout the years resulted in the evolution of two distinct cooking styles—Hungarian and Hungarian-Jewish. Eventually, the Jewish influence even began to infiltrate the eating habits of all of Hungary. I remember such Jewish foods as matzoh ball soup and fladen (a dense, sweet cake made with fruits and nuts) being served in restaurants in Budapest when I was a child.

Like its neighbor, Austria, Hungary has a well-deserved reputation for its wonderful pastries and baked goods. It is actually Hungarian wheat that is milled into the flour that, in turn, is responsible for the delicate but sturdy strudel dough, elegant cakes, feathery dumplings, and ultrathin filled pancakes known as palacsinta. Other natural resources include an assortment of tree fruit (pears, apples, sour cherries, apricots, and plums in particular); such freshwater fish as carp and perch; and winter vegetables such as cabbage and potatoes. Seeds are commonly used for seasoning, caraway and poppy being the most prevalent, and nuts are often incorporated into cake batters to add body and flavor.

Although Hungary does have a vibrant Jewish community, the Jews have been well assimilated into Hungarian life. However, there is still a very observant Orthodox sect and rabbis are available to oversee the kashering process at some markets. My family and other assimilated Jews have had a tendency to cook "kosher style," meaning we forbade the eating of pork and pork products, nonkosher meat cuts, catfish, and any mixture of dairy and meat. Nevertheless, Edward Weiss and I have tested all our recipes according to the stringent kosher guidelines of the 92nd Street Y Kosher Cooking School. The menus we've included reflect the most typical and delectable dishes in the Hungarian cooking repertoire. As a third-generation owner of the food importing company Paprikas Weiss, and a noted gourmet, Ed Weiss has contributed the rich, home-cooked favorites of his childhood—well seasoned with warm memories and his grandfather's famous spices. And I have perfected the desserts and baked goods, including the classic flourless tortes, the pride of Hungarian pastry-making and my trademark.

—André Balog

André Balog

If you ask André Balog where he spent a good part of his childhood, he will answer, "In the kitchen." He was raised by his Hungarian mother and grandmother, both of whom naturally gravitated toward the kitchen, and it was there that young André learned to walk, talk, and cultivate his palate. Visits to his great-grandparents' country house in Debrecen, Hungary, further enriched his culinary education. This summer home had a reputation as a great place to eat, and as many as fifteen to twenty people would drop by at lunchtime to enjoy the Hungarian-Jewish specialties that were always served.

Since his father was a journalist, André traveled a great deal as a child. In addition to Budapest, he lived in Paris, Rome, Stockholm, and London, frequently eating his meals in restaurants. Although he was raised primarily on Hungarian dishes, this exposure to different types of international cuisine broadened his horizons and piqued his interest in foreign foods.

André didn't realize he had absorbed much of his family's food knowledge or skill until he found himself living in Israel in a school dormitory. He started to cook out of necessity, duplicating his mother's and grandmother's recipes. It was then that he decided to learn as much as he could about cooking.

While in Israel, he studied with Devorah Wigoder, the author of Garden of Eden cookbook (Harper & Row, 1988). From there, he came to New York City, where he apprenticed with the pastry chef at a downtown restaurant called the Wise Maria. During this stint, André says he perfected his dessert-making skills. But he still wanted to brush up on French cooking techniques, so he traveled to Europe to take classes with Roger Vergé, the famed chef and restaurateur. Upon his return to the States, André joined Paprikas Weiss, an importer of fine food products, where he is now employed.

Although he no longer works as a chef on a daily basis, André Balog teaches cooking, caters dessert parties, and still travels to France every year to take classes, gather ideas, and sample European cooking. He also writes a column in Hungarian for a weekly cultural newspaper published in his homeland.

André's repertoire of Hungarian dishes includes the ones passed down from his grandmother and mother as well as those recipes he has developed with Edward Weiss, a fellow Hungarian and owner of Paprikas Weiss. On several occasions, these two exceptional cooks have communicated their expertise in and affection for Hungarian food to students enrolled in the 92nd Street Y Cooking School. On his own, André Balog has taught classes at the Y devoted to French cooking, chocolate, pastry, and desserts.

Edward Weiss

When Edward Weiss's grandfather emigrated to New York City from Hungary, good paprika was not available in the States. So Mr. Weiss wrote to Szeged, the town in Hungary where the climate, water, and soil produce the finest paprika anywhere, and ordered a shipment of 200 pounds of the spice. With that ample supply, Grandmother Weiss was content—she had plenty of paprika to prepare her goulashes and other specialties, and there was enough to lend to her Hungarian neighbors when they needed a pinch or two. Soon Grandpa began selling paprika directly to the Hungarian housewives, toting a basket up and down the sidewalks of the Yorkville section of Manhattan where they lived. His success eventually led to the establishment of a small grocery store featuring paprika and other Hungarian staples. Naturally, he named the store Paprikas Weiss.

Now, almost a hundred years later, Paprikas Weiss is a culinary haven known for its fine foods, cookware, and thousands of unique items, many still imported from Hungary and others from all over the globe. As president of Paprikas Weiss Importer, Edward Weiss has expanded the company to meet the needs of today's gourmet shopper while preserving the Old World charm of the original store. In addition to running the company, he has written several cookbooks and dictionaries, showcasing his talents as food expert and linguist respectively. The Paprikas Weiss Hungarian Cookbook (Morrow, 1979) is a classic.

Although Edward grew up in the food business, he studied political science and law in college and graduate school, earning a doctorate in international law. He has always had a natural flair for languages as well, and is fluent in both Hungarian and German. As an international food importer, Edward Weiss draws on his diverse background in business, government, law, and linguistics all the time. In his travels overseas, the day-to-day operation of the store, or his work as a food consultant, he makes the most of his skills—especially the keen sense of taste he acquired in his mother's and grandmother's kitchens.

Caraway Soup—*Köménymagos Leves*
Chicken Paprikas—*Csirke Paprikás*
Cucumber Salad—*Uborka Sálata*
Hazelnut Torte—*Mogyoró Torta*

Caraway Seed Soup

Köménymagos Leves

MAKES 4 TO 6 SERVINGS

*This soup is permeated with the distinctive flavor of caraway seed,
a seasoning used extensively in Hungarian cooking.*

4 cups water
4 teaspoons caraway seeds
3 tablespoons margarine
3 tablespoons all-purpose flour
1 tablespoon Hungarian sweet paprika
  Salt and ground black pepper to taste
¾ cup thin egg noodles (optional)
2 eggs
1 cup croutons

1. In small saucepan, bring 2 cups water to a boil over high heat. Add caraway seeds; reduce heat to low and simmer 30 minutes. Strain, reserving liquid; discard caraway seeds.
2. In large saucepan, melt margarine over medium heat. With wire whisk, blend in flour; cook until mixture browns slightly, stirring constantly. Stir in paprika, reserved caraway-flavored water, salt and

pepper to taste, and an additional 2 cups water. With wire whisk, beat until smooth. Add noodles, if desired; simmer 5 minutes. Reduce heat to low.

3. In small bowl, beat eggs slightly. Add $\frac{1}{2}$ cup hot soup mixture to eggs, stirring to combine. Pour egg mixture back into hot soup in saucepan. Whisk gently over low heat until just heated through; do not boil. (If soup boils after eggs are added, the mixture will curdle and become lumpy, so make sure the saucepan is kept over very low heat.)

4. To serve, ladle hot soup into warm bowls; garnish with croutons.

Chicken Paprikas

Csirke Paprikás

MAKES 4 TO 6 SERVINGS

Sweet Hungarian paprika is the ingredient that imparts a true native taste to this dish. We have found many brands to be widely available in supermarkets and specialty food shops.

$\frac{1}{4}$ cup chicken fat or vegetable oil
1 onion, peeled and finely chopped
One 3- to 3$\frac{1}{2}$-pound chicken, cut into pieces
1 green bell pepper, cored, seeded, and finely chopped
1 tomato, peeled, seeded, and chopped
1 tablespoon sweet Hungarian paprika
Salt and freshly ground black pepper to taste
Hot cooked rice or Hungarian noodles or dumplings
(nokkedli or tarhonya)

1. In large skillet, heat chicken fat or oil over medium heat until hot. Add onion; sauté 2 minutes. Stir in $\frac{1}{4}$ cup water. Cover skillet and

reduce heat as low as possible. Steam onion 1 hour, adding more water if necessary.

2. Add chicken pieces, green pepper, tomato, and paprika. Sprinkle with salt and pepper to taste; stir in an additional $\frac{1}{2}$ cup water. Cover and cook 35 to 45 minutes longer, until chicken is tender.

3. Serve chicken and sauce with rice, noodles, or dumplings.

NOTE: Steaming the onion for 1 hour is the best way to obtain its maximum flavor, which would not develop during the relatively short cooking time characteristic of this dish. With meat that cooks for a longer time period, this step isn't necessary, since the onion simmers along with the other ingredients.

Wine note: This and beef goulash have more in common than being evenly matched in the competition to be Hungary's national dish. Both are potted and have some of the same ingredients. More to the point, one of the most well-known Hungarian red wines complements both: Egri Bikavér, meaning bull's blood. Once a very full and powerful wine, in its current incarnations, both kosher and nonkosher, it has been toned down significantly. Egri (the kosher version has dropped the Bikavér) varies little from the nonkosher and is a good match for either of these dishes. It's moderate in most aspects, and allows the dishes to stand out against a smooth background.

Cucumber Salad

Uborka Sálata

MAKES 4 SERVINGS

In some Hungarian kitchens, this dish is prepared with sour cream. You might want to experiment with that version for a dairy meal, but we consider the recipe as given to be the more authentic one.

2 large cucumbers, peeled and thinly sliced
1 tablespoon salt
1 small onion, peeled and thinly sliced
1 clove garlic, peeled and finely chopped
3 tablespoons white vinegar
1 teaspoon sugar
1 teaspoon Hungarian sweet paprika
  Freshly ground black pepper to taste
$\frac{3}{4}$ cup sour cream (optional)
1 tomato, cut into wedges
$\frac{1}{2}$ green bell pepper, cored, seeded, and cut into strips

1. In medium bowl, toss cucumbers with salt. Cover and refrigerate 30 minutes, or until most of the liquid has drained off. Squeeze remaining liquid from cucumber slices and pat dry on paper towels.
2. In salad bowl, combine cucumber slices, onion, garlic, vinegar, 2 tablespoons cold water, and sugar. Season with paprika and black pepper; stir in sour cream, if desired.
3. To serve, garnish with tomato wedges and julienned green pepper.

Hazelnut Torte

Mogyoró Torta

MAKES 8 TO 10 SERVINGS

Most of the cakes we bake are done in the Austro-Hungarian tradition, using beaten egg yolks and ground nuts rather than flour to provide texture and body. This torte takes a bit of time, but the results are well worth the effort. By the way, it makes an excellent Passover dessert.

CAKE

- 8 eggs, separated
- $\frac{1}{2}$ cup sugar
- $\frac{1}{4}$ cup orange juice
- $\frac{3}{4}$ cup ground hazelnuts
- $\frac{1}{4}$ cup matzoh meal

HAZELNUT CREAM

- $\frac{3}{4}$ cup sugar
- $\frac{1}{3}$ cup water
- 8 egg yolks
- 1 cup (2 sticks) margarine, softened
- $\frac{1}{2}$ cup ground toasted hazelnuts
- 12 whole shelled hazelnuts for garnish (optional)

1. Preheat oven to 350°F. Grease a 9-inch springform pan.
2. Prepare the cake batter: In medium bowl with electric mixer at medium speed, beat egg yolks and sugar about 10 minutes, or until smooth and pale yellow. Whisk in orange juice until blended; add ground hazelnuts and matzoh meal, stirring to combine.
3. In another medium bowl with clean beaters and electric mixer at high speed, whip egg whites until stiff peaks form. With rubber spatula or wire whisk, gently fold beaten whites into yolk mixture until blended.
4. Pour batter into prepared springform pan. Bake 35 minutes, or until top springs back when lightly touched. Cool on wire rack.

5. Prepare hazelnut cream: In small saucepan, stir together sugar and water until sugar dissolves. Place over high heat and bring to a boil; boil until mixture reaches soft-ball stage (see Note).

6. Meanwhile, in medium bowl with electric mixer at medium speed, beat egg yolks 3 minutes, or until foamy. Gradually add boiling sugar syrup, a little at a time; beat 2 to 3 minutes longer, or until cool. Reduce speed to low; add margarine and continue beating 5 minutes longer. Stir in ground toasted hazelnuts.

7. To assemble cake: Slice cooled cake horizontally into 2 or 3 layers with long serrated knife. Spread each layer evenly with hazelnut cream; stack layers and frost top and sides with remaining cream. Garnish with whole hazelnuts, if desired.

N O T E : To test sugar-water mixture for the soft-ball stage, drop a small amount into a bowl of cold water. Take the bit of mixture from the water and roll it between your fingers; a small, soft ball should form. Or test the boiling liquid with a candy thermometer. When it reaches the soft-ball stage (238°F) calibrated on the thermometer, it's ready.

Wine note: A lively and lightly sweet white wine is just the ticket for this torte. An Asti would do nicely, either the sparkling or still variety. So, too, would a Vouvray or a semidry New York, Bordeaux, or Israeli white. Wines that are sweeter would tend to cloy, not complement.

Peppers with Tomatoes—*Lecso*
Beef Goulash—*Marha Gulyas*
Pancakes for Sweet Fillings—*Palacsinta*
Fruit Compote—*Kompót*
Noodles with Poppy Seeds—*Makos Metelt*

Peppers with Tomatoes

Lecso

MAKES 4 SERVINGS

There are many varieties of this very popular Hungarian dish. In our homeland, it is most often served with a type of firm Hungarian smoked pork sausage. About half a pound of thinly sliced kosher beef or veal sausage or even frankfurters would substitute nicely for the pork. Or prepare the recipe vegetarian style for a lighter appetizer or side dish.

2 tablespoons vegetable oil
1 onion, peeled, halved, and sliced into crescents
4 large green peppers (about 2 pounds), cored, seeded, and cut into strips
1 tomato, peeled, seeded, and cut into wedges
$1\frac{1}{2}$ teaspoons sweet Hungarian paprika
$\frac{1}{2}$ teaspoon salt
$\frac{1}{2}$ pound smoked sausage or frankfurters, sliced $\frac{1}{4}$-inch thick (optional)
2 eggs

1. In large heavy saucepan, heat oil over medium-low heat. Add onion and sauté 5 minutes, stirring frequently. Add green peppers; continue sautéing 5 minutes longer, stirring occasionally.

2. Stir in tomato, paprika, and salt; reduce heat to low. Add sausage or frankfurters, if desired; cover and cook 15 minutes.

3. In small bowl, beat eggs slightly; add to hot vegetable mixture, stirring gently until eggs have scrambled. Serve immediately.

Wine note: The red Hungarian wine, Egri, would wash this down well, but in looking at the tomato and sausage, Chianti also comes to mind. A light and fruity Beaujolais from France would also help overcome any eggy quality. Make sure it's cool.

Beef Goulash

Marha Gulyas

MAKES 4 SERVINGS

People disagree as to whether goulash or chicken paprikas is considered the national dish of Hungary. We take no sides, cooking and enjoying both! For extra zing, you might want to use a pinch of hot paprika in your goulash.

3 tablespoons vegetable oil
$1\frac{1}{2}$ pounds boneless chuck steak, trimmed of fat and cut into 1-inch cubes
1 onion, peeled and chopped
1 clove garlic, peeled and finely chopped
1 tablespoon sweet Hungarian paprika
1 green bell pepper, cored, seeded, and quartered
1 ripe tomato, peeled, seeded, and quartered
$\frac{1}{4}$ teaspoon caraway seeds
Salt and freshly ground black pepper to taste
5 medium potatoes, peeled and diced
Hot cooked noodles

1. In dutch oven or large heavy saucepan, heat oil over medium-high heat. Add beef, a few pieces at a time; brown well on all sides. Remove beef and set aside.

2. To drippings in dutch oven, add onion and garlic; sauté 3 minutes. Return beef to pot; add paprika, stirring to coat the meat evenly.

3. Stir in 1 cup water, or enough to cover beef. Add green pepper, tomato, caraway seeds, and salt and pepper to taste. Reduce heat to very low; cover and cook $1\frac{1}{2}$ to 2 hours.

4. Add potatoes; cover and cook 30 minutes longer, or until potatoes and beef are tender. Serve with noodles.

Wine note: The wine suggestion on page 188 for chicken paprikas applies here.

Pancakes for Sweet Fillings

Palacsinta

MAKES 6 TO 8 SERVINGS

Fill these crêpelike pancakes with any thick, sweet mixture for a classic Hungarian dessert. We prefer a fruit compote or thick apricot or cherry preserves, while some of our countrymen favor apricot butter (lekvar) or a sweet cheese filling.

3 eggs
$1\frac{1}{3}$ cups club soda or seltzer
$\frac{1}{3}$ cup orange juice
$1\frac{1}{4}$ cups all-purpose flour
2 tablespoons granulated sugar
1 teaspoon vanilla extract
$\frac{1}{2}$ teaspoon salt
2 tablespoons margarine
Confectioners' sugar
Fruit Compote (recipe follows) or fruit-flavored jam or filling

1. In medium bowl, beat eggs slightly with wire whisk. Gradually beat in club soda or seltzer and orange juice, a little at a time. Beat in flour, granulated sugar, vanilla, and salt until mixture forms a smooth batter.

2. In 8- or 9-inch skillet, heat 1 teaspoon margarine over medium-high heat. With ladle, add enough batter to coat bottom of skillet in a thin, even layer. Cook pancake 2 minutes; turn it and cook $1\frac{1}{2}$ minutes on second side, or until lightly browned.

3. Remove pancake to warm plate and keep warm while repeating Step 2 with remaining batter.

4. To serve, fill pancakes with fruit compote or jam; roll up, jelly roll style, and sprinkle with confectioners' sugar.

Wine note: A sweet pancake poses problems for the wine. There is some question whether wine is the correct beverage; a cup of coffee or tea might be more satisfactory. For those special times when a wine would set off the occasion, try a sweet sparkling wine, perhaps Asti Spumante; a sweet sherry; one of the late harvest wines; a Sauternes; even a sweet wine made in the old style from a New York winery might do. The idea is not so much to match sweet to sweet, but to let the wine add a twist of something new, an added dimension of pungency, sourness, or fruit of such a character that the wine and the dessert highlight each other.

Fruit Compote

Kompót

In Hungary, where tropical fruits are scarce, hard winter fruits such as apples and pears make up the bulk of a compote. Other seasonal fruits can also be added when available, including the small oval variety of plum, sour cherries, apricots, or quince. Sugar is used sparingly so as not to make the compote cloyingly sweet.

> 2 pounds fresh seasonal fruit (apples, pears, plums, apricots, and/or cherries)
> $\frac{1}{4}$ to $\frac{1}{2}$ cup sugar
> $\frac{1}{2}$ unpeeled lemon, squeezed (reserve juice)
> 4 whole cloves

1. Peel, core, and quarter the apples and pears. Cut plums, apricots, and cherries in half and remove pits.
2. In large saucepan, combine prepared fruit, sugar, reserved lemon juice, lemon half, cloves, and enough water to cover. Place over medium heat and bring to a boil.
3. Reduce heat to low; cover and simmer 30 minutes, or until fruit is fork-tender. (Do not cook until fruit falls apart.)
4. Discard lemon and cloves. Use as a filling for palacsinta (see preceding recipe) or serve warm in small dessert dishes.

Noodles with Poppy Seeds

Makos Metelt

MAKES 4 SERVINGS

This combination makes a surprisingly sweet and light finale to a meal that's on the heavy side. It is true Hungarian comfort food!

One 8-ounce package wide egg noodles
1 teaspoon salt
1 teaspoon vegetable oil
$\frac{1}{2}$ cup ground or crushed poppy seeds
2 tablespoons sugar
$1\frac{1}{2}$ tablespoons melted margarine

1. In large saucepan, bring 3 quarts water to a boil over high heat. Add noodles, salt, and oil; cook 8 minutes, or until noodles are tender.
2. Drain noodles and rinse under cold running water. Return noodles to saucepan. Add poppy seeds, sugar, and margarine; stir to coat noodles evenly with mixture. Cook over low heat 3 minutes, or until noodles are heated through. Serve hot.

Chinese

a traveler going from one end of China to the other would be impressed by the vastness of the country and the startling differences in climate and geography. In smaller, more homogeneous nations, a cook in the northeast corner might prepare the same meal for dinner as does her counterpart in the southwest. But that duplication could almost never occur in China. Let's take a short journey through the country to get a taste of its diversity.

The northern part, centering around Beijing (Peking) has a cool climate hospitable to the cultivation of wheat. While rice is the staple crop and starch of choice in other parts of China, here noodles, dumplings, and steamed buns take its place. Mongolia, China's neighbor to the north, has also had an impact on the cuisine. Beef, lamb, and duck are often barbecued Mongolian style or dipped in hot broth to simmer along with cut-up vegetables. As a rule, the dishes prepared in northern China are light and subtle, with small amounts of garlic, scallions, leeks, and wine the preferred flavorings. In prerevolution Peking, the presence of the Imperial Palace exerted influence: Dishes prepared for the emperor and his entourage were expected to be the most delicately seasoned and prestigious in all the land, often containing rare and costly ingredients.

The southern section of China, containing Kuang-Chou (Canton), is almost subtropical in climate and very productive agriculturally. Fruit grows in abundance here, the coastal waters and rivers offer an ample supply of seafood, and livestock thrive in the fertile fields. Stir-frying and steaming are the traditional cooking methods, with soy sauce and fermented black beans two favored seasonings. Flourishing trade has created a wealthy economy and an adventurous spirit, reflected in a cooking style that's innovative and exciting.

The eastern part of China encompasses Shanghai, probably the most cosmopolitan and westernized city in the country. The Yangtze River flows into the sea just north of Shanghai, irrigating lush rice fields along the way. All this water means a steady influx of fresh fish and bumper crops of vegetables, including bamboo shoots, bok choy, napa cabbage, a wide variety of mushrooms, and many types of greens. Consequently, vegetables and rice are mainstays of the diet. Ingredients are sometimes flavored with dark soy sauce and braised over low heat, or stir-fried with milder sauces and modest quantities of spices, producing a more refined cuisine than that found to the west and south. The people around Shanghai also seem to have a collective sweet tooth, so some of their dishes are a bit sweeter than those in other parts of China.

The Hunan and Szechuan provinces in the western region are known for their hot, spicy fare. The steamy climate and fertile land around the upper basin of the Yangtze River foster the growth of many types of peppers and spices, which give this cuisine its great variety and fiery reputation. Some of the regional cooking methods tend to increase the hotness of the food. In stir-frying, for example, the hot spices are often cooked in oil first to seal in their flavor. Then scallions and ginger might be added to intensify the combination. And it's customary to serve a spicy sauce with a dish that already has some heat of its own. Because this part of China is landlocked, fresh seafood does not figure prominently. Chicken, venison, and pork are used more frequently, as are countless species of mushrooms that grow in the rich, moist soil. Pickled vegetables and dried foods are also much more common here than in the other provinces.

Although each of these major regions has its own distinct culinary style, Chinese cooking as a whole is characterized by certain similar threads. First of all, meals are always tremendously varied; each consists of several dishes, which in turn can contain a large number of ingredients. Like most Chinese cooks, I try to provide contrasts of taste, texture, color, size, and shape in every dish, aided greatly by a wide selection of oriental vegetables, often combined with small amounts of meat or fish.

The soybean has always been an important part of the Chinese diet, too. A valuable and inexpensive protein source, it has many uses, including bean curd (tofu), bean curd skins, soybean milk, and soybean sprouts. In fact, bean curd and soybean milk are vegetarian or pareve substitutes for the dairy products that never found their way into Chinese cuisine. The absence of milk, cheese, and cream eases the transition of Chinese food into kosher.

Lack of refrigeration and scarcity of fuel also affected the development of China's culinary tradition. My resourceful Chinese ancestors dried an assortment of vegetables and seafood to keep them from spoiling, creating an array of food products that are still widely used. On the other hand, two common cooking methods that evolved—stir-frying and steaming—highlighted the freshness of the fresh ingredients while maximizing available fuel. Although these limitations may seem inhibiting, I believe they have made the Chinese cuisine one of the most flexible in the world.

This flexibility also makes it relatively simple to cook Chinese dishes in accordance with the dietary laws. Although authentic Chinese cooking does make frequent use of pork and shellfish, I have found that dark-meat turkey and veal make acceptable substitutes for pork when seasoned properly, and such fish as salmon and halibut can stand in for shrimp, scallops, and lobster meat, on occasion.

While the fresh vegetables, fruits, nuts, rice, and noodles used in Chinese dishes are all pareve and pose no problem to the kosher cook, some of the dried and processed ingredients can be a little controversial. Many oriental food products are imported from China, Japan, and other Far Eastern countries. While more and more are being stamped with a ⓤ or other symbol of kashrut, others have not yet received rabbinical approval, even though they contain only pure vegetable ingredients, such as black beans or dried mushrooms. However, since these foods are processed in nonsupervised plants overseas, they cannot always be approved. I have also discovered that from one shopping trip to the next, an approved oriental product can lose its kosher insignia, while a formerly banned food may have gained one! I find it safest to check products continually for their kosherness, and consult with a rabbi if there's a question of purity.

Surprisingly enough, Chinese and kosher cooking share some comparable roots. For example, the Jewish dietary laws are based, in part, on a reverence for life, as are the prohibitions against eating animals developed by the early Chinese Buddhists and Taoists. Furthermore, a Jewish tribe made its home long ago in the Chinese city of Kaifeng in Hunan province, blending into the culture and contributing some traditions of its own. Perhaps this cohabitation is responsible for the resemblance between kreplach and wontons!

In the menus that follow, I've carefully developed recipes that preserve the taste of genuine Chinese cuisine but strictly adhere to kosher guidelines. I've also tried to provide a representative sampling of each of China's regional cooking styles. Wherever it's eaten, a typical Chinese meal usually starts with a soup or appetizer, followed by several main dishes that are served together. Although the recipes in these menus were designed to complement each other nicely, they can be interchanged without adversely affecting the balance and contrast of the meal.

—*Millie Chan*

Millie Chan

M illie Chan was born to second-generation Chinese-American parents in San Antonio, Texas. In this city near the Mexican border, her mother and father ran a large, elegant Chinese restaurant and several groceries, so Millie got into cooking at an early age. She and her family frequently gathered with other Chinese families in the area for big, communal meals featuring a variety of dishes contributed by each. During her childhood, she developed quite a taste for Tex-Mex food as well!

Although Millie's natural culinary talents were being nurtured by her parents and grandmother (another excellent cook), she decided to study music, eventually gaining a degree in music education. Soon after graduation, she married and moved to New York City, where her husband pursued his career in architecture and Millie became a full-time mother. While her children were growing up, she cooked a lot of traditional Chinese family meals and learned new techniques in cooking classes at the China Institute. Here she met Florence Lin, the renowned Chinese cooking teacher and author, who became her mentor.

Eventually, Millie felt she was able to share her impressive culinary skills by teaching her own cooking classes at the China Institute. Her kosher expertise, however, was not developed until later. At a fundraiser for her children's school, she donated Chinese cooking lessons. Helen Nash, a kosher cookbook author, bought the lessons, and the two women ended up teaching each other. Millie quickly recognized the wonderful compatibility of Chinese food with the dietary laws, and she soon turned this insight into a whole new cooking course. In 1981, she established the first Chinese kosher cooking class at the 92nd Street Y.

These days, Millie serves on the board of the China Institute and works there part-time in an administrative position. She is also in great demand as the only kosher Chinese cooking teacher in New York City, and has compiled a cookbook of her favorite recipes, titled Millie Chan's Chinese Kosher Cookbook (Harmony/Crown, 1990). One Chan son is now a medical student, the other is an architect, and Millie's daughter is carrying on her family's food heritage as a restaurant manager in Vermont.

New-style Egg Drop Soup—*Dun Hwa Tong*
Stir-fry Beef with Leeks—*Tsung Bau Niu-Rou*
Chicken and Cucumber Salad—*Liang Ban Huang Gwa*
Chicken in Casserole—*Hong Sau Gee*
Steamed Fillets of Sole—*Zheng Yu*
Banana Fritters—*Zha Shiang-Jau*

New-style Egg Drop Soup

Dun Hwa Tong

MAKES 4 TO 6 SERVINGS

I developed this recipe as a heart-healthy alternative to traditional egg drop soup, which uses whole eggs. The elimination of the yolks cuts out the cholesterol without losing the traditional texture and taste of this Cantonese favorite.

  5 cups chicken broth
  2 teaspoons kosher (coarse) salt
  1 tablespoon soy sauce
  1 tablespoon rice wine
  2 tablespoons cornstarch
  4 egg whites, well beaten
  2 teaspoons oriental sesame oil
  2 teaspoons finely chopped scallions for garnish

1. In large saucepan, bring chicken broth to a boil over high heat. Add salt; stir well. Stir in soy sauce and rice wine; reduce heat to medium and simmer 30 seconds.

2. In a cup, combine $\frac{1}{2}$ cup water and cornstarch; blend well. Gradually add cornstarch mixture to boiling broth, stirring constantly until broth thickens. Return broth to a boil.

3. Remove saucepan from heat. Immediately and gradually add beaten whites in a slow, thin stream, stirring gently and constantly in a circular motion until set.

4. To serve, ladle soup into individual bowls; add drops of sesame oil to each serving and garnish with chopped scallions. Serve immediately.

Stir-fry Beef with Leeks

Tsung Bau Niu-Rou

MAKES 4 SERVINGS

Ask your butcher for London broil to use in this recipe—I've found this kosher cut of beef round to be best for stir-fry recipes. The secret to successful stir-frying is to cut the meat and vegetables into pieces of uniform size so they will cook evenly and look wonderfully Chinese in the finished dish.

1 bunch leeks
$\frac{1}{2}$ pound London broil or minute steak
2 teaspoons cornstarch
$\frac{3}{4}$ teaspoon sugar
1 tablespoon dark soy sauce
$\frac{1}{4}$ cup (4 tablespoons) corn oil or peanut oil
1 teaspoon salt, or more to taste

1. Cut leeks in half lengthwise. Rinse under cold running water to remove all sand. Cut each half leek into 2-inch lengths; shred white and light green parts into thin strips. Reserve dark green tops for stock, if desired.

2. With sharp knife, thinly slice beef across grain; cut slices into thin shreds. In shallow bowl, combine 1 teaspoon cornstarch, $\frac{1}{4}$ teaspoon sugar, soy sauce, and 1 tablespoon water. Add beef, tossing to coat well. Cover and refrigerate 20 minutes.

3. Place a wok or large skillet over medium-high heat; heat until hot. Add 2 tablespoons oil; heat until hot. Toss in leeks; stir-fry until coated with oil. Add salt and $\frac{1}{2}$ teaspoon sugar; stir-fry 3 to 4 minutes, until leeks are just wilted. Transfer to warm serving platter; wipe out wok with paper towels.

4. Place the same wok over medium-high heat; heat until hot. Add remaining 2 tablespoons oil; heat until very hot. Add beef; stir quickly to separate pieces. Cook 3 to 5 minutes, until beef is cooked through, stirring constantly. Add leeks; stir to combine. Make a well in center of mixture.

5. In a cup, blend remaining 1 teaspoon cornstarch with 1 tablespoon water; stir into well in center of wok. Cook over medium heat until sauce forms a glaze over the ingredients, stirring constantly.

6. Taste for seasoning, adding more salt if necessary. Transfer to warm serving platter and serve at once.

N O T E : Cuts of meat have different names in different parts of the United States. To make sure you get the appropriate kosher cut, it's best to tell your butcher what kind of recipe you'll be preparing.

Wine note: A fruity and light red wine would pair well with this dish—the fruitiness of the wine playing off the oil, sugar, and soy sauce. Try a Beaujolais or Gamay.

Chicken and Cucumber Salad

Liang Ban Huang Gwa

MAKES 4 SERVINGS

I find it easier to slice the chicken if the raw meat is partially frozen first.

1 boneless, skinless chicken breast half
1 egg white
2 teaspoons rice wine
2 tablespoons plus 2 teaspoons corn oil
1 teaspoon cornstarch
$\frac{1}{4}$ teaspoon kosher (coarse) salt
2 medium seedless cucumbers, peeled
1 teaspoon oriental sesame oil

1. Slice chicken breast crosswise as thinly as possible. Cut slices into lengthwise shreds about $1\frac{1}{2}$ inches long.
2. In shallow bowl, beat egg white with rice wine, 2 teaspoons corn oil, cornstarch, and salt. Add chicken to this marinade mixture; toss to coat thoroughly. Cover and refrigerate at least 1 hour, or overnight.
3. Cut cucumbers crosswise on a slight diagonal into slices about 1 inch long; cut slices lengthwise into shreds. Set aside.
4. Place a wok over medium-high heat; heat until hot. Add 2 tablespoons corn oil; heat until hot. Add shredded chicken. Quickly stir-fry to separate shreds; continue stir-frying 2 to 3 minutes longer, until chicken turns white. Stir in cucumber. Transfer mixture to large bowl; cool to room temperature.
5. Stir in sesame oil. Serve at room temperature.

Wine note: Cucumber has a cooling and refreshing effect on the palate and this dish seems just right for a spring lunch on porch or patio. A light, unassertive white wine could wash it down well without destroying the sprightliness of the food. A dry Riesling or Pinot Blanc from Israel would be just the ticket.

Chicken in Casserole

Hong Sau Gee

MAKES 4 SERVINGS

Marinating the chicken before cooking gives it a flavor assertive enough to stand in for pork. This dish is a good one to include in a menu of stir-fried recipes, since it doesn't have to be done at the last minute—the chicken braises gently.

1 tablespoon soy sauce
1 tablespoon rice wine
1 tablespoon cornstarch
$\frac{1}{2}$ teaspoon salt
$\frac{1}{2}$ teaspoon sugar
$\frac{1}{2}$ pound boneless, skinless chicken (breasts or thighs), cut into 1-inch chunks
1 tablespoon corn oil
2 scallions, chopped
2 cups chicken broth
4 dried black mushrooms, soaked, stems removed, and caps cut into quarters
2 peeled slices fresh gingerroot, each about the size of a quarter
Hot cooked rice

1. In shallow bowl, combine soy sauce, rice wine, cornstarch, salt, and sugar. Add chicken chunks; toss to coat well. Cover and refrigerate 1 hour.
2. In large saucepan or heatproof casserole dish, heat oil over medium-high heat. Add scallions; stir-fry 30 seconds. Stir in chicken broth, mushrooms, and gingerroot; bring to a boil. Add chicken; return to a boil.
3. Reduce heat to low; cover and simmer 10 minutes, or until chicken is tender. Serve with rice.

Wine note: This dish gives a lot of leeway as far as wine goes—red or white, dry or slightly sweet. Riesling in most of its many manifestations would be an ideal match for the ginger and soy sauce. Gewürztraminer would add another dimension, while Chenin Blanc would provide a nice touch. In red wine, a young Coteaux du Tricastin, Minervois, Beaujolais, or Côtes du Rhône from France; or a Merlot from Israel.

Steamed Fillets of Sole

Zheng Yu

MAKES 4 SERVINGS

$\frac{3}{4}$ pound gray sole fillets or flounder fillets
3 tablespoons corn oil
1 tablespoon light soy sauce
2 teaspoons shredded scallions
1 teaspoon peeled, finely minced fresh gingerroot
1 teaspoon rice wine
$\frac{1}{4}$ teaspoon kosher (coarse) salt
Dash of white pepper
2 dried black mushrooms, soaked, stems removed, and caps slivered
4 thin slices bamboo shoot, slivered
Cilantro sprigs for garnish (optional)

1. Cut fillets in half lengthwise. If fillets are very long, cut in half crosswise.
2. In shallow bowl, combine 1 tablespoon oil, soy sauce, scallions, gingerroot, rice wine, salt, and pepper. Add fish fillets, coating well with marinade. Cover and refrigerate 1 hour.

3. At narrow end of each fish fillet, place a few pieces of bamboo shoot and mushrooms. Roll up fillet, jelly roll style. Place fish rolls on a large round plate with a 2-inch rim.

4. In large skillet or dutch oven, bring 2 inches water to a boil over high heat. Place the plate of fish on a wire rack or steamer over the boiling water. Cover and steam 7 minutes, or until fish turns opaque.

5. In small skillet, heat remaining 2 tablespoons oil over high heat until almost smoking. To serve, pour hot oil over fish; garnish with cilantro, if desired.

N O T E : Cilantro is also known as coriander or Chinese parsley. Its flat leaves resemble Italian parsley, but its aroma and flavor are more pungent.

Wine note: A wide range of dry white wines would marry well with this strong dish characterized by the aromas of cilantro and ginger. Choices abound—Chablis, Macon, Pinot Grigio, Seyval Blanc, or Fumé Blanc are some.

Banana Fritters

Zha Shiang-Jau

MAKES 4 SERVINGS

This deep-fried confection is a favorite dessert in restaurants serving spicy Chinese food.

4 firm, ripe bananas
¾ cup all-purpose flour
2 tablespoons cornstarch
2 teaspoons baking powder
2 cups corn oil
¼ cup superfine sugar

1. Peel bananas and cut into 2-inch pieces.
2. In medium bowl, combine flour, cornstarch, and baking powder. Add ¾ cup water; stir to make a thick batter.
3. Place wok or large saucepan over medium-high heat; heat until hot. Add oil; heat until temperature reaches 325°F on deep-fat thermometer. Dip banana pieces into batter, allowing excess to drip off. Carefully add bananas, 6 or 7 pieces at a time, to hot oil. Deep-fry about 2 minutes, or until golden brown, turning several times during cooking. Remove from oil and drain on paper towels; keep warm. Repeat with remaining banana pieces until all are cooked.
4. To serve, transfer banana fritters to serving platter; sprinkle with sugar. Serve warm.

Stuffed Mushrooms—*Shiang Dong-Gu*
Salmon Steaks with Spicy Sauce—*Sh-Tse Yu*
Sesame Chicken—*Zhi-Ma Gee*
Watercress Salad—*Liang Ban Shee-Yang-Tsai*
Sesame Cookies—*Zhi-Ma Bien*

Stuffed Mushrooms

Shiang Dong-Gu

MAKES 4 TO 6 APPETIZER OR MAIN-DISH SERVINGS

If fresh water chestnuts are difficult to find, you can substitute fresh jicama. I recently discovered this Latin or Mexican vegetable—it looks a bit like a turnip but has a sweet taste and crunchy texture similar to water chestnuts. Drained, canned water chestnuts can be used as well. The ground turkey in the stuffing makes an excellent substitute for pork.

1 cup ground turkey
$\frac{1}{4}$ cup finely minced scallions
$\frac{1}{4}$ cup finely minced bamboo shoots
3 fresh water chestnuts, peeled and finely minced
   (about $\frac{1}{2}$ cup)
1 tablespoon light soy sauce
1 tablespoon dark soy sauce
1 tablespoon corn oil
1 teaspoon cornstarch
$\frac{1}{2}$ teaspoon peeled and finely minced fresh gingerroot

$\frac{1}{2}$ teaspoon kosher (coarse) salt

$\frac{1}{2}$ teaspoon sugar

Dash of white pepper

20 dried black mushrooms, each about the size of a quarter, soaked overnight and stems removed

1. In large bowl, combine turkey, 7 tablespoons water, and remaining ingredients except mushrooms. With spoon, stir in one direction until mixture becomes light and fluffy.
2. Drain mushrooms and squeeze water from each cap. Spread the underside (inside) of each mushroom cap with about 1 tablespoon turkey mixture, mounding it slightly in center.
3. Oil a large round plate with a rim; arrange stuffed mushrooms on plate. Pour 2 inches of water into large deep skillet or dutch oven. Place over high heat and bring to a boil. Set plate of mushrooms on wire rack or steamer over the boiling water; cover and steam 15 minutes.
4. Pour off liquid accumulated on plate and reserve. Serve mushrooms as an appetizer, or accompany with liquid to serve as a main course.

N O T E : The reserved liquid can be refrigerated and added as needed to flavor stir-fried vegetables, or it can be used as a base for a vegetarian broth.

Most oriental-style mushrooms are sun-dried and therefore kosher. If there's a doubt about the product you intend to use, consult your rabbi.

Wine note: Mushrooms are magic with wine, and the stuffing here does nothing to detract from that. Let's go for a light wine for this appetizer—Cabernet Blanc or rosé, a young light red from Burgundy, a Beaujolais, or one of the generic reds from Israel.

Salmon Steaks with Spicy Sauce

Sh-Tse Yu

MAKES 4 SERVINGS

The black beans are listed as optional in the ingredients because I have not found a brand that is approved and stamped with a kosher symbol. Black beans are a pure vegetable product, but are processed in a foreign plant. Therefore, your individual rabbi should be consulted as to their purity. In any case, this dish will taste terrific with or without black beans.

1 tablespoon light soy sauce
1 teaspoon rice wine
Dash of sugar
2 thin slices peeled fresh gingerroot, finely shredded
1 scallion, finely shredded
2 large salmon steaks
2 tablespoons cornstarch
3 tablespoons corn oil

SPICY SAUCE
1 clove garlic, peeled and finely minced
1 teaspoon salted black beans, coarsely chopped (optional)
2 teaspoons hot chili sauce, or to taste
$\frac{1}{2}$ teaspoon kosher (coarse) salt
$\frac{1}{4}$ teaspoon sugar
$\frac{1}{4}$ cup chicken broth, fish broth, or water
$\frac{1}{2}$ teaspoon cornstarch

1. In shallow bowl, combine soy sauce, rice wine, dash of sugar, gingerroot, and scallion; mix well. Add salmon and turn to coat well with marinade. Cover and refrigerate 1 hour.
2. Dust salmon steaks on both sides with cornstarch. Place medium skillet over medium-high heat; heat until hot. Add corn oil; heat until oil is hot. Add salmon steaks; sauté about 2 minutes, or until browned on underside. Turn steaks over and sauté on second side 2

minutes longer, until salmon is browned and cooked through. Transfer to serving platter and keep warm. Leave oil in skillet.

3. Prepare sauce: Add garlic and black beans, if desired, to the hot oil in the skillet; stir well. Stir in chili sauce, salt, and $\frac{1}{4}$ teaspoon sugar. Blend broth and cornstarch in a cup; stir into skillet. Cook over medium heat about 2 minutes, or until sauce thickens, stirring constantly.

4. Pour sauce over salmon and serve immediately.

Wine note: Salmon is a fish that goes well with red wine. In this case, try a light red—Chianti would do well, as would a young Barbera or Israeli generic. Because of the spicy sauce, one of the whites made from red grapes also might appeal, such as a Cabernet Blanc. A less exciting and more classical match would be the Israeli or Californian Sauvignon Blancs or Chardonnays—wines that have sufficient weight to meet the salmon and sauce on even terms.

Sesame Chicken

Zhi-Ma Gee

MAKES 4 SERVINGS

This recipe was popular at my parents' restaurant in San Antonio. Although the cooking procedure may seem a little repetitive, deep-frying the chicken twice gives this dish its authentic taste and look.

2 tablespoons plus ½ teaspoon cornstarch
2 tablespoons soy sauce
1 teaspoon oriental sesame oil
½ teaspoon sugar
¾ pound boneless chicken (thighs or breasts)
1 tablespoon chicken broth
1 tablespoon rice wine
2 cups corn oil
1 bunch cilantro (fresh coriander), rinsed and dried
2 tablespoons sesame seeds

1. In shallow bowl, combine 2 tablespoons cornstarch, 1 tablespoon soy sauce, sesame oil, and sugar; mix well. Cut chicken into pieces about 1 inch long by ½ inch wide; add to soy mixture, coating well with marinade. Cover and refrigerate at least 1 hour.
2. In small bowl, combine chicken broth, rice wine, remaining 1 tablespoon soy sauce, and remaining ½ teaspoon cornstarch; mix well. Place wire strainer over saucepan; keep near stove.
3. Place wok over high heat and add oil; heat until very hot. Add cilantro to hot oil; deep fry 1 to 2 minutes, or until crisp. Remove and drain. Pat with paper towels to remove excess oil.
4. Return wok to high heat and reheat oil until very hot. Drain chicken from marinade and add to hot oil; deep-fry about 2 minutes or just until it changes color. With slotted spoon, transfer chicken to wire strainer set over saucepan to drain. Reheat oil again until very hot. Return chicken to hot oil and deep-fry about 2 minutes more, or until chicken is crispy around the edges. Pour chicken and oil into strainer set over saucepan and allow to drain.

5. Return wok to medium heat; add 2 tablespoons drained oil and heat until medium-hot. Stir broth mixture in small bowl; add to hot oil and cook 1 to 2 minutes, or until slightly thickened, stirring constantly. Add cooked chicken; cook until sauce coats chicken with a clear glaze, stirring constantly. To serve, sprinkle with sesame seeds and transfer to serving plate. Garnish with fried cilantro and serve immediately.

Wine note: The double-dip deep-frying rules out the bigger red wines, while giving light reds and whites a chance to shine. How about a Chenin Blanc, Riesling, semidry white from Bordeaux, or one of the young, red Bordeaux or Gamays?

Watercress Salad

Liang Ban Shee-Yang-Tsai

MAKES 4 SERVINGS

2 bunches watercress
$\frac{1}{4}$ cup sliced bamboo shoots, finely minced
$\frac{1}{4}$ cup seasoned pressed bean curd, cut into cubes
2 teaspoons oriental sesame oil
$\frac{1}{2}$ teaspoon kosher (coarse) salt
$\frac{1}{2}$ teaspoon sugar

1. Wash watercress and shake dry. In large saucepan, bring 8 cups water to a boil over high heat. Add watercress and let steep 10 seconds. Drain; rinse with cold water until cool to the touch.
2. Squeeze out as much water as possible from watercress, and chop it until finely minced; there should be about 1½ cups.
3. In medium bowl, combine watercress, bamboo shoots, and bean curd; toss well. In cup, combine sesame oil, salt, and sugar. Add sesame dressing to watercress mixture just before serving.

NOTE: Tomsum and Azumaya brands of bean curd are both certified as kosher and are available in the produce section of the supermarket, as well as in oriental markets and some health-food stores. There might also be local approved brands sold in your area—they would have a Ⓤ or Ⓚ and will probably be labeled "pareve" as well.

Sesame Cookies

Zhi-Ma Bien

MAKES 5 DOZEN

Fruit is usually the preferred dessert after a Chinese family meal. At banquets and special occasions, however, a more elaborate sweet might be served. Although these crisp cookies do not originate from China, I developed the recipe with ingredients that impart an oriental flavor. This dough can be prepared up to 1 week in advance, then sliced and baked when needed.

6 tablespoons ($\frac{3}{4}$ stick) margarine
$\frac{3}{4}$ cup packed brown sugar
1 egg
1 teaspoon vanilla extract
1 cup all-purpose flour
$\frac{1}{4}$ teaspoon kosher (coarse) salt
$\frac{1}{4}$ teaspoon baking powder
$\frac{3}{4}$ cup toasted sesame seeds

1. In large bowl with electric mixer at medium speed, or with wooden spoon, beat margarine and brown sugar until blended. Add egg and vanilla; continue beating until light and fluffy.
2. In medium bowl or on waxed paper, sift together flour, salt, and

baking powder. Add flour mixture and sesame seeds to sugar mixture; stir until thoroughly blended into a soft dough.

3. Shape dough into a roll about $1\frac{1}{2}$ inches in diameter; wrap in waxed paper and chill several hours, or up to 1 week.

4. When ready to bake, preheat oven to 350°F. Grease cookie sheets. With a long, sharp knife, slice dough into thin rounds about $\frac{1}{8}$ inch thick. Place rounds on cookie sheets about 1 inch apart. Bake 8 minutes, or until light brown around the edges.

5. Remove cookies from cookie sheets and cool on wire racks.

NOTE: For a dairy meal, these cookies can be prepared with butter instead of margarine.

Wine note: These would make a nice nibble with a sipping wine that's just a mite sweet, yet not as sweet or unctuous as a Sauternes. Some suggestions: a sweet Gewürztraminer or Vouvray, or a demi-sec from Israel.

Italian

*t*he culinary heritage of Italy dates back over two thousand years, making Italian cuisine as we know it today one of the oldest in the world. It started when the Greeks conquered Sicily and remained there to partake of lavish meals prepared from an abundance of locally available foods. A few centuries later came the legendary feasts of the Roman Empire, renowned for their extravagant and exotic dishes consumed in large quantities in sumptuous surroundings.

After the decline of the empire, Italy was at a culinary standstill of sorts until the Middle Ages, when Arab invaders, and later the Crusades, introduced new food products and preparation techniques from the East. This period was followed by the Renaissance —a rebirth of all the arts, including the art of fine cooking. Today, Italy is recognized the world over for its significant culinary contributions.

As in France and China, much of Italy's national cuisine has evolved from several regional styles. Until a little over a hundred years ago, the country was divided into many small, independent states, each with its own food products and culinary traditions. In addition, there has always been an economic division in Italy between the more prosperous north and the poorer south, further influencing the development of food patterns. Modern transportation, better food distribution, and increased travel have recently made Italian cuisine more uniform and consistent. But happily, some regional differences do remain, preserving the diversity and freshness that are trademarks of Italian cooking.

In the northeastern area around Venice, for example, fish from the Adriatic Sea, wild mushrooms, and local Parmesan cheese enliven the table. Tuscany is known for its olive oil, bread, beans, beef, and game, while the Piedmont region near Milan boasts excellent risotto, polenta, mush, veal, and truffles. Bologna is justly famous for its sausages, hams, and the robust meat sauce that tops egg-enriched ribbons of pasta. From Naples south, on the other hand, tubular, eggless macaroni is often served, accompanied by fish and vegetable sauces. Tomatoes, eggplant, zucchini, sweet peppers, and all kinds of seafood are plentiful here. The southern part of the country is also the birthplace of pizza, now an international treat.

Rome's history as a religious and political center has also given it an eclectic diet, but certain foods stand out as quintessentially Roman. These include artichokes, celery, tripe, and lamb, as well as stews and other dishes flavored with mint, cloves, and sage. Rome was also home to a large Jewish community, from which the unique Judeo-Roman culinary style developed.

Although regional distinctions continue to some degree, many foods are more universally Italian. Fish and pasta, for instance, are cooked in kitchens from Milan to Palermo. Almost every province in Italy touches the sea, providing the country with a huge variety and quantity of fish. Pasta originated in southern Italy before it infiltrated other parts of the land, but today every section of Italy has its favorite shape and method of preparation for this national passion, ranging from a simple topping of garlic and olive oil to an elaborate stuffed and layered casserole.

Among the great natural resources of Italy are its fruits, vegetables, and herbs. Marketplaces offer a profusion of fresh produce, including broccoli, spinach, asparagus, fennel, garlic, citrus fruits, figs, grapes, and all the regional crops. Bunches of oregano, sweet basil, rosemary, parsley, thyme, and other fresh herbs are usually close by, ready to perfume and flavor the humblest of dishes. As far as meats go, chicken and veal are eaten more often than beef or lamb—cows and sheep are raised primarily for dairy products. And

Italians are regarded as expert cheese-makers, creating a large assortment of cheeses for cooking and eating, among them mozzarella, ricotta, Gorgonzola, provolone, Parmigiano, fontina, and Bel Paese.

Jews have lived in various parts of Italy for many centuries. Before World War II, when a large number were forced to flee, several Jewish families could trace their roots back as far as ancient Roman times. Others arrived from the Middle East, North Africa, and Spain during and after the fifteenth century. Jewish settlements thrived in such major cities as Rome, Milan, and Florence, as well as in a few smaller villages scattered throughout the countryside.

The cuisine that emerged from Jewish kitchens was a blend of old and new—cooks adapted the dishes of their homeland to the products and customs of Italy, and changed the traditional Italian recipes to conform with dietary laws. In fact, quite a few foods with Jewish origins are considered to be typically Italian. These include eggplant, fennel, and artichokes cooked in the style of the Roman Jews (neatly trimmed and flattened, then braised in olive oil and lemon juice). Two other familiar menu offerings from the Judeo-Roman culinary legacy are caponata (marinated eggplant and olive appetizer) and focaccia (a flat, round yeast bread flavored with rosemary and garlic). The Jews also passed down a number of dishes prepared with vinegar. It both flavored and preserved foods, allowing observant cooks to prepare a recipe in advance and let it stand at room temperature until it was eaten for the Sabbath meal.

Since the Jews have inhabited Italy through so many generations, much of the work of translating dishes from Italian to kosher has already been done. Nevertheless, modern Jewish cooks may need some guidance in making kosher adaptations of Italian-American favorites, many of which combine dairy and meat products, or use pork. One way around this dilemma is to prepare an all-dairy menu, as New York City's kosher-Italian restaurant Va Bene does.

One of the menus that follows was developed from Va Bene's carefully tested recipes. Chef Paolo Lattanzi uses all Cholov Yisroel products in his kitchen except for the Parmigiano cheese. Although kosher, the Parmigiano is kept in a small vestibule outside the kitchen to be freshly grated at the table. On shopping trips, you might find some canned and packaged imported items, such as dried porcini mushrooms and olive oil, that have arrived on these shores without certification. Consult your rabbi before using these products.

It's also possible to create a meat-based meal that's truly Italian, kosher, and very tasty, as Esther Shear did with our first menu. Although Italian-Jewish families like hers did eat a lot of vegetarian and fish dishes, their cooking also included a number of savory main courses centering on veal, beef, or chicken. And since Italian Jews followed the Sephardic tradition, the hindquarter of the animal was kashered and used. This made way for recipes using leg of lamb and veal rump, in addition to the usual kosher cuts.

As it turns out, eliminating sausages, ham, and cheese-and-meat combinations still leaves room for a lot of delicious Italian cooking. Besides, native Italians don't sprinkle grated Parmigiano cheese on everything, even though waiters in Italian-American restaurants might lead you to believe otherwise!

Paolo Lattanzi

*P*aolo Lattanzi's childhood home was close to the old Jewish quarter of Rome. Even though his family wasn't Jewish, his mother liked to cook many of the typical Roman-Jewish dishes. So it wasn't unusual for the Lattanzi kids to feast on caponata, marinated artichokes, fish with raisins and pine nuts, focaccia, and the other simple but delectable foods created by Jewish cooks. A wonderful cook, Mama Lattanzi's repertoire also included various other specialties, all prepared with the freshest local ingredients.

When the Lattanzi family—four brothers, a sister, and mama—came to the United States in 1968, it was natural to go into the restaurant business. "My mother's kitchen was always like a restaurant anyway," recalls Paolo, and he found it easy to land a job as a chef. Then in 1979, the family opened the first Lattanzi restaurant, serving up basic Italian fare, lovingly and deliciously cooked according to family recipes. In 1983, after vacationing in Rome and becoming reacquainted with Roman-Jewish cuisine, the brothers decided to introduce some of these dishes to their customers. They instituted a weekly nonkosher Roman-Jewish dinner at their Lattanzi restaurant in New York City's theater district. It immediately caught on and grew in popularity.

Two years ago, Paolo decided the time was right to start a kosher Italian restaurant. So he developed a meat-based kosher menu at Trastevere 84—a well-liked Lattanzi dining spot on Manhattan's Upper East Side—and applied for rabbinical supervision. The menu was approved, and a large clientele was soon enjoying the glatt kosher Roman-style specialties. When several diners began requesting fish and dairy dishes, Paolo opened Va Bene around the corner from Trastevere 84. The menu here features such items as tortellini with wild mushrooms, snapper with garlic, olive oil, and tomatoes, and Italian cheesecake. At least four soups are included every day, and an impressive selection of kosher wines is always on hand. At both restaurants, the menus are now rounded out with northern and southern Italian food. And on holidays, like Chanukah, Paolo can be found cooking up such traditional recipes as potato latkes and apple doughnuts. All the cooking and baking is done with ⓤ approved ingredients.

There are now five New York City restaurants owned by the Lattanzis, and every family member is involved in one or another. Paolo Lattanzi considers himself the "traveling chef" of the family—he's the one who usually starts up a new venture and keeps it rolling for a while. He divides his free time between an apartment in Manhattan and a home in Tarrytown, New York.

◆ ◆ ◆

For biographical note on Esther Shear, see page 108.

Roasted Peppers with Anchovies and Olives—
Peperoni Arrostiti con Acciughe
Veal Stew—*Spezzatino di Vitello Milanese*
Risotto
Broccoli with Garlic and Oil—*Broccoli all'aglio*
Whipped Wine Custard—*Zabaglione*

Roasted Peppers with Anchovies and Olives

Peperoni Arrostiti con Acciughe

MAKES 6 SERVINGS

I like to roast or broil peppers to bring out their flavor. The anchovies and olives offer a nice salty contrast to the sweetness of the peppers.

    4 large red bell peppers
    3 tablespoons olive oil
        Juice of 1 lemon
    1 tablespoon finely chopped peeled onion (optional)
    8 canned anchovies, drained
    8 pitted black olives, halved

1. Preheat broiler. Place whole peppers on broiler pan and broil about 4 inches from heat source 10 to 15 minutes, or until charred on all sides and softened. Turn them frequently.
2. Transfer peppers to brown paper bag; fold top over to close. Leave peppers in bag 10 to 15 minutes.
3. Peel skin from peppers and remove membranes and seeds. Cut peppers into thin strips; arrange on serving plate. In small bowl, mix

well oil, lemon juice, and onion; pour evenly over peppers. Garnish with anchovies and olives.

NOTE: Placing hot broiled peppers in a closed paper bag makes it much easier to peel them. As they steam, their skins loosen.

Veal Stew

Spezzatino di Vitello Milanese

MAKES 6 TO 8 SERVINGS

This boneless veal stew is a take-off on ossobuco, a northern Italian veal dish made with veal shanks and sprinkled with gremolata—a heavenly mixture of lemon peel, garlic, and fresh parsley. The version that follows is quicker and easier to prepare; a perfect main course for a company dinner.

2 to $2\frac{1}{2}$ pounds boneless veal stewing meat, cut into chunks
    Salt and ground black pepper to taste
  3 tablespoons all-purpose flour
  3 tablespoons vegetable oil
  2 medium onions, peeled and chopped
  3 carrots, peeled and finely diced
  1 rib celery, finely diced
  4 to 5 cloves garlic, peeled and minced
One 8-ounce can stewed tomatoes
  1 cup white wine
  $\frac{1}{2}$ cup tomato sauce
  2 bay leaves
    Pinch of dried thyme
  $\frac{1}{4}$ cup chopped parsley
  1 tablespoon grated lemon peel

1. Sprinkle veal with salt and pepper to taste; dust pieces evenly with flour. In dutch oven, heat oil over medium-high heat. Add veal; cook about 10 minutes or until well browned on all sides, turning often. Stir in onions, carrots, celery, and 3 minced garlic cloves; cook 3 minutes, stirring often.

2. Stir in tomatoes with their liquid, the wine, tomato sauce, bay leaves, and thyme; bring to a boil. Reduce heat to low; cover and simmer 1 to $1\frac{1}{2}$ hours, or until veal is tender.

3. Meanwhile, combine parsley, lemon peel and remaining garlic for gremolata. To serve, remove bay leaves; ladle veal mixture onto plates and sprinkle with gremolata.

NOTE: The veal may have to be browned in several batches. If so, return all the veal to the pot before adding onions and other vegetables. Once all the ingredients are added, the stew can simmer, covered, in a 350°F oven, instead of on top of the stove, for the same amount of time.

Wine note: This classic Italian dish deserves a classic Italian red wine. A Chianti or Valpolicella would go nicely, as would a Barbera. If you want to go with an Israeli wine, try a Merlot or proprietary red. All of these wines could be poured along with the appetizer as well.

Quick Risotto

MAKES 6 TO 8 SERVINGS

In northern Italy, rice is an important part of the cuisine, and this creamy, golden rice dish is traditionally served with veal. Risotto usually takes a lot of patience and care to cook correctly. I've shortened and simplified the process by eliminating the slow, gradual stirring in of the broth—instead, all the broth is added at once and the rice is covered to cook until tender. The results are more like a pilaf than a classic risotto in texture, but the saffron taste is authentic.

$\frac{1}{4}$ cup margarine
1 medium onion, peeled and chopped
1 teaspoon saffron threads
2 cups converted rice
2 cups chicken broth
1 cup dry white wine
Salt

1. In large saucepan, melt margarine over medium heat. Add onion; sauté 2 or 3 minutes. Stir in saffron; cook 1 minute longer, stirring constantly.
2. Stir in rice until well coated with margarine and onion. Add broth and wine, stirring to combine; bring to a boil. Reduce heat to low; cover and simmer 20 to 25 minutes, until all liquid has evaporated and rice is tender.

Broccoli with Garlic and Oil

Broccoli all'aglio

MAKES 4 TO 6 SERVINGS

1 bunch broccoli (about $1\frac{1}{4}$ pounds)
2 tablespoons olive oil
2 cloves garlic, peeled and minced
$\frac{1}{2}$ cup chopped parsley
1 large tomato, peeled, seeded, and diced
Salt and freshly ground black pepper

1. Cut off and discard tough ends of broccoli. Cut stems into $\frac{1}{4}$-inch-slices. Cut florets into bite-sized pieces.
2. Heat oil with garlic in large skillet over medium heat. Add broccoli; stir to coat with oil and garlic. Stir in parsley, tomato, and salt and pepper to taste. Cover and cook 10 to 15 minutes, until broccoli is tender-crisp, stirring occasionally.

Whipped Wine Custard

Zabaglione

MAKES 6 SERVINGS

This frothy dessert is usually prepared with marsala wine and real whipped cream. However, kosher sherry is more readily available and nondairy whipping cream makes the dessert pareve and acceptable as a finale for this menu.

6 egg yolks
⅔ cup sherry or marsala wine
½ cup sugar
1 teaspoon grated lemon peel
2 cups nondairy liquid creamer

1. In top of double boiler set over simmering water, whisk egg yolks, sherry, sugar, and lemon peel until blended. Continue whisking mixture over simmering water 15 to 20 minutes, or until it becomes thick, light, and custardlike; remove from heat.
2. In small bowl with electric mixer at high speed, beat creamer until stiff peaks form. With rubber spatula, gently fold into egg yolk mixture until blended.
3. To serve, spoon into wine goblets, champagne glasses, or dessert dishes. Serve warm or refrigerate until well chilled.

NOTE: Whip Rich brand is a nondairy whipping cream substitute that beats up like real whipped cream.

Wine note: A slightly sweet sipping sherry would accent the wine used in this airy dessert. If sherry is hard to find, go back to the popular sweet Muscat—a very versatile dessert wine.

Pasta with Chickpeas—*Pasta e Ceci*
Fillet of Sole with Raisins and Pine Nuts—*Sogliola di Rolatine*
Veal Cutlets with Artichokes—*Scaloppine di Vitello al Carciofi*
Lemon Tart—*Torta di Limone*

Pasta with Chickpeas

Pasta e Ceci

MAKES 6 TO 8 SERVINGS

Combining pasta with dried beans is an Italian custom that goes back thousands of years. The smart peasant cooks probably knew that the proteins in the pasta and beans complemented each other, resulting in a nutritious vegetarian dish. This recipe is like a thick soup in consistency, and should be served in bowls with plenty of crusty Italian bread.

    1 pound chickpeas (garbanzo beans)
       Salt
 1½ teaspoons tomato paste
   ½ pound small pasta (macaroni, shells, or the like)
    2 tablespoons olive oil
    3 cloves garlic, peeled and crushed
    1 sprig fresh rosemary, chopped, or ½ teaspoon dried
       Freshly ground black pepper to taste

1. Soak chickpeas in 8 cups cold water to cover overnight; drain.
2. In dutch oven or large saucepot, combine chickpeas and 12 cups hot water. Place over high heat and bring to a boil; add 2 teaspoons

salt or to taste. Reduce heat to low; cover and simmer 1 to $1\frac{3}{4}$ hours, until chickpeas are almost tender, stirring occasionally with wooden spoon.

3. Stir tomato paste into chickpeas; increase heat to high and bring to a boil, adding more hot water if necessary. Add pasta; cook 10 minutes, or until pasta is tender.

4. Meanwhile, in small skillet or saucepan over medium-high heat, heat olive oil. Sauté garlic and rosemary in hot oil 3 to 5 minutes, until garlic is tender. Stir into chickpea–pasta mixture.

5. To serve, ladle into individual soup bowls. Sprinkle each serving with freshly ground pepper.

NOTE: It's important to use a wooden spoon rather than a metal one when stirring the chickpeas or any dried beans. Metal will affect the texture and cooking properties of the beans.

Wine note: A light or medium-bodied red wine is a classic match for pasta and chickpeas. Chianti, of course, or Barbera—might as well stick with Italian wines.

Fillet of Sole with Raisins and Pine Nuts

Sogliola di Rolatine

MAKES 4 TO 6 SERVINGS

In the old Roman-Jewish ghetto Portico d'Ottavia, this fish dish was frequently prepared for Shabbat. The vinegar in the sauce acted as a preservative of sorts, so the recipe could be cooked ahead of time and eaten at room temperature for the Sabbath meal. The raisins counteract the acidity of the vinegar, and in combination they produce that sweet-sour flavor common to many Jewish-style dishes.

$\frac{1}{2}$ cup bread crumbs
$\frac{1}{3}$ to $\frac{1}{2}$ cup olive oil
2 cloves garlic, peeled and finely chopped
2 tablespoons chopped parsley
2 tablespoons golden raisins, soaked in water to soften and drained
2 tablespoons pine nuts
2 tablespoons cider vinegar
Salt and freshly ground black pepper to taste
2 pounds sole fillets
1 cup white wine

1. Preheat oven to 450°F.
2. In small bowl, combine bread crumbs, $\frac{1}{4}$ cup olive oil, garlic, parsley, raisins, pine nuts, vinegar, and salt and pepper to taste; mix well. Add more olive oil, if necessary, to hold mixture together.
3. Spread a little of the bread crumb mixture on each sole fillet. (Reserve some mixture for topping.) Roll up or fold over fillets to enclose filling; place in 2-quart oblong baking dish. Pour wine into baking dish; add about $\frac{1}{2}$ cup water, if necessary, to cover bottom of baking dish with $\frac{1}{2}$ inch of liquid. Sprinkle remaining bread crumb mixture on top of fish rolls; drizzle with a little olive oil.
4. Bake fish 10 to 15 minutes, until it flakes when touched with a fork. Serve fish hot, or let cool to room temperature.

Wine note: Many purists would choose not to drink wine with this course because of the vinegar in the recipe. But there's wine in it, too. Try to make both the cooking and drinking wine Sancerre from the Loire. Though it's a bit expensive for cooking, a cup in the pot will leave ample wine for drinking. Sancerre has that lemony sour twist that not only partners most fish nicely but will accommodate the sour flavor derived from the vinegar in this dish.

Veal Cutlets with Artichokes

Scaloppine de Vitello al Carciofi

MAKES 6 SERVINGS

Veal cutlets or "scallops" are the basis for many Italian dishes. Each region prepares these thin slices of veal in its own manner, personalized with local ingredients and seasonings. Here, the veal is cooked with baby artichokes in the Roman style.

6	small (baby) artichokes
1	lemon, halved
$\frac{1}{4}$	cup olive oil
1 or 2	cloves garlic, peeled and minced
1	medium onion, peeled and chopped
1	cup fresh mushrooms, sliced
1	bay leaf
$\frac{1}{4}$	cup white wine
	Salt and freshly ground black pepper to taste
8	veal cutlets for scaloppine, pounded thin
1	sprig parsley, finely chopped (leaves only)

1. Trim thorny tips and stems of artichokes; cut artichokes in half, if necessary. Rub artichokes with lemon.
2. In large skillet, heat 2 tablespoons olive oil over medium heat. Add garlic, onion, mushrooms, bay leaf, and artichokes. Sauté 10 to 15 minutes, until artichokes are tender.
3. Add wine; simmer until wine is reduced by half. Remove from heat; stir in salt and pepper to taste. Cover and keep warm.
4. In another large skillet, heat remaining 2 tablespoons olive oil over medium-high heat. Sauté veal in hot oil about 3 minutes on each side, or until cooked through. Season with salt and pepper to taste and transfer veal to warm platter.
5. To serve, remove bay leaf; spoon artichoke mixture over veal and sprinkle with parsley.

Wine note: Artichokes could easily anchor the list of foods least amenable to wine. Here, however, the wine in the recipe and the great affinity of veal to wine creates an exception to the rule. A full-blown Chardonnay would do well. The dish is elegant enough for a Meursault, but a California Chardonnay would be just as good at a quarter of the expense, as would an Israeli Chardonnay from the Golan Heights/Mt. Hermon.

Lemon Tart

Torta di Limone

MAKES 6 SERVINGS

Fresh fruit is usually served after most Italian meals, but special occasions call for a slightly fancier dessert. I created this lemon tart as a light but sweet ending for a festive meal. Since it uses pareve ingredients, it can be served after a meat or dairy dinner.

SWEET PASTRY

2 eggs, beaten
$\frac{1}{2}$ cup sugar
Pinch of salt
$1\frac{1}{2}$ cups sifted all-purpose flour
$\frac{1}{2}$ cup (1 stick) margarine, cut into small pieces

LEMON FILLING

2 eggs
$\frac{1}{2}$ cup sugar
Juice and grated peel from $1\frac{1}{2}$ lemons
$\frac{1}{2}$ cup ground almonds
$1\frac{1}{2}$ tablespoons whole blanched almonds

1. Prepare pastry: In medium bowl, mix eggs, sugar, and salt with wooden spoon until well blended. Gradually add flour, a little at a time, mixing well after each addition. With fingers or pastry blender, work in margarine until dough forms.

2. Roll dough into ball; wrap in waxed paper and refrigerate 1 hour.

3. Preheat oven to 375°F. On lightly floured board, roll out dough into 11-inch circle. Fit pastry into 9-inch tart pan or pie plate. With fork, prick pastry all over. Bake in oven 15 minutes.

4. Meanwhile, prepare filling: In medium bowl, beat eggs and sugar with wire whisk or electric mixer until light and creamy. Mix in lemon juice and peel; stir in ground almonds. Pour mixture into partially baked pastry shell; arrange whole almonds on top.

5. Bake tart 30 minutes longer, or until set and golden. Remove from oven and cool on wire rack. Serve at room temperature.

Wine note: Sip a cream sherry from Spain or Israel, a Sauternes from France, an Asti Spumante from Italy, or a Niagara from New York, complementing both the sweetness and tartness of this dessert.

Caribbean

Color and spice define the cooking of the Caribbean Islands and the Latin countries of the western hemisphere. While each nationality has made its unique contributions to the world of food, the area as a whole shares similar ancestry, climate, and geography.

When Christopher Columbus accidentally sailed into the Caribbean Sea in 1492, he was searching for a route to India. What he found instead was a chain of islands fringed by pristine beaches and surrounded by brilliant blue waters. The inhabitants were mostly South Americans and American Indians who subsisted on a diet of starchy cassava roots, yams, corn, peanuts, and fish, enlivened by chile peppers and native seasonings like ginger and allspice.

Columbus's voyage opened up the Caribbean Islands to the prominent world powers of the time. Spain, Portugal, France, Britain, and the Netherlands began to vie for control of this tropical paradise, and each left its political and culinary mark. Later came African slaves and servants from India, both groups adding their own food customs and ingredients to the Caribbean cooking pot. These influences, coupled with the lush produce and plentiful seafood indigenous to the region, eventually blended into a vibrant and diverse cooking style.

The cuisine of the islands and other Latin countries takes full advantage of the multihued fruits and vegetables that thrive in the warm, humid climate. Maria Colon Goldman, my colleague in creating these recipes, remembers her grandmother going right to her own backyard in Puerto Rico to pick fruits and vegetables for the dinner table. Mangoes, coconuts, papayas, bananas, breadfruit (used more as a vegetable than a fruit), pineapples, passion fruit, and cherimoya (similar to a custard apple) are among the fruit offerings. The starchy vegetables that grow in abundance include the widely used plantain and a varied group of roots, tubers, and squashes.

Green plantains look like long unripe bananas, and although they have a hint of sweetness, they're usually cooked much like potatoes. Islanders typically enjoy sliced plantains fried in lard or oil, a dish that resembles French fries. Ripe yellow plantains are sweeter, but also need to be cooked before eating—they're sometimes fried into crispy chips or simmered in syrup for dessert. Other starchy native vegetables are yucca, pumpkin, yams, cassava, chayote (a type of squash), and a selection of misshapen tubers collectively called "viandes" in Hispanic markets or bodegas here and in the Spanish-speaking islands. Avocados, tomatoes, all kinds of peppers, and a variety of dried beans are also used extensively in Caribbean cuisine. In fact, few meals are complete without an accompaniment of rice and beans served together.

Island cooks have tended to focus on this large assortment of starchy plant foods that grows all around them, creating a carbohydrate-based cooking style. Small amounts of pork, beef, goat, and chicken are incorporated in the menu when available, and fish from nearby waters make their way into many dishes. The catch can be stewed, fried, or pickled with vinegar and spices into an escabeche.

The inventive use of island seasonings turns even the humblest ingredients into savory, memorable fare. Little red annatto seeds (from the Caribbean tree of the same name) are sautéed until they give up their color. The resulting orange substance is achiote, which imparts a characteristic deep yellow color to many Hispanic dishes. Onions, garlic, and hot and/or sweet peppers are another trio of ingredients that form a zesty base for many recipes. Sofrito, for example, is a garlicky mélange of fried peppers, onions, tomatoes, cilantro, oregano, and other herbs. Maria's mother and aunt make up big batches of this mixture, freeze it in small jars, and send her off with a stockpile whenever she visits them in Brooklyn. Maria still enjoys cooking traditional Puerto Rican foods, but as a working mother, finds it a bit too time-consuming to prepare sofrito and other favorites that require a lot of preparation by hand. In a pinch, the food processor or blender can stand in without too much loss of authenticity.

There are obvious components of island cuisine that would be taboo in a kosher kitchen—lard, ham, pork, sausages, and shellfish, for instance. With Maria's help, however, I have developed some very tasty renditions of classic Caribbean dishes that use only kosher ingredients in permitted combinations.

This is really fairly simple. Fresh produce, natural dried beans, and rice are all allowed, and very few recipes call for mixing meat or poultry with dairy products. In fact, coconut milk is used quite a lot, especially in desserts, so it's even possible to end a meat meal with a creamy custard or pudding. I've even created a kosher sofrito!

All the food products we've used are easy to obtain in most large supermarkets. If you're thinking of expanding your Caribbean cooking repertoire beyond our menu, it would probably be necessary to explore the Hispanic markets in larger cities.

To the best of my knowledge, the only Jewish settlement in the West Indies was established in Curaçao in 1651. That same year, the Mikve Israel-Emanuel Synagogue was founded in Willemstad. The fourth building housing this synagogue, dating from 1732, is still standing, and is a major tourist attraction for visitors to Curaçao.

More Jews and islanders have lived side by side in New York City, the latter sometimes replacing the former in certain neighborhoods. In the South Bronx, the Williamsburg section of Brooklyn, or the Lower East Side of Manhattan, it's not unusual for a bodega to occupy the space recently vacated by a Jewish delicatessen. In some cases, it's even possible to buy a knish and an order of fried plantains in the same establishment!

Maria and I worked very closely developing the recipes that follow —her goal was to preserve the true flavor of the islands, and mine to adhere to the dietary laws. We're both very pleased with the results.

—*Mimi Olanoff*

Mimi Olanoff

Like many Jewish girls, Mimi Olanoff grew up in a home that centered around the kitchen. Her Austrian-Jewish mother was a superb cook and baker, easily able to duplicate dishes she had tasted at other people's tables and in restaurants. Dinner was always a special event in the household, filled with a tempting assortment of interesting foods.

While she was growing up in Brooklyn, New York, Mimi learned to appreciate fine cooking by watching and sampling. But the kitchen was strictly her mother's domain, and she never actually got any hands-on experience until she married and began cooking on her own. By then, she was anxious to go full steam ahead. Much to her husband's delight, she became an excellent and adventurous cook, creating a varied repertoire of international specialties. Frequent trips to England, Italy, France, and the Caribbean always sparked new ideas, and, like her mother, Mimi was able to re-create some of the dishes the Olanoffs enjoyed in their travels.

Her knowledge of Latin cooking came from several sources. Mimi's husband spent part of his youth in Mexico, and he brought his mother's authentic recipes for Spanish rice and baked fish to the marriage. Vacations in the Caribbean added more recipes to the file. Then Maria Colon Goldman, a secretary from Puerto Rico, joined the office staff where Mimi worked as a systems analyst. The two quickly formed a mother-daughter-type relationship, sharing cooking secrets and friendship.

Now "retired," Mimi still does plenty of work—volunteering both through the 92nd Street Y Talks and Tours Program and in an adult literacy project. She and her husband continue to travel, constantly replenishing her culinary ideas for the classes she teaches on Caribbean cooking, Mediterranean cuisine, and English afternoon tea.

Maria Colon Goldman

There aren't many people around who are comfortable with and adept at cooking both Jewish and Hispanic food, but Maria Colon Goldman is one. Born in the southern Puerto Rican city of Ponce, Maria spent the first part of her childhood enjoying the native dishes her mother and grandmother prepared, some with fruits and vegetables picked right from her backyard.

When she was eight, the Colon family moved to New York City. The Latin markets in the neighborhood where they lived offered many familiar Caribbean ingredients, enabling Mrs. Colon to continue cooking her Puerto Rican specialties. Maria was educated in the city's public schools and went on to become a statistical typist and secretary. She now works at Hofstra University on Long Island.

Along the way, Maria met and married her Jewish husband. Wishing to learn as much as she could about Judaism, she did a lot of research into the customs and foods of the Jews. A firm believer in carrying on traditions, Maria took a great interest in making the Jewish holidays as festive as possible for her husband and two children. With a little help from her mother-in-law, she taught herself how to prepare the typical dishes that went with each holiday, and can now whip up a wonderful Passover or Rosh Hashanah feast.

Nevertheless, many meals in the Goldman home still have a strong Puerto Rican accent. The family loves her rice and beans, fried plantains, and empanades, as well as the coconut rice pudding and pasteles contributed every so often by Grandmother Colon. Maria's mother buys the ingredients for these and other recipes in a five-block-long Hispanic marketplace in Brooklyn, which specializes in foods from the Caribbean Islands.

At one of her first jobs, Maria met Mimi Olanoff, whose olive complexion and dark hair and eyes led her to believe that Mimi was "one of her own." Although she was wrong, the two developed a close bond over the years, strengthened by their mutual interest in cooking and their similar outgoing personalities. Each has enlightened the other about her respective culinary heritage, and their families spend several holidays together.

Avocado Dip—*Guacamole*
Pita Crisps
Caramel Chicken—*Pollo Caramelado*
Rice and Black Beans—*Moros y Cristianos*
Veal Chops Tropical Style—*Carne de Ternera Tropical*
Fried Plantains—*Plantanos Fritos*
Sweet Pastry Turnovers—*Empanades de Dulce*

Avocado Dip

Guacamole

MAKES 8 SERVINGS

We prefer a little zing in our guacamole, so we call for the addition of 1 or 2 chopped hot chile peppers, such as jalapeños. If you like a milder taste, either omit the chiles altogether or use less fiery peppers. Markets in the States offer California or Florida avocados. These make great guacamole, but the avocados from the islands are even more flavorful, if you can find them here.

$\frac{1}{2}$ cup finely chopped peeled red onion
$\frac{1}{2}$ cup finely chopped cilantro (fresh coriander)
2 medium tomatoes, peeled, seeded, and finely chopped (optional)
1 to 2 fresh green chiles, seeded and chopped
4 ripe avocados
About $\frac{1}{4}$ cup virgin olive oil
Kosher (coarse) salt to taste
Freshly ground black pepper to taste
Juice of $\frac{1}{2}$ lime or lemon
Pita Crisps (recipe follows) or tortilla chips

1. In medium bowl, combine chopped onion, cilantro, tomatoes, and chiles.
2. Halve avocados and remove pits. Reserve 1 pit. With tip of small

knife, cut avocadoes into $\frac{1}{2}$-inch pieces. With teaspoon, lift pieces out of peel to avoid mashing.

3. Add avocado pieces to vegetable mixture in bowl; mix ingredients gently until combined but not mushy. (Visible bits of avocado should remain.) Stir in enough oil to moisten, and season to taste with salt and pepper. Squeeze lime or lemon juice on top; place 1 avocado pit in center to prevent discoloration.

4. Cover guacamole with plastic wrap against surface and refrigerate 1 hour. Serve with pita crisps or tortilla chips.

NOTE: An avocado is ripe when you are able to press it gently with your thumb and an indentation remains. Ripe avocados should be refrigerated until ready to use. To prevent discoloration during preparation, halve, pit, and cut up avocados one at a time.

Wine note: An avocado dip per se would not necessarily call for wine, except that it so often is served at aperitif time. Then, whether the guacamole is heated up with chile peppers or is mild, a cold, sparkling wine is especially welcome. In the case of this spicy guacamole, opt for one of the many slightly sweet bubblies; those from New York State would serve admirably.

Pita Crisps

MAKES 4 DOZEN

4 pita breads, split in half
Corn oil

1. Preheat oven to 250°F. Cut each pita bread half into 8 wedges. With knife, trim off outer edge of each wedge. Separate wedges into triangles.

2. Place triangles on cookie sheet, insides facing up; brush lightly with oil. Bake 15 minutes, or until crisp.

Caramel Chicken

Pollo Caramelado

MAKES 8 SERVINGS

On my first trip to the Caribbean, I visited Puerto Rico and stayed in a hotel run by a former pro-Castro newscaster. The restaurant there offered several Cuban specialties, this chicken dish among them. I found its flavors so intriguing that I tried to duplicate the recipe upon my return to New York. This version comes very close, especially when served with the traditional Rice and Black Beans (recipe follows).

Two 3-pound chickens, cut into pieces
       Juice of 3 lemons
    5 cloves garlic, peeled and minced
    2 medium onions, peeled and chopped
    1 medium green bell pepper, grated or finely minced
    ½ teaspoon dried thyme
    ½ teaspoon curry powder
       Salt and freshly ground black pepper to taste
    ½ cup corn oil
    2 tablespoons sugar
    1 large tomato, peeled, seeded, and diced
       Sliced cooked mushrooms, pimiento strips, cooked peas, and/or artichoke hearts, for garnish

1. Rinse chicken and pat dry. In large bowl, combine lemon juice, garlic, onions, green pepper, thyme, curry powder, and salt and pepper to taste for marinade. Add chicken; cover and refrigerate at least 5 hours or overnight.

2. Drain chicken on a wire rack set over a large bowl, scraping off any vegetables or spices that may stick to its surface. Dry chicken thoroughly with paper towels. Strain marinade; reserve vegetables and liquid separately.

3. In dutch oven, heat oil over medium-high heat until very hot. Stir in sugar; cook until sugar turns golden brown, stirring often. Add

chicken pieces and brown well on all sides, about 10 minutes. Stir in reserved vegetables from marinade; cook 3 minutes, or until vegetables are translucent.

4. Add reserved marinade liquid and tomato. Reduce heat to low; cover and simmer 50 minutes to 1 hour, or until chicken is tender.

5. To serve, top with any or all of the garnishes and accompany with rice and black beans.

Wine note: Don't reach for the driest of wines for this one. Fruit is the answer, and an undertone of sweetness necessary. In red, a cool Beaujolais or a light, fruity red from the Samson region of Israel. Cold white Gamay or white Zinfandel might do for those with a slightly sweeter tooth. In white, choose either a Riesling from any one of several places—California, New York, Israel—or perhaps a Vouvray.

Rice and Black Beans

Moros y Cristianos

MAKES 6 TO 8 SERVINGS

The Latins call this combination Moors and Christians because of the contrast of the black beans (African Moors) with the white rice (Christians). The sautéed onion–green pepper–garlic–tomato mixture forms a kosher sofrito that can easily stand in for the Puerto Rican original.

1 cup dried black turtle beans
1¼ medium onions, peeled
2 cloves garlic, peeled
2 tablespoons olive oil
1 small green bell pepper, seeded and finely chopped
2 medium tomatoes, peeled, seeded, and chopped
Salt
Freshly ground black pepper to taste
1 cup raw long-grain white rice

1. Sort beans carefully to remove all foreign matter and damaged beans. Rinse thoroughly.

2. In large saucepan or dutch oven, combine beans and enough water to cover by 1 inch. Bring to a boil over high heat; boil 2 minutes. Remove from heat; cover and let stand 1 hour.

3. Drain beans and rinse. Add enough fresh hot water to cover beans by 1 inch. Bring to a boil over high heat. Add ¼ onion and 1 garlic clove. Reduce heat to low; partially cover and simmer 1 to 2 hours, or until beans are tender, adding more hot water if necessary. Drain beans, reserving cooking liquid.

4. Finely chop remaining onion and mince remaining garlic clove. Heat oil in large saucepan over medium heat. Add chopped onion, garlic, and green pepper; sauté 5 minutes, or until onion is translucent. Add tomatoes and cook about 10 minutes, or until sofrito mixture is quite thick and well blended, stirring often. Season with salt and pepper to taste.

5. Stir 2 cups cooked black beans into sofrito; mix well. Add raw rice, 1 teaspoon salt, and 2 cups reserved cooking liquid from beans; bring to a boil. Reduce heat to low; cover and cook 17 minutes, or until rice is tender. Stir gently to fluff, and serve with chicken.

NOTE: Any remaining cooked beans can be stored, covered, in the refrigerator and reheated.

Wine note: Put the Moors and the Christians together and we're speaking of Spain. Add the classic combination of onion, garlic, and tomatoes and we're talking about a well-made young red kosher Spanish wine. Any that can be found is worthy of trying here.

Veal Chops Tropical Style

Carne de Ternera Tropical

MAKES 4 SERVINGS

This dish can be an alternative to caramel chicken or a second main dish for a Caribbean-style buffet.

4 veal shoulder chops (about 2 pounds)
Salt and freshly ground black pepper to taste
2 teaspoons dry mustard
$\frac{1}{4}$ cup vegetable oil
2 to 3 cloves garlic, peeled and minced
$\frac{3}{4}$ cup dry white wine
$\frac{3}{4}$ cup freshly squeezed orange juice
$1\frac{1}{2}$ cups thinly sliced peeled onions
2 green bell peppers, cored, seeded, and cut into thin strips
Hot cooked rice

1. Wipe chops dry with paper towels. Sprinkle them evenly on both sides with salt and pepper to taste and dry mustard.
2. In large skillet, heat oil over medium-high heat. Add garlic; cook 2 to 3 minutes, or until softened but not brown.

3. Add seasoned chops; cook 3 to 5 minutes on each side, or until browned, turning once.

4. In small bowl, combine wine and orange juice; pour over chops. Increase heat to high; boil until liquid is slightly reduced.

5. Scatter onions and green peppers over chops; reduce heat to low. Cover and simmer 1 hour, or until chops are tender. To serve, arrange chops over rice and spoon sauce on top.

Wine note: As a dry white wine is among the ingredients, let's think along that line. Gewürztraminer immediately comes to mind. Since a typical taste component of Gewürztraminer is grapefruit, this wine would accommodate the orange juice in the recipe. A couple of nice, dry Gewürztraminers are imported from Alsace, and a couple of nice sweet ones are distributed out of California. Failing that, an Emerald Riesling would be an interesting match.

Fried Plantains

Plantanos Fritos

MAKES 8 SERVINGS

The plantains for this recipe should be ripe—on the soft side with a brown-spotted yellow skin. Different cooks have different techniques for preparing this traditional dish, so we've included two variations here. Plantains can also be sliced paper-thin and fried in hot oil until crisp, like potato chips, or shaped into a ring around a meat stuffing, dipped in egg, and fried.

    5 to 6 ripe plantains
        Corn oil

1. Peel plantains as you would bananas. Or, using a small sharp knife, cut through skins lengthwise on ridges; remove peel.

2. In large skillet, heat $\frac{1}{4}$ inch oil over medium-high heat until hot.

3. Cut peeled plantains into diagonal slices, about $\frac{1}{4}$ to $\frac{3}{8}$ inch thick. Slip them into hot oil and fry about 3 to 4 minutes on each side, until tender and lightly browned.

4. With slotted spoon, remove to paper towels to drain. Serve immediately.

VARIATION 2

3. Slice plantains into chunks about 1 by $1\frac{1}{4}$ inches. Place in hot oil and fry 3 to 4 minutes on each side, until tender and lightly browned.

4. With slotted spoon, remove from oil. Stand plantain pieces between 2 sheets of aluminum foil, with cut ends touching foil. With rolling pin, mallet, or palm of hand, flatten plantain pieces between sheets of foil.

5. Return to hot oil and fry 1 minute longer on each side, or until golden brown. With slotted spoon, remove to paper towels to drain. Serve immediately.

Wine note: Any white or rosé wine with a little zip and sweetness would partner this dish when it's served as a snack. Serve the wine cold. Among the contenders: white Zinfandel, white Gamay, Cabernet Blanc, rosé of Cabernet, Chenin Blanc, Riesling, Gewürztraminer, Niagara, and California or New York sparklers.

Sweet Pastry Turnovers

Empanades de Dulce

MAKES 4 DOZEN

In the Colon family, cinnamon and cloves are often used to flavor desserts. Both spices grow on several of the Caribbean islands and are in plentiful supply. Here these tiny pies are filled with a tropical blend of yams, coconut, and pineapple, but you may want to try a different sweet or savory filling.

$\frac{1}{2}$ cup mashed cooked yams
$\frac{1}{2}$ cup grated or flaked coconut
$\frac{1}{2}$ cup canned crushed pineapple, drained
Pastry (see page 21 or page 268)
1 egg
$\frac{1}{3}$ cup sugar
1 tablespoon ground cinnamon

1. Preheat oven to 400°F. In small bowl, combine yams, coconut, and crushed pineapple; set aside.
2. Prepare pastry: On lightly floured board with lightly floured rolling pin, roll out pastry $\frac{1}{8}$ inch thick. With 3-inch-round cookie cutter or a glass, cut pastry into circles. Place dough circles on ungreased cookie sheets.
3. Fill center of each dough circle with scant teaspoon of yam mixture. Lightly moisten edges of pastry with water. Fold circle in half over filling to form a semicircular turnover. With fork, press edges firmly to seal. (If tines of fork stick to dough, dip in flour occasionally.)
4. In cup, beat egg with 1 teaspoon water; brush mixture on top of each turnover. Place turnovers in oven; bake 15 to 18 minutes, until golden brown. (Halfway through baking time, turn cookie sheet around to distribute heat evenly.)
5. With spatula, remove turnovers from cookie sheets to wire racks. In cup, combine sugar and cinnamon; sprinkle on turnovers while still warm. Serve warm or cool.

NOTE: Empanades can be baked ahead and frozen. To serve, thaw and reheat briefly in 350°F oven.

Wine note: It is time for a dessert wine. Sauternes would be super—the real stuff from France—or a late-harvest wine from Israel or California, or a sweet Gewürztraminer. Stay away from the "traditional" sweet kosher Concords and such—the flavors would clash.

Mexican

*t*he spirited, flavorful fare of Mexico is deeply rooted in that country's history and culture. Long before the European explorers "discovered" the New World, Mexico was inhabited by the Aztec and Mayan Indians. These tribes successfully lived off the land for centuries, beginning with the cultivation of squash, beans, avocados, and peppers in the fertile Valley of Mexico. Around 5000 years ago, corn became an important crop as well. Supplemented by wild edible plants, these staples were turned into such simple dishes as the tortillas and tamales familiar to many Americans today. Eventually, these foods were joined by a greater variety of chile peppers, potatoes, tomatoes, and an assortment of tropical fruits, resulting in new combinations of ingredients and a more varied cuisine.

By the time the Spaniards arrived at what is now Mexico City in A.D. 1519, they found tables set with an array of colorful and exotic foods. The Spanish conquerer Cortés and his soldiers reported that the lavish, multicourse meals served at the Emperor Montezuma's palace included a variety of game birds, fish from local waters, and strange fruits and vegetables, often enlivened with sauces made from chiles and/or tomatoes. A mixture of cocoa and water filled royal goblets with a bitter drink the Aztecs called "chocolate." Much of what they saw and tasted was completely foreign to the Spaniards.

Spanish ships returned to their native ports carrying many of these new discoveries. Seeds and cuttings from Mexican crops were planted in European soil, and the bitter chocolate beverage was cut with sugar to make it more appealing to European tastes. On their return to Mexico, the conquerers took some of the foods and cooking techniques characteristic of their own cuisine. Included in the cargo were cattle, sheep, hogs, and chickens. Soon Mexican cooks incorporated the meats of these domesticated animals into their meals. Wheat, rice, almonds, and such fruits as peaches, limes, oranges, and grapes also made their way to the New World, adding a bit more diversity to the Mexican diet. Close behind were the seasonings brought by European spice traders—cinnamon, cloves, thyme, marjoram, and bay leaves.

The Spanish nuns who settled in Mexico were largely responsible for spreading their culinary customs throughout their adopted country. For example, they showed the native women how to use oil, wine, and the "new" spices to enhance their cooking. In turn, the nuns created a number of exciting dishes by combining familiar Spanish ingredients with those the Indians grew and used. A unique and vibrant national cuisine evolved from this mélange of simple Indian cooking, dazzling Aztec royal fare, and Spanish ingenuity.

In the years that followed, other foreigners came and went, influencing Mexican cooking in the process. French, Austrian, and Italian dishes were introduced in the mid-nineteenth century, and the enduring interchange with neighboring North America began about the same time. Later on, Middle Eastern emigrés came to Mexico, and an Arabic influence appeared in the food.

When I came to the States in 1982, I was surprised to see how many Americans thought that authentic Mexican food was limited to saucy enchiladas, fiery chili con carne, or overstuffed tacos, all accompanied by piles of refried beans and corn chips. The delicious dishes of my childhood, marked by their subtle contrasts of texture and flavor, were very few and far between. Classic Mexican cuisine from every region goes way beyond the familiar Tex-Mex dishes. Wheat and cattle are the major resources of the north; grains, produce, and other types of livestock thrive in the central valley; all kinds of seafood are harvested from the coastal areas; and exotic fruits flourish in the tropical region.

A trip through a Mexican marketplace can reveal the diversity of ingredients that go into my country's meals. As in ancient times, corn, beans, squash, and peppers still grow abundantly and play an important role in the cuisine. Mexican cooks grind dried corn into masa just as their Indian ancestors did. The masa is then transformed into tortillas, tamales, and other traditional dishes. Beans and squash come in many colors and shapes, a number of which are available in U.S. produce markets and ethnic groceries. And, of course, peppers are used extensively to give Mexican food its zesty personality. These range from tiny, fiery-hot chiles to fat, sweet yellow peppers to dark reddish purple types. Used in fresh, dried, or pickled form, each imparts its own taste and pungency to a dish.

Although some unusual fruits, vegetables, and herbs figure prominently in the cooking of Mexico, the menus I have developed use readily available produce. Such items as chayote (a pear-shaped light green squash), jicama (a brown turniplike vegetable with sweet, crunchy flesh), epazote (a fragrant, flavorful herb), and achiote seeds (a distinctive spice) may sound a bit exotic, but many large supermarkets and small specialty stores now carry them.

Based on the standard Americanized Mexican food served in the United States, one would think it difficult to prepare this cuisine in accordance with the dietary laws. Often, meat and poultry are rolled in tortillas and topped with cheese or sour cream, and several typical recipes are fried in lard and/or prepared with pork. However, few of the dishes passed down through my family and eaten in Mexican homes rely on these combinations. In my restaurant and kitchen, I use primarily vegetable oil instead of lard for frying and sautéing, and I rarely combine meat and dairy products in the same dish. While no recipes start out with the intention of being kosher, several do turn out that way. It is not difficult to enjoy Mexican fare while following the dietary laws.

The menus I've developed have been perfected through years of cooking experience at my restaurant, Mi Cocina, in New York's Greenwich Village and others in the city. Several of the recipes that follow I learned in my grandmothers' kitchens, where I spent many hours of my childhood. This is classical Mexican cooking at its best, translated into kosher and passed down from my family to yours.

—*José Prud'homme*

José Prud'homme

With his French surname, José Prud'homme doesn't sound like the born-and-bred Mexican chef he is. This paradox of sorts came about because his paternal grandfather came to Mexico from France, and subsequently raised his family in his adopted land. José's father then married into a Mexican family that went back many generations, and the Prud'homme children were brought up in a traditional Mexican home.

José's two grandmothers came from different parts of Mexico, and each was skilled at cooking the dishes of her particular region. As a young boy, José enjoyed staying close by their sides during meal preparations, picking up a good deal of culinary expertise in the process. He was especially interested in the way unrelated ingredients could be transformed into intriguing sauces.

At the age of sixteen, José began taking technical courses in Mexico, expecting to pursue a career in engineering. In 1982, he came to the United States to study English. While here, he also enrolled in Peter Kump's New York Cooking School to polish his culinary techniques. He soon discovered that cooking was his true passion, and quickly switched the direction of his career from engineering to food. So he became a chef at a restaurant featuring the increasingly popular foods of his homeland.

When Cinco de Mayo opened in New York City's Soho neighborhood, the menu focused on the Tex-Mex dishes Americans seemed to crave. The menu was successful, but José soon felt it was time to branch out and familiarize New Yorkers with the lighter, subtler classical Mexican cuisine he grew to love in his grandmothers' homes and through his childhood travels. José recently started his own restaurant, Mi Cocina. Here he is constantly experimenting with new dishes, changing the menu frequently to expose his patrons to the many different regional cooking styles of his native country.

He further spreads the word about Mexican cuisine through classes he teaches at Peter Kump's Cooking School, Kings Supermarket in New Jersey, the New School for Social Research, and the 92nd Street Y. He lives in New York City with his wife, Marzena.

Mushroom Soup—*Sopa de Hongos*
Pompano in Papillote Yucatan Style—
Pampano Empapelado Yucateco
Roasted Onions Yucatan Style—*Cebollas Asadas à la Yucateca*
Fresh Tomato Relish—*Xnipec*
Almond Flan—*Flan Yucateco or Queso de Napoles*

Mushroom Soup

Sopa de Hongos

MAKES 6 SERVINGS

This light, refreshing soup originated in the Mexican state of Querétaro, where I grew up. It's an area in which a certain type of large, flavorful mushroom grows in abundance and gives character to a number of traditional native dishes. Although this mushroom is not available in the States, shiitake mushrooms make an excellent substitute. Be sure to provide diners with the suggested garnishes so they can personalize their bowls of soup. A squeeze of lime juice is an especially nice addition—I find it helps marry the different flavors. I frequently offer this easy-to-prepare recipe as the "soup of the day" on my restaurant menu.

2 tablespoons vegetable oil
$\frac{1}{2}$ cup finely chopped onion
2 small cloves garlic, peeled and finely chopped
1 pound shiitake mushrooms, sliced
6 cups vegetable or chicken broth
   Salt and freshly ground black pepper to taste

GARNISHES
$\frac{1}{2}$ cup finely chopped onion
$\frac{1}{3}$ cup roughly chopped coriander leaves
2 jalapeño peppers, seeded and finely chopped
1 lime, cut into 6 wedges

1. In large saucepan, heat oil over medium heat. Add chopped onions and garlic; cook 5 minutes, or until tender-crisp.
2. Add mushrooms; cook 5 minutes longer, or until softened.
3. Add broth; bring to a boil. Reduce heat to low and simmer 10 minutes. Add salt and pepper to taste.
4. To serve, ladle hot soup into bowls. Top with choice of garnishes and a squeeze of lime juice.

NOTE: Since this is a dairy menu, vegetable broth should be used in the preparation of the soup. If serving a meat meal, you may use chicken broth instead.

Pompano in Papillote Yucatan Style
Pampano Empapelado Yucateco

MAKES 4 SERVINGS

Large schools of pompano make their home in the Gulf of Mexico. Therefore, these fish frequently show up on dinner tables in the Yucatan Peninsula—that part of Mexico that juts out into the Gulf. In this recipe, the mild pompano is rubbed with assertive seasonings and left to marinate. When ready to cook, the Mexicans usually wrap the fish in banana leaves, then bake it to a moist turn. I've substituted the more easily obtainable parchment paper. Whichever you choose, the fish will turn out succulent and delicious.

4 pompano fillets (7 to 8 ounces each)
4 teaspoons Recado Rojo (recipe follows)
2 tablespoons olive oil, plus additional for coating
   parchment paper
1 large onion, peeled and thinly sliced
$1\frac{1}{2}$ pounds tomatoes, peeled, seeded, and sliced $\frac{1}{4}$ inch thick
   (strain juice and set aside)
1 small cayenne pepper or other fresh hot pepper, roasted
   and peeled
1 small green bell pepper, peeled and finely chopped
   Salt
6 tablespoons Seville orange juice (see Note)
   Hot tortillas
   Cebollas Asadas à la Yucateca (see page 260)
   Xnipec (see page 260)

1. Rub the fillets with 1 tablespoon recado rojo and let stand at room temperature or in the refrigerator at least 2 hours.

2. In medium skillet, heat olive oil over medium heat. Add onion slices; sauté about 5 minutes, until softened but not browned. Stir in remaining 1 teaspoon recado rojo.

3. Add tomatoes, reserved tomato juice, and peppers; cook about 4 minutes, or until vegetables are softened. Add salt to taste and 2 tablespoons orange juice; remove from heat.

4. Preheat oven to 450°F. Cut out four 16- by 12-inch rectangles of parchment paper; fold each in half to measure 8 by 12 inches. With scissors or knife, start cutting from one corner of folded side, following an imaginary line that resembles a question mark (fig. A). (Resulting papillote should resemble a heart.)

5. With pastry brush, paint a light coating of olive oil on both sides of each parchment "heart." Using half the tomato mixture, spread some on one side of each opened paper. Top each with a fish fillet and a quarter of the remaining tomato mixture (fig. B). Sprinkle 1 tablespoon orange juice and a pinch of salt on each. Fold other side of heart over fish. Starting at the folded side, fold down open edge, overlapping the fold as you go along to secure it (fig. C). Fold tip of papillote several times to secure the closing (fig. D).

6. Place papillotes on baking sheet and bake 12 minutes. To serve, carefully open parchment hearts to allow steam to escape. Serve with hot tortillas, cebollas asadas, and xnipec.

NOTES: To roast hot pepper, place in lightly greased skillet over high heat. Cook, turning frequently, until slightly charred and softened.

Only the juice squeezed from Seville oranges will give this and other Mexican dishes their characteristic sour flavor—Florida or California oranges are too sweet. If Seville oranges are unavailable, you may substitute a mild oriental rice wine vinegar.

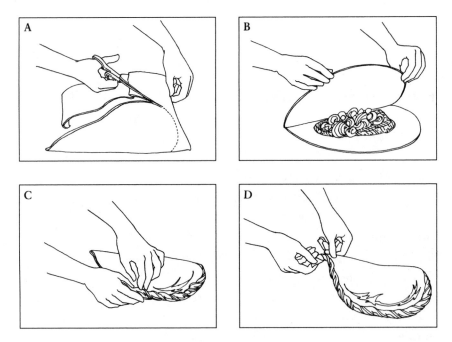

FISH PAPILLOTE

RECADO ROJO (RED SEASONING)

MAKES ¼ CUP

1 tablespoon achiote seeds
1 teaspoon salt
¼ teaspoon cumin seeds
¼ teaspoon dried oregano
¼ teaspoon whole black peppercorns
3 whole allspice
⅛ teaspoon paprika
4 cloves garlic, peeled and mashed
3 tablespoons Seville orange juice or mild white vinegar

In spice grinder or electric blender, combine all ingredients except garlic and orange juice; grind or blend to a fine powder. Transfer to small bowl; stir in garlic and orange juice to form a paste.

NOTE: Achiote seeds are available in Latin or Hispanic markets. Consult with your rabbi if there's a question about their purity.

Wine note: This is a dish just calling for wine—but what kind? The fish is mild but the seasonings are assertive. A hefty white or a red is needed. If white, look to Burgundy for a Meursault, if it can be afforded. Otherwise, try a Macon-Villages on the edge of Burgundy; a Chardonnay from California or the Golan Heights (Mt. Hermon), or a lovely Gavi from Italy. All should have the muscle to tame the tomatoes and other seasonings. If red is the choice, an Israeli Merlot, a blended Israeli red of character, or a cool rosé from Israel or California would be fine with this fish.

Roasted Onions Yucatan Style

Cebollas Asadas à la Yucateca

MAKES 2 CUPS

1 pound red onions, peeled
1 cup Seville orange juice
1 whole cayenne or other hot pepper, roasted and peeled
Salt and freshly ground black pepper to taste

1. Place whole onions on broiler pan or baking sheet. Broil onions or bake in 450°F oven until soft, turning occasionally. Let cool to room temperature.
2. Into medium bowl, roughly chop cooled onions into large pieces. Stir in juice, whole cayenne pepper, and salt and pepper to taste.
3. Marinate onions at room temperature at least 1 hour to blend flavors, stirring occasionally. Remove hot pepper, if desired. Serve onions with pompano.

NOTE: In Latin or Hispanic markets, canned or bottled Seville orange juice is sometimes available under the name Naranja Agria. For this recipe, you may substitute a combination of $\frac{1}{2}$ cup regular orange juice, $\frac{1}{4}$ cup grapefruit juice, and $\frac{1}{4}$ cup lime juice for the Seville orange juice.

Fresh Tomato Relish

Xnipec

MAKES 1$\frac{1}{2}$ CUPS

1 large tomato, peeled, seeded, and chopped
$\frac{1}{4}$ cup chopped red onion
1 chile habanero or whole cayenne pepper, seeded and minced

Juice of 2 Seville oranges
2 tablespoons chopped cilantro (coriander)
Salt to taste

In small bowl, combine all ingredients except cilantro and salt. Let stand 1 hour at room temperature. Just before serving, stir in cilantro and salt to taste.

NOTE: A chile habanero is a Mexican hot pepper that is not widely available in many parts of the United States. You may use any small hot fresh pepper instead—cayenne or jalapeño both work well. Remove seeds very carefully before chopping—these are the hottest part of the pepper! Wear rubber gloves, if possible, when peeling and seeding very hot peppers.

Almond Flan

Flan Yucateco or Queso de Napoles

MAKES 6 TO 8 SERVINGS

This rich-tasting custard dessert is actually quite light and relatively low in cholesterol. While most flans use whole eggs or egg yolks, this one uses only the whites of the eggs. The almonds in the recipe reflect the strong Middle Eastern influence on Mexican cooking. The Yucatan Peninsula actually has a significant Lebanese population, and many of the dishes in that part of my country exemplify this Arabic-Mexican mix.

CARAMEL
1½ cups sugar
½ cup water

CUSTARD

2 cups milk

$\frac{1}{2}$ cup sugar

$\frac{1}{4}$ cup ground blanched almonds

$\frac{1}{2}$ cup (about 4) egg whites

1. Prepare caramel: In medium-sized heavy saucepan, combine sugar and water. Place over high heat and bring to a boil. Continue boiling until light brown in color. Pour caramel syrup into 6-cup rectangular mold or baking dish; set aside to cool.

2. Preheat oven to 350°F. Prepare custard: In small saucepan over high heat, combine milk, sugar, and almonds; bring to a boil.

3. Meanwhile, in large bowl, whisk egg whites lightly. With ladle, gradually add hot milk mixture, stirring until well incorporated into egg whites.

4. Pour milk mixture into caramel-lined mold; cover with foil. Place mold in larger baking pan or roasting pan. Pour enough boiling water around mold to reach halfway up sides.

5. Place pan in oven and bake $1\frac{1}{4}$ hours, or until flan is firm.

6. Remove mold from baking pan or roasting pan. Refrigerate at least 8 hours or overnight, until very well chilled.

7. To unmold, run blade of small knife around edge of mold. Place serving platter over mold and, holding with both hands, invert flan onto platter. Spoon any syrup remaining in mold onto flan.

Wine note: Light and lively are the descriptions for wine to accompany flan. Though sweet dessert wines abound, few would seem as well qualified as those from the Muscat grape, and none could match the delicacy and elegance of Muscats from the Asti region of Italy. That means either Asti Spumante, the sparkling version, or a Muscato d'Asti, a still wine. At least two Israeli brands also include a Muscat.

Zucchini Flower Soup—*Sopa de Flor de Calabaza*
Wild Mushroom Turnovers—*Quesadillas de Hongo Silvestre*
Ranch Sauce—*Salsa Ranchera*
Lime and Coconut Pie—*Pay de Limon y Coco*

Zucchini Flower Soup

Sopa de Flor de Calabaza

MAKES 8 SERVINGS

The blossoms from the zucchini plant have been used since Aztec times, when, along with corn and beans, squash was revered as one of the "sacred trio" of crops. The Indians made use of every part of the zucchini squash—flesh, seeds, and flowers—and were probably responsible for inventing a soup similar to this one. In any case, this recipe originated in the fertile central section of the country, near Mexico City, close to the legendary gardens of Xochimilco where many fruits and vegetables flourish.

3 tablespoons corn oil
1 medium onion, peeled and finely chopped
3 cloves garlic, peeled and finely chopped
1 large tomato, peeled, seeded, and chopped
1 pound zucchini flowers
$\frac{1}{2}$ cup fresh or defrosted frozen corn kernels
1 sprig epazote (optional)
8 cups vegetable broth or chicken broth
  Salt to taste

1. In large saucepan, heat oil over medium-high heat. Add onion; cook 5 minutes, or until transparent, stirring frequently. Add garlic and tomato; cook 3 minutes longer.
2. Stir in zucchini flowers, corn, and epazote, if desired. Add broth

and bring to a boil. Reduce heat to low; cover and simmer about 12 minutes, or until vegetables are tender. Add salt to taste. Serve hot.

NOTES: The seasons for zucchini flowers are spring and summer—that's when they're available in specialty produce markets and some large supermarkets. If you're growing zucchini in a backyard garden, allow it to flower and use the blossoms in this recipe.

Epazote is a fragrant herb that is starting to become available in North American markets.

Wild Mushroom Turnovers

Quesadillas de Hongo Silvestre

MAKES 6 SERVINGS

Quesadillas are turnovers made from corn dough (masa) that is filled with a variety of ingredients. These use wild mushrooms, vegetables, and cheese, but other versions might contain brains, zucchini flowers, or chiles. My grandmothers used to prepare a "kids' quesadilla" filled with chiles, cheese, and chopped epazote leaves. Almost every quesadilla filling contains a little cheese.

While it's possible to make quesadillas with packaged tortillas, the authentic Mexican taste can only be achieved by using a masa dough to enclose the filling. Balls of masa are typically flattened in a tortilla press, then filled and folded. If you don't have a tortilla press, use a rolling pin to flatten the masa into pancake shapes (place each ball of dough between sheets of waxed paper to prevent sticking).

FILLING

- 3 tablespoons butter, margarine, or corn oil
- 1 large onion, peeled and finely chopped
- 3 cloves garlic, peeled and finely chopped
- 1 jalapeño pepper, seeded and finely chopped
- 1 pound shiitake mushrooms, sliced
- 1 large tomato, broiled, peeled, seeded, and finely chopped
  Salt to taste
- 8 ounces white Cheddar cheese, crumbled
- 2 tablespoons chopped epazote leaves (optional)

MASA

- $1\frac{1}{2}$ cups warm water
- 2 teaspoons salt
- 2 cups (8 ounces) masa harina
- 2 to 3 cups corn oil, for frying

CONDIMENTS

Salsa Ranchero (recipe follows)
Sour cream

1. Prepare filling: In large skillet over medium heat, melt butter or margarine or heat oil. Add onion, garlic, and jalapeño; sauté 5 minutes, or until tender-crisp but not brown. Add mushrooms; cook 5 minutes longer, stirring often. Add tomato and salt to taste; cook 3 minutes longer. Remove from heat and let cool. Stir cheese and epazote leaves into cooled mixture.

2. Prepare masa: In large bowl, combine water and salt. Gradually stir in masa harina until a ball forms.

3. Transfer ball of dough to work surface; knead 1 minute. Cover with damp cloth.

4. Remove a piece of masa about the size of a large cherry tomato. Form masa into a ball. Line tortilla press with two 6-inch rounds of plastic wrap. Place ball of masa between pieces of plastic; flatten with press into $\frac{1}{8}$-inch-thick disk. Peel off top piece of plastic wrap; place

about 1½ tablespoons mushroom-cheese filling in center of masa circle. Fold masa over to enclose filling, forming a semicircle; press edges lightly to seal. Peel off plastic wrap. Repeat with remaining masa dough and filling.

5. In deep-fryer or dutch oven, heat oil over medium-high heat until hot.

6. Fry quesadillas, a few at a time, in hot oil about 2 to 3 minutes, until lightly browned. Transfer to paper towels to drain.

7. Serve quesadillas hot, accompanied by salsa ranchero and sour cream.

NOTE: Masa harina is available in Latin and Hispanic grocery stores, or in gourmet shops where specialty food products are sold.

Wine note: Mushrooms and wine—red wine—are a perfect match. Given the Lebanese connection, the one red kosher wine from Lebanon would be ideal—but try to find it! Good choices would be a regional wine from France, perhaps a Rhône; a proprietary blend from Israel (a few of which are made for mushrooms and can stand up to the seasonings here); or one of the Italian varietals such as Valpolicella, which would act more as a background for the food.

RANCH SAUCE

Salsa Ranchera

MAKES 1 CUP

This recipe is served as an everyday table sauce in Mexican homes. It adds a bit of zip to quesadillas or grilled meat, fish, or poultry. It can also be used as a dip for tortilla chips.

- 1 pound ripe tomatoes
- 4 serrano chile peppers
- 1 clove garlic, peeled
  Salt to taste

1. Preheat broiler. Place tomatoes and peppers on broiler pan. Broil 4 inches from heat source, turning frequently, until skins are blistered and slightly charred.

2. Let stand at room temperature until cool. Remove peel and seeds from tomatoes and peppers.

3. Meanwhile, place peeled garlic clove in small skillet. Place over low heat and heat garlic just until warm; do not brown or soften. (Warming the garlic removes some of its bite.)

4. In food processor, process peppers and garlic until chopped. Add tomatoes and salt to taste; pulse on and off until chopped (do not purée). Let stand at room temperature until ready to use.

NOTE: To make it easier to peel roasted peppers, enclose them in a brown paper bag while they're cooling.

Lime and Coconut Pie

Pay de Limon y Coco

MAKES 6 TO 8 SERVINGS

I created this dessert to satisfy the collective sweet tooth of my steady customers. Since limes and coconuts grow prolifically in my homeland, these are the fruits I chose to flavor this recipe. The popularity of this pie confirms my feeling that these tropical tastes go well with a Mexican meal.

CRUST

- $2\frac{1}{4}$ cups all-purpose flour
- $\frac{3}{4}$ cup confectioners' sugar
- $\frac{1}{4}$ teaspoon salt
- $\frac{1}{2}$ cup (1 stick) butter or margarine
- 6 tablespoons vegetable shortening
- 2 egg yolks
- $\frac{1}{4}$ teaspoon vanilla extract

EGG WASH

- 1 egg
- $\frac{1}{2}$ teaspoon milk

FILLING

- 5 extra-large eggs
- $\frac{3}{4}$ cup granulated sugar
- Grated peel from 4 large limes
- $\frac{3}{4}$ cup lime juice
- $\frac{3}{4}$ cup grated fresh coconut
- $\frac{3}{4}$ cup heavy cream
- Additional confectioners' sugar (optional)

1. Prepare crust: Sift flour, confectioners' sugar, and salt into a medium bowl. With pastry blender or 2 knives, cut in butter or margarine and shortening until coarse crumbs form.
2. Combine yolks and vanilla; stir into flour mixture until dough

forms. With hands, press dough together into a flat disk about $\frac{3}{4}$ inch thick. Cover and refrigerate about 30 minutes.

3. On lightly floured work surface with floured rolling pin, roll out dough to a $\frac{1}{4}$-inch-thick circle about 10 inches in diameter. Transfer to 9-inch pie plate; trim off excess dough and flute edges. Cover and freeze pie crust about 15 minutes.

4. Preheat oven to 425°F. In small bowl, beat egg and milk for egg wash. Bake pie crust 10 minutes. Brush with egg wash; bake 5 minutes longer.

5. Meanwhile, prepare filling: In large bowl, mix eggs, granulated sugar, grated lime peel, lime juice, and grated coconut until well blended. Stir in cream until well incorporated.

6. Pour filling mixture into partially baked crust. Reduce oven temperature to 300°F and bake $1\frac{1}{4}$ hours, or until filling is set.

7. Remove pie to wire rack to cool. Serve at room temperature, or refrigerate to serve chilled. To serve, dust with confectioners' sugar, if desired.

Vietnamese

ost Americans grew to know Vietnam as the war-torn country portrayed on television during the sixties and seventies. Fortunately, this image is being rectified today, as more and more Vietnamese like myself settle in the States and introduce people to our unique culture and exciting cuisine.

To understand how the culinary customs of my birthplace have evolved, it's best to start with a short lesson in geography and history. Vietnam is an S-shaped country about three-fourths the size of California. Laos and Cambodia are to the west, China to the north, and the South China Sea and Gulf of Thailand to the east and south respectively. At the top of the S is the Red River Delta, and at the bottom, the Mekong Delta, the two separated from each other by a narrow spine of mountainous coastal land. Natives often describe my country as "a bamboo pole holding a bucket of rice on each end." The buckets are an apt description of the lush delta areas, where rice paddies thrive and most of the Vietnamese people live.

The first settlers probably came to the Red River section more than two thousand years ago from Indonesia, southern China, Thailand, and other Asian lands. In 111 B.C., the Chinese conquered what was then called "Nam Viet," and ruled there for ten centuries. The Chinese cultural, religious, and culinary influence was strong during this long period of rule, but the Vietnamese were selective in adopting new traditions and were able to preserve a good part of their own heritage. By A.D. 939, in fact, the Vietnamese had set up their own dynasties, and the country was relatively independent for the next nine hundred years or so.

During this "age of independence," Mongolian invasions from the north, close contact with Indian-influenced Laos, Cambodia, and Thailand, and trade with European explorers all had an impact on Vietnamese cuisine. Then from 1859 to 1954, France ruled the country, acquainting the Vietnamese with refinements of French cooking. What finally emerged from this foreign domination was a Vietnamese cuisine with a very distinctive blend. The Chinese contributed such elements as stir-frying and deep-frying in a wok, a great variety of Buddhist-inspired vegetarian dishes, and eating food with chopsticks. From the Mongolians came the inclusion of beef in a number of North Vietnamese specialties, and a type of Mongolian hot pot called *lau*. Asian neighbors introduced the Vietnamese to curries and Indian spices, and the French brought asparagus, pastries, long, crusty loaves of bread, café au lait, pâté, and ice cream. The result is a delicious union of Asian and European culinary styles.

Geography has also played a role in the evolution of Vietnamese cooking, with each of the three regions contributing its own dishes. In the north, where the Chinese influence is strongest and the climate cool and dry, stir-fries, soups, and stews are prevalent. The mountainous central part of the country serves up the most delicate, sophisticated fare. Hue, the major city in this area, was at one time the imperial capital of Vietnam, and many of the dishes known here were created for the royal table. The tropical south features the simplest but spiciest foods. Hot, sunny weather is conducive to growing many kinds of produce, including pineapples, mangoes, durian (a spiky breadfruit-shaped plant with creamy yellow flesh), chile peppers, and coconut. Fruits and vegetables are either eaten raw, pickled, or tossed into quickly prepared stir-fries and boldly spiced curries that help beat the heat. Barbecuing with sweet-sour sauces is also a popular cooking technique here.

Despite regional distinctions, certain common elements exist in the cooking of my homeland. Nuoc mam, Vietnamese fish sauce, is probably the most important. This universal ingredient is used to flavor the majority of Vietnamese dishes and usually takes the place of salt at the table. Nuoc mam is made by layering fermented ancho-vies and salt, then draining off the accumulated liquid to use as a sauce. Sometimes this liquid is mixed with lime juice, chiles, sugar, garlic, and vinegar to create nuoc cham, a lively hot sauce used to spice up recipes or added as a condiment to cooked foods. Other flavors that often show up in our cooking are lemon grass, coriander, and mint—providing a cool counterpoint to all that heat.

Contrasting different textures in the same dish is another classic Vietnamese trait. A number of recipes pair cooked ingredients with raw or very crisply cooked fresh vegetables. Because Vietnamese cooking uses little fat, the cuisine is generally light and nutritious. Even the popular stir-fried dishes require much less oil than similar Chinese versions, and lard never appears in the cooking pot.

The food of Vietnam is not difficult to prepare according to kosher guidelines, but some changes do need to be made. Let's start with the fish sauce, an integral ingredient in many recipes. Although bottled nuoc mam doesn't include any nonkosher ingredients, it's processed in Asian plants that haven't been certified and approved. I've care-fully worked out my recipes using a combination of soy sauce and salt in place of the forbidden fish sauce. The results are slightly different from the originals but quite authentic-tasting.

Pork and shellfish are the only other difficult foods for the kosher Vietnamese cook. I've found that veal makes an excellent substitute for pork in most recipes, and many seafood dishes can be prepared with a firm, white-fleshed fish.

The mixing of milk and meat is hardly ever an issue in the Viet-namese kitchen. Since the cow was long considered sacred in my country, only goat's milk was used—and sparingly. Other dairy products did not even enter into the diet until the arrival of the French. Beef was eventually included in meals, but only on special occasions—lack of refrigeration kept it scarce. Therefore, typical Vietnamese dishes never combined dairy products and meat.

The influx of immigrants from Southeast Asia to the United States has made Vietnamese ingredients much more accessible here in re-cent years. Farmers who settled in California, Florida, Texas, and Hawaii have planted seeds they brought with them from their native lands. Now, exotic fruits and vegetables flourish in these states, finding their way into oriental groceries and supermarkets across the country. Just a few years ago I had difficulty finding some of the ingredients essential to my cooking, but today food shopping is a much easier task. Even so, the recipes that follow use the most basic ingredients in fairly uncomplicated preparations. My personal mission is to give you a small taste of Vietnamese cuisine and show you how wonderful it can be!

—*Nicole Routhier*

Nicole Routhier

*N*icole Routhier's love of cooking began during her childhood in Vietnam, grew during her travels as a teenager throughout Southeast Asia and Europe, and deepened during her student years at the Culinary Institute of America (CIA). Today, she shares this love through her roles as caterer, cooking teacher, and award-winning cookbook author.

Nicole was born in 1956 in Saigon, now called Ho Chi Minh City, to a Vietnamese mother and French father. As a child, she was happiest helping out in the kitchen, watching her mother and nanny cook. In the process, she learned North Vietnamese–style cooking from her mother, originally from Haiphong, and Central Vietnamese dishes from her nanny, who was from Hue. Since the family was living in South Vietnam, young Nicole was exposed to all three of the cooking styles of her homeland.

Nicole's repertoire expanded as the Routhiers moved throughout Laos, Cambodia, and Thailand in the years that followed. In 1970, when Mrs. Routhier opened a French-Vietnamese restaurant in Laos, Nicole found herself in the midst of the professional food scene and enjoying every minute of that hectic life. "From that time on, I was hooked on cooking," she says.

In the early seventies, Nicole's stepfather took the family to live in France, and then Belgium. Here, Nicole picked up many of the western-style techniques that she later integrated into her own cook-

ing. Knowing that she wanted to pursue a career in food, she arrived in New York in 1982 and soon entered the program at the CIA, graduating in 1985. The few years after graduation were spent working in Manhattan restaurants and perfecting and writing down the recipes that had been passed down verbally from mother to daughter. Her ultimate goal was to write a cookbook in which she could "share the traditions and tastes of Vietnam with as many people as possible." That goal was reached with the 1989 publication of The Foods of Vietnam *(Stewart, Tabori & Chang).*

Now out of the restaurant business for the time being, Nicole spreads the joys of the Vietnamese table through her cooking classes at the New School and 92nd Street Y in New York City, and her catering business, Asiana Ltd.

Lime Chicken Brochettes—*Ga Nuong Voi*
Soybean and Ginger Sauce—*Nuoc Tuong*
Vietnamese-style Barbecued Veal Chops—*Thit Be Nuong*
Pickled Cabbage or Mustard Greens—*Dua Cai*
Crisp-fried Bean Curd in Tomato Sauce—*Dau Phy Sot Ca Chua*
Rice and Black Mushrooms in a Clay Pot—*Com Nam Huong*
Black Bean Dessert—*Che Dau Den*

Lime Chicken Brochettes

Ga Nuong Voi

MAKES 4 SERVINGS

In this recipe, boneless chunks of chicken are marinated in a lime-shallot mixture, then skewered and broiled over charcoal. The combination of flavors reflects the blend of cultures in Vietnam—shallots are part of the French legacy, while the citrus juice and peel shows a Thai influence. Serve these clean-tasting brochettes as an appetizer or snack (as the Vietnamese street vendors do) or as an entrée with rice, a vegetable, and a soup.

$1\frac{1}{2}$ pounds chicken thighs
4 shallots, peeled and thinly sliced
$\frac{1}{2}$ teaspoon sugar
$\frac{1}{4}$ teaspoon salt
$\frac{1}{2}$ cup vegetable oil
2 tablespoons soy sauce
Juice of 1 lime (about 2 tablespoons)
Grated peel of 1 lime (about 1 tablespoon)
Freshly ground black pepper to taste
24 white pearl onions, unpeeled

1. Bone chicken thighs; remove and discard any excess fat, leaving skin attached. Cut chicken into 1-inch chunks and set aside.
2. In blender or with mortar and pestle, grind or pound shallots,

sugar, and salt to a fine paste. Transfer to large bowl; stir in oil, soy sauce, lime juice, lime peel, and pepper. Add chicken pieces, tossing well to coat with marinade. Cover loosely and marinate in refrigerator 1 to 2 hours.

3. Meanwhile, in large saucepan over high heat, bring 2 quarts water to a boil. With sharp knife, cut a small X in the root end of each onion. Drop onions into gently boiling water and cook 3 minutes. Drain, rinse under cold water, and peel. Add onions to chicken mixture and toss well to coat with marinade.

4. Prepare outdoor grill for cooking, or preheat broiler. On each of 12 wooden skewers, alternately thread 3 to 4 pieces of chicken and 2 onions. Place skewers 3 inches from hot coals or 6 inches from broiler heat source. Grill 6 to 8 minutes, until chicken is cooked through, turning once and occasionally brushing with marinade.

NOTE: The bamboo skewers should be soaked in a bowl of cold water for at least 30 minutes before using to prevent burning.

Wine note: The mélange of tastes in this recipe calls for a wine that can marry them all, while providing refreshment. The sweet, sour, and salty combination would blend companionably with a fruity, sweet Concord. A fruity rosé would fill the bill as a drier wine, as would a grassy and cold Sauvignon Blanc from Israel or California.

Soybean and Ginger Sauce

Nuoc Tuong

MAKES $\frac{2}{3}$ CUP

I use this flavorful mixture as a dipping sauce for cooked or uncooked vegetables and broiled or grilled meats. Even though it doesn't contain nuoc mam, the classic Vietnamese fish sauce, it imparts a distinct Vietnamese character to food.

2 cloves garlic, peeled and crushed
1 fresh hot red chile pepper
4 teaspoons sugar
1 tablespoon grated peeled fresh gingerroot
$\frac{1}{4}$ cup freshly squeezed lemon juice
$\frac{1}{4}$ cup yellow soybean sauce
1 tablespoon light soy sauce

1. In blender or with mortar and pestle, blend or pound garlic, chile pepper, sugar, and gingerroot to a fine paste.
2. Add remaining ingredients and $\frac{1}{4}$ cup water; mix well. Use immediately or let stand at room temperature for flavors to blend.

NOTE: Yellow soybean sauce is available at oriental markets and gourmet specialty stores. Consult with your rabbi if there is a question about its purity.

Vietnamese-style Barbecued Veal Chops

Thit Be Nuong

MAKES 4 SERVINGS

Marinating meats in a caramel-based sauce is an age-old Vietnamese tradition. Pork spareribs are typically used with this sweet marinade, but I've adapted the recipe for veal chops. The sauce is made by caramelizing sugar, and it reflects my country's love of sweets. After marinating, the meat may either be simmered in the sauce or drained and grilled. If possible, grill the chops over a medium-hot charcoal fire to give the meat a distinctive and delicious smoky taste.

Lemon grass, a common Vietnamese aromatic herb, is used in this recipe to flavor the marinade. You may substitute grated fresh gingerroot for the lemon grass; in this case, omit the chile peppers.

$\frac{1}{2}$ cup sugar
$\frac{1}{4}$ cup light soy sauce
$\frac{1}{4}$ cup minced fresh lemon grass, or 2 tablespoons grated peeled fresh gingerroot
4 shallots, peeled and minced
4 cloves garlic, peeled and minced
2 small fresh hot chile peppers, minced
  Freshly ground black pepper to taste
4 veal chops, cut about $\frac{3}{4}$ inch thick and trimmed of fat

1. Place sugar in small heavy saucepan over low heat. Cook 5 to 10 minutes until golden brown, occasionally swirling the pan. (Sugar will smoke slightly.) Immediately remove from heat; stir in soy sauce and 2 tablespoons water. (Mixture will boil vigorously; be careful to guard against splattering.)
2. Return caramel mixture to low heat and boil gently about 3 minutes, or until sugar is completely dissolved, occasionally swirling pan. Add lemon grass, shallots, garlic, chile peppers, and black pepper to taste; stir to combine. Remove from heat and let sauce cool.
3. Pour sauce into large shallow non-metal dish. Add chops, coating well with marinade. Cover with plastic wrap and refrigerate several hours, occasionally turning chops.
4. Preheat broiler or prepare outdoor grill for cooking. Bring veal chops to room temperature; drain chops, reserving marinade.
5. Grill chops over medium-hot coals 15 minutes, or to desired doneness, turning once and basting occasionally with marinade. To serve, sprinkle with additional ground black pepper.

Wine note: A sparkling wine that is not too dry is a delicious compromise for a dish with such a mix of sweetness, saltiness, and hotness. The bubbles improve the bite of ginger and pepper, and the lightly sweet fruitiness harmonizes the whole. Most such wines are native New Yorkers, but Spain and Italy also provide contenders.

Pickled Cabbage or Mustard Greens

Dua Cai

MAKES 4 TO 6 SERVINGS

In Vietnam, pickled cabbage is often served with grilled or simmered foods to perk up the meal. A true brine contains just water and salt, and the pickling process could take up to a week (that is, if the weather is hot!). To accelerate this process, I have reduced the amount of salt and added extra vinegar. This way, your cabbage can be pickled in a couple of days.

Once pickled, the cabbage turns the color of a pickled green olive, becomes crunchy, and develops a sour tang. It's usually eaten as a side dish, but you may also combine it with meat or seafood in stir-fries. Before serving or cooking the cabbage, rinse it well in water. During cooking, season it with a pinch of sugar to offset the acidity.

1 pound green or white cabbage or mustard greens
1 bunch scallions, cut into 2-inch lengths
$\frac{1}{2}$ cup distilled white vinegar
1 tablespoon salt

1. If using cabbage, shred coarsely. If using mustard greens, cut crosswise in pieces 2 inches long and $\frac{1}{2}$ inch wide. In large bowl, combine cabbage or greens with scallions.
2. In small saucepan over high heat, bring 4 cups water, vinegar, and salt to a boil. Remove from heat; cool until warm to the touch. Pour brine mixture over vegetables. Place a small plate or dish on top of vegetables to weight them and immerse them in brine.
3. Let vegetables stand at room temperature 2 to 3 days, until they turn a yellowish color and taste sour. Drain before serving and rinse well with cold water.

Wine note: Any light red wine would go nicely, with a nod, perhaps, to the Italian reds such as Chianti, Valpolicella, or Barbera. Israel also produces a host of lesser reds that could accommodate this vegetarian dish.

Crisp-fried Bean Curd in Tomato Sauce

Dau Phy Sot Ca Chua

MAKES 4 SERVINGS

This is one of the tastiest vegetarian dishes ever invented by Vietnamese cooks.

1 pound firm bean curd (tofu)
  Peanut oil for frying
4 shallots, peeled and thinly sliced
4 cloves garlic, peeled and thinly sliced
4 large ripe tomatoes (1½ pounds), peeled, seeded, and diced
2 tablespoons light soy sauce
1 teaspoon sugar
½ cup chicken broth or water
2 scallions, thinly sliced
2 tablespoons chopped cilantro (fresh coriander)
  Freshly ground black pepper to taste
  Hot cooked rice

1. Cut bean curd into 1-inch cubes. Drain on a double thickness of paper towels.
2. Pour ½ inch peanut oil into large skillet and place over medium heat. Heat oil until hot. Add bean curd cubes in batches; fry about 8 minutes, or until crisp and golden brown on both sides, turning several times. With slotted spoon, remove bean curd and drain on paper towels.
3. Remove all but 2 tablespoons oil from skillet. Place skillet over medium heat and heat remaining oil until hot. Add shallots and garlic to hot oil; sauté 1 minute. Add tomatoes, soy sauce, and sugar; cook 1 minute longer. Reduce heat to low and simmer 15 minutes.
4. Increase heat to medium-high; add chicken broth or water and bring to a boil. Add reserved fried bean curd to skillet and toss well. Reduce heat to low; cook 5 minutes longer, or until heated through. Add scallions and cilantro; stir to blend.
5. To serve, sprinkle with freshly ground black pepper and accompany with rice.

Rice and Black Mushrooms in a Clay Pot
Com Nam Huong

MAKES 4 SERVINGS

This dish resembles a pilaf in its cooking technique and appearance, but the black mushrooms give it a decidedly oriental twist.

8 Chinese dried black mushrooms
3½ cups chicken broth
1 tablespoon light soy sauce
3 tablespoons vegetable oil
1 cup finely chopped onions
½ cup finely chopped celery
2 cups long-grain rice (preferably Jasmine rice)

1. Soak mushrooms in hot water to cover for about 30 minutes, or until soft and pliable. Squeeze out excess water; cut off and discard woody stems. Cut mushroom caps into julienne strips and set aside.
2. In medium saucepan, combine chicken broth and soy sauce over high heat; bring to a boil. Reduce heat to low (liquid should maintain just a bare simmer).
3. In ovenproof clay pot or heavy 2-quart saucepan, heat oil over medium heat. Add onion and celery; sauté 5 minutes, or until vegetables are softened but not browned. Add mushrooms; cook 1 minute, stirring constantly. Add rice; stir with wooden spoon to coat grains evenly with oil. Cook about 3 minutes, or until rice turns opaque, tossing constantly.
4. Remove rice from heat and stir in hot broth until well combined. Return to very low heat; cover and cook 20 minutes, or until rice is tender and liquid is absorbed. Serve immediately.

NOTE: Chinese dried black mushrooms and Jasmine rice are available at oriental grocery stores.

Black Bean Dessert

Che Dau Den

MAKES 4 TO 6 SERVINGS

In Vietnam, this dessert is most popular during the long, hot days of summer. It's similar to a sweetened cold soup, and when not eaten after a meal, is often enjoyed as an afternoon treat, especially upon awakening from a nap! Fresh fruit is actually the most common after-dinner dessert, but this makes a refreshing alternative.

    1 cup dried black turtle beans
    $\frac{1}{2}$ teaspoon baking soda
    2 cups coconut milk
    1 cup sugar
    Crushed ice

1. In medium bowl, combine beans and enough water to cover. Soak overnight at room temperature.
2. Rinse beans with several changes of water to remove all impurities; drain.
3. In large saucepan, bring 6 cups water to a boil over high heat. Add beans and baking soda. Reduce heat to low; simmer 30 to 45 minutes, until beans are tender but not mushy, occasionally skimming off foam that rises to the surface.
4. Stir in coconut milk and sugar; continue simmering 5 minutes longer. Remove from heat and cool to room temperature.
5. To serve, ladle bean mixture into individual cups or bowls. Top with crushed ice.

NOTE: Use dried black turtle beans in this recipe, not salted Chinese black beans.

Russian-Polish
(Eastern European)

*a*s this book demonstrates, Jews have scattered around the world. But in the recent past until the end of World War II, the largest numbers lived in Eastern Europe, particularly Russia and Poland. (Poland was under Russian rule during most of this period.) It was primarily in the *shetls* or villages of these countries that Jewish families of the Ashkenazic faith carried on their traditions. And it was here that the dishes we think of as typically "Jewish" were born—dishes such as gefilte fish, blintzes, chopped liver, and chicken soup.

During the late nineteenth and early twentieth centuries, droves of Ashkenazic Jews emigrated from Eastern Europe to North America to escape the tyranny of czarist rule. In the small bundles of belongings these immigrants carried, there were almost always a few well-worn cooking pots. And in the memories of the Ashkenazic housewives, there were familiar combinations of ingredients that eventually formed the backbone of Jewish-American cooking. Many were either scrawled into vague recipes or verbally passed down from mother to daughter to granddaughter and beyond, and are still being cooked in Jewish-American homes today.

While the Sephardic Jews left Spain and settled in the nearby Mediterranean and North African countries, the Ashkenazim (which means "German" in Hebrew) traveled from the Germanic countries east, taking up residence in lands of similar geography and climate. German Jews actually entered Eastern Europe in force after the persecutions by the Crusades in the Middle Ages. By the fifteenth century, about 5 million Ashkenazim called Russia, Poland, and to a lesser extent, Romania, home.

The staples of the Russian and Polish table were not unlike those the Jews left behind in Germany. Potatoes, cabbage, beets, and wheat were the main agricultural crops, and a variety of fish, fowl, and meats provided more nourishment. Until the First World War, there were two distinct classes in these countries—the nobility and the peasantry—each of which translated these ingredients into their own cuisine. For the most part, the Jews were relegated to the peasant class, and developed an assortment of dishes well suited to the cold climate, available food products, and the laws of kashrut. Religious persecution also played a big part in the evolution of a Jewish culinary style. From the late 1700s until the Russian Revolution of 1917, most Jews were restricted by "The Pale of Settlement." This edict confined them in isolated shetls throughout the Russian and Polish countryside, or in ghettos within the larger towns and cities. Although The Pale greatly inhibited freedom, it did work to bind the Jews together and preserve their customs and rituals.

Eating was a main focus of Jewish shetl life, even when food was scarce. Through the years of confinement, Jewish housewives learned to make do with very little. Most kept chickens in their yards, and almost every part of the bird found its way onto the table. The fat and skin were rendered into schmalz and gribenes. Chicken feet, necks, backs, and assorted scraps were thrown into the soup pot along with greens and root vegetables for every Jewish mother's famous chicken soup. And as a luxury, the whole bird would be roasted to a golden turn for a special Shabbat or holiday dinner.

One-dish meals featuring small amounts of meat were also popular. Beef brisket or flanken was typically pot-roasted or braised for several hours along with potatoes and vegetables. As for fish, the local herring, pike, whitefish, and other freshwater species were turned into Jewish specialties as well. Favorites were gefilte fish and pickled or creamed herring.

In most families, however, meat, fish, and poultry were not everyday foods. More often, root vegetables and grains were the mainstays of the Jewish peasant diet. Thrifty housewives prepared hearty hot soups based on beets, cabbage, potatoes, turnips, carrots, and/or onions—the only vegetables abundant enough to use freely. In warmer weather, cucumbers and sorrel went into cold soups. To preserve the cucumbers of summer, Polish and Russian Jews stored them in a brine seasoned with garlic and dill, giving birth to the world-renowned kosher pickle of today.

Although the climate and soil of Eastern Europe were not hospitable to many fruit and vegetable crops, wheat, rye, barley, and similar grains thrived. These grains were milled into flour and baked into dark, chewy loaves of pumpernickel, rye, and black bread. Along with potatoes, these breads appeared at almost every peasant meal. Doughs made from the softer flours were formed into noodles, dumplings, and wrappers for a variety of starchy fillings. The pirogen, knishes, blintzes, and kugels we now love resulted from a blend of peasant ingenuity and an abundance of grains. On other occasions, the grains were cooked whole, incorporated into such savory classics as mushroom-barley soup and kasha varnishkes.

Most of the foods prepared by the Eastern European Jews were similar to traditional Russian and Polish dishes and fit into the Jewish dietary laws. Several dishes, however, had to be changed a bit. Borscht made with beef, for example, couldn't be topped with its typical dollop of sour cream at a meat meal, and cheese-filled pirogen would never accompany roast chicken. In other cases, Jewish cooks invented their own versions of Eastern European specialties.

Many of these dishes and adaptations made their way across the Atlantic, where they survived and flourished in the neighborhoods settled by Eastern European Jews. But the Jewish Ashkenazic cooks also enriched and enlarged their cuisine with the plentiful ingredients they found in America. Beef hot dogs and salami, lox, bagels, thick corned beef and pastrami sandwiches, and cheesecake are all Jewish-American creations born in the kitchens, delicatessens, and appetizing stores of the New World. When you cook the recipes in this chapter, you will get that unique mixture of Polish, Russian, and Romanian influences, seasoned with a "bissel" of New York City's Lower East Side and other early Jewish-American neighborhoods.

—*Leila Hirsch*

Leila Hirsch

*A*s the mother of ten children, Leila Hirsch has cooked her share of family and holiday meals! Her culinary experience began when she married her husband, Irving, more than thirty-five years ago, and set up a kosher home. Through trial, error, and sketchy directions from her mother-in-law, Leila learned to cook the Eastern European dishes familiar to her Russian grandparents and Polish in-laws. Although her repertoire has now expanded to include many international cuisines, Leila is still famous for her mouth-watering chicken soup, challah, chopped liver, and other Jewish delights.

Leila was born in the Bronx to second-generation Jewish-American parents. In college, she took a number of biology, chemistry, and math courses in anticipation of a career in medicine. This preparation, along with her natural instinct for combining ingredients, provided an excellent background for becoming an accomplished cook. Her talent for improvisation has put her personal stamp on traditional dishes, enlivening and enriching them.

Leila still loves preparing typical Jewish foods for Shabbat dinner and festive occasions. Holidays often find thirty or more relatives around the table, looking forward to such Hirsch family traditions as stuffed veal birds or capon, mushroom-barley soup, sweet potato-apple-carrot kugel, apple cake, and rugelach—plus the platters of fresh vegetables that were the one element missing from most old-style Eastern European meals. Passover is an especially joyous celebration. In addition to the two seders Leila makes, she also hosts a blintz party during the week. For this event, three generations of cousins and their children are invited to dig into Leila's special blintzes, cheesecake, and strawberry shortcake—all kosher for Passover.

Leila's well-deserved reputation as an expert cook earned her the privilege of editing two cookbooks for Hadassah, and several of her recipes have been featured in the food section of Long Island's Newsday. She has passed her culinary skills onto her children, most of whom are now cooking on their own with wonderful results. "Each has his or her own area of expertise," says Leila.

These days, cooking isn't always the prime focus of Leila's busy life. She also spends a good amount of time in her administrative job at the 92nd Street Y, and frequently travels here and abroad with her husband.

Mushroom-Barley Soup
Chopped Liver—*Gehakte Leber*
Chicken Fat and Cracklings—*Schmalz and Gribenes*
Pot Roast
Groats and Noodles—*Kasha Varnishkes*
String Beans with Garlic
Noodle Pudding—*Lokshen Kugel*
Apple Cake

Mushroom-Barley Soup

MAKES 6 SERVINGS

This is one of those hearty soups that helped Russian and Polish peasants make it through many a cold, long winter night. Born of necessity in the Jewish ghettos of Eastern Europe, mushroom-barley soup was a tasty way to stretch a few staples into a filling meal. In my Jewish-American version, I take advantage of the agricultural bounty in this land of plenty. I start with homemade chicken soup, then add chunks of veal and fresh vegetables for a real stick-to-your ribs dish. By double-batching my chicken soup every Shabbat, I always have enough golden broth to use as a base for other recipes like this one.

   1 large onion, peeled and diced
   2 cups diced carrots
   2 cups diced celery
   1 tablespoon vegetable oil
   1 pound veal stew meat, cubed
   1 pound fresh mushrooms, thinly sliced
One 1-pound package pearl barley, soaked overnight in water to cover by 1 inch
   4 quarts chicken broth, preferably homemade chicken soup

1. In dutch oven or large saucepot, combine onion, carrots, celery, and oil. Place over medium heat and sauté 5 to 10 minutes, until onion is tender.

2. Add veal and remaining ingredients; bring to a boil.

3. Reduce heat to low; cover and simmer 2 hours, or until veal is tender and soup is thickened.

Wine note: Considering the weight of this soup, head directly for the red wine section. Geographically closest to Russia, for kosher wine purposes, is Hungary, with a serviceable red. The proprietary red wines of Israel (dry reds) also would be powerful enough to accompany this recipe.

Chopped Liver

Gehakte Leber

MAKES 6 TO 8 SERVINGS

Many serious eaters feel that chopped liver is the true test of a good Jewish cook. I prepare mine in a wooden bowl with an old-fashioned metal chopper, never in a food processor or blender. Chopping by hand gives the liver the right texture—coarse but not chunky. A processor or blender would make the mixture too smooth, more like a French pâté than a Jewish chopped liver.

<blockquote>

1 pound chicken livers or steer liver

3 to 4 tablespoons Schmalz (recipe follows)

3 medium onions, peeled and finely chopped

2 hard-cooked eggs

Chopped Gribenes (recipe follows) (optional)

Salt and freshly ground black pepper to taste

</blockquote>

1. Broil the livers thoroughly until no trace of pink remains.
2. In medium skillet, heat 1 tablespoon schmalz over medium-low heat. Add onions; sauté 5 to 10 minutes, until soft but not brown.
3. In wooden bowl with metal chopper, coarsely chop liver and eggs together. Add onions and drippings from skillet; chop a little longer until well combined. (Do not form a paste.) Add 1 or 2 tablespoons chopped gribenes and enough schmalz to moisten. Season to taste with salt and pepper.

NOTE: When I don't have schmalz on hand, I sometimes substitute an equal amount of mayonnaise. Either should be mixed in just until the liver reaches the right consistency—it's more a question of "feel" than exact measurements. While the mayonnaise is an adequate stand-in, only the rich, golden chicken fat will give the chopped liver its authentic taste.

CHICKEN FAT AND CRACKLINGS

Schmalz and Gribenes

$\frac{1}{2}$ pound chicken fat (from 2 or 3 chickens or 1 large fowl)
$\frac{1}{4}$ pound chicken skin, cut into small pieces

1. In large heavy skillet, combine chicken fat and skin over medium-low heat. Cook slowly for 35 to 45 minutes, until fat liquefies and skin becomes golden and crisp.
2. Strain liquid fat into a glass jar. Store in refrigerator. Reserve gribenes to eat as a snack, toss into chopped liver mixture, or use as a garnish for mashed potatoes or noodles.

Wine note: Many red wines like liver. They should have weight and substance, as a little tannin would not be amiss with this. Cabernet

Sauvignon from California or Israel, a St. Emilion from France or another chateau-bottled Bordeaux would stand up to the richness of this dish.

Pot Roast

MAKES 6 SERVINGS

Pot roast was once part of every Jewish woman's repertoire, and I was no exception. When I was first married, my mother-in-law sent over a piece of brisket one Friday and told me to cook it up with onions in a large pot. Never having cooked this cut of meat before, I improvised a little and added some herbs and flavorings I liked to the cooking pot. I then called my own mother to find out at what point I should stop cooking the meat so it wouldn't fall apart. I followed her advice, slicing the meat while it was still firm, then serving it with the hot gravy. If you prefer pot roast that turns into shreds at the touch of a fork (my family doesn't), just return the sliced meat to the gravy in the pot and cook until soft.

        Vegetable oil
   1 large onion, peeled and sliced
        Garlic powder
        Dried parsley flakes
        Dried basil leaves
One 4½-pound first cut brisket of beef
  12 medium potatoes, peeled and quartered
        Salt to taste

1. Heat oil in dutch oven over medium heat. Add onion; sauté 10 minutes, or until golden brown. Sprinkle onion evenly with garlic powder, parsley flakes, and basil; push onion to one side of pot.
2. Increase heat to medium-high. Sprinkle both sides of brisket with garlic powder. Add brisket to dutch oven and brown on both sides.

3. Reduce heat to low. Add enough water to just cover brisket; bring to a simmer. Add potatoes and salt; cover and cook $1\frac{1}{2}$ hours, or until meat is fork-tender but still firm.

4. Remove potatoes and brisket from pot. Cover brisket and let stand 15 to 30 minutes for easier slicing.

5. With sharp knife, thinly slice meat. Serve sliced brisket with potatoes and cooking liquid from pot as gravy.

NOTE: I generally sprinkle in enough garlic powder, parsley flakes, and basil to completely cover the bottom of the pot.

Wine note: Is there a better dish for a big red wine than pot roast? No! So dig deep into the wine cellar or under the galoshes in the hall closet for a hearty red wine. Eschew the lesser wines and go for the biggest Bordeaux, Burgundy, or Cabernet that can be found. A kosher red Zinfandel should be on the market shortly—that would go nicely too.

Groats and Noodles

Kasha Varnishkes

MAKES 4 TO 6 SERVINGS

Kasha is milled from buckwheat, one of the few crops that could thrive on the barren, chilly fields of Eastern Europe. Jewish housewives paired the nutty, assertive flavor of kasha with the blander taste of bow-tie noodles to come up with this classic dish, kasha and bows.

One 8-ounce box bow-tie noodles
   1 cup kasha (buckwheat groats)
   1 egg, lightly beaten
  $\frac{1}{4}$ cup ($\frac{1}{2}$ stick) margarine
    Salt to taste

1. Cook bow-tie noodles in boiling, salted water according to package directions; drain. Run cold water over noodles to stop the cooking; drain again and set aside.

2. In small bowl, mix kasha with egg until all grains are evenly coated.

3. Place medium skillet over medium-high heat; heat until hot. Reduce heat to very low; add kasha mixture. With fork, break up kasha to separate grains. Cook kasha 5 to 10 minutes, until grains are roasted, shaking skillet as kasha cooks.

4. In large saucepan over high heat, bring 2 cups water, margarine, and salt to a boil. Add kasha; reduce heat to medium. Cover and cook about 20 minutes, or until all water is absorbed.

5. Stir bows into hot kasha to heat through. To serve, moisten kasha and bows with pot roast gravy.

String Beans with Garlic

MAKES 4 TO 6 SERVINGS

I often prepare this simple dish to go along with the pot roast on Shabbat.

- 1 pound green beans
- $\frac{1}{4}$ cup ($\frac{1}{2}$ stick) margarine
- 3 cloves garlic, peeled and pressed

1. Cut green beans in half. In large saucepan over high heat, combine beans and enough water to cover; bring to a boil. Reduce heat to low; cover and cook 5 to 8 minutes, until beans are fork-tender.

2. Drain beans and return to saucepan. Add margarine and garlic; toss to combine. Cook over low heat until margarine melts, stirring often.

Noodle Pudding

Lokshen Kugel

MAKES 6 TO 8 SERVINGS

Through countless Shabbat dinners, Ashkenazic Jews have eaten some type of kugel, the Yiddish term for pudding. It can be made from noodles, potatoes, apples, carrots, rice, or even matzoh, all held together by eggs and then baked golden brown. Lokshen, or noodle kugel, has always been a mainstay on my family's dinner table. Although some cooks enrich their lokshen kugels with cottage cheese, cream cheese, and/or sour cream, I offer a pareve version here to go with a meat-based menu.

One 16-ounce package broad egg noodles
1 cup (2 sticks) margarine, melted
1 cup sugar
4 eggs, beaten
1 apple, peeled and grated
$\frac{1}{2}$ cup golden raisins
1 tablespoon orange marmalade
1 teaspoon vanilla extract
Ground cinnamon

1. Cook noodles in boiling, salted water according to package directions; drain.
2. Preheat oven to 375°F. Grease 13- by 9-inch baking dish.
3. In large bowl, combine drained noodles with remaining ingredients except cinnamon; mix well. Pour into prepared dish, smoothing top. Sprinkle with cinnamon.
4. Bake kugel about 1 hour, or until golden and set. To serve, cut into squares.

Apple Cake

MAKES 8 SERVINGS

Apples were among the few fruits cultivated in the colder European countries in which the Ashkenazic Jews settled. Therefore, it's no surprise that many Jewish-style desserts are based on apples. This cake probably evolved from the Germanic tradition.

Vegetable cooking spray
3 cups peeled and diced apples (Cortland, McIntosh, or Rome Beauty)
2 cups plus 2 tablespoons granulated sugar
4 to 5 teaspoons ground cinnamon
3 cups all-purpose flour
1 tablespoon baking powder
1 teaspoon salt
1 cup vegetable oil
4 eggs, lightly beaten
$\frac{1}{4}$ cup orange juice
1 teaspoon vanilla extract
Confectioners' sugar for dusting

1. Preheat oven to 375°F. Spray a 10- or 12-cup bundt pan or tube pan with vegetable cooking spray, or grease lightly.
2. In medium bowl, toss apples with 2 tablespoons granulated sugar and all the cinnamon; set aside.
3. In large bowl, combine flour, remaining 2 cups granulated sugar, baking powder, and salt; mix with a wooden spoon.
4. Make a well in center of flour mixture; add oil, eggs, orange juice, and vanilla. With wooden spoon, stir liquid ingredients in well, then blend thoroughly into flour mixture.
5. Spoon one-third of the batter into prepared bundt pan; spread half the apple mixture evenly over batter. Repeat layers, ending with batter.

6. Bake cake 1 to 1¼ hours, until toothpick inserted in center comes out clean. Cool cake in pan on wire rack.

7. To serve, invert cake onto plate; invert again onto cake plate so cake is right side up. Dust cake lightly with confectioners' sugar.

Wine note: Apple cakes and pies fit so well with dessert wines. A real French Sauternes would be marvelous; so would a New York honey wine. A medium-sweet Muscat would fit right in, as would a New York Port or a late-harvest or naturally sweet wine from California.

Beet Soup—*Borscht*
Vegetarian Chopped Liver
Little Pies—*Pirogen or Piroshki*
Potato Kneidlach
Rugelach

Beet Soup

Borscht

MAKES 4 SERVINGS

The original borscht was made from beets, which grew abundantly in Russia and Eastern Europe. Inventive cooks eventually added more ingredients to the soup pot, including other root vegetables and even beef. Now there are two main types of borscht in the traditional Jewish recipe file—a dairy version and a meat version. I enjoy both kinds, but this dairy recipe is what most people picture when they think of borscht. It's usually served cold over boiled potatoes.

    8 beets, peeled and grated or cut into julienne strips
    2 small onions, peeled and diced (optional)
    2 tablespoons sour salt, vinegar, or lemon juice (see Note)
One 16-ounce container sour cream
    4 medium potatoes, peeled

1. In large saucepan or dutch oven, combine beets, onions, sour salt, and 8 cups water. Place over high heat and bring to a boil.
2. Reduce heat to medium; cover and cook 30 minutes, or until beets are tender. Remove from heat and cool to room temperature.
3. Remove 1 cup beet mixture from pot to small bowl and stir in sour cream. Return sour cream mixture to pot and stir thoroughly to blend. Refrigerate borscht until well chilled.

4. Meanwhile, in medium saucepan, combine potatoes and enough water to cover. Place over high heat and boil 15 to 20 minutes, until tender.

5. To serve, ladle cold borscht into bowls; add 1 hot potato to each bowl.

N O T E : Sour salt is not the same as table salt—it is a special seasoning that can be found in Eastern European groceries or gourmet shops. If it is not available, you may substitute vinegar or lemon juice, but add these ingredients at the end of the cooking time for the soup.

Vegetarian Chopped Liver

MAKES 6 SERVINGS

This is an American invention, created as an appetizer or side dish to serve with a dairy meal. It resembles the real thing in texture, but the taste is noticeably different.

 2 tablespoons vegetable oil
 2 medium onions, peeled and finely chopped
 1 pound green beans, cooked and chopped
 6 hard-cooked eggs, chopped
 $\frac{1}{2}$ cup finely chopped walnuts (optional)
 3 tablespoons mayonnaise

1. In medium skillet, heat oil over medium heat. Add onions; sauté 5 to 10 minutes, until soft but not brown.

2. In medium bowl, combine onions, green beans, eggs, and walnuts. Add mayonnaise; mix until ingredients bind together.

Little Pies

Pirogen or Piroshki

MAKES 4 SERVINGS

The word pirog *comes from the Russian word* pir, *which means "feast." As a category, pirogen resemble small turnovers filled with meat, cheese, potatoes, mushrooms, or cabbage—all staples of the Eastern European kitchen. In the nineteenth century, pirogen sometimes appeared on appetizer trays served by the Russian aristocracy. But these turnovers were probably a peasant dish originally, especially appropriate for a dairy meal when stuffed with cheese. I prefer to cook my pirogen in boiling water, but they can also be fried.*

DOUGH
- 2 cups all-purpose flour
- 2 eggs, lightly beaten
- $\frac{1}{2}$ teaspoon salt

FILLING
- 1 medium onion, peeled and diced
- 1 tablespoon melted butter, plus additional for tossing (optional)
- 1 cup cottage cheese or pot cheese
- 1 egg, beaten
- 3 tablespoons sugar
- $\frac{1}{4}$ teaspoon ground cinnamon

1. Prepare dough: Measure flour into large bowl. Form well in center; add $\frac{1}{2}$ cup water, 2 eggs, and salt. With wooden spoon, mix liquid into dry ingredients until soft dough forms. Transfer dough to floured work surface; knead until smooth. Cover with warm bowl and let dough rest 10 minutes.

2. Meanwhile, prepare filling: In small skillet over medium heat, sauté onion in 2 teaspoons melted butter for 5 minutes, or until golden. Remove from heat; let cool slightly. Stir in cottage cheese, 1 teaspoon melted butter, egg, sugar, and cinnamon until well blended.

3. On floured surface with floured rolling pin, roll out dough, one-half at a time, to $\frac{1}{4}$-inch thickness. With 2- to 3-inch round cookie cutter, cut out circles of dough. Put a spoonful of cheese filling in center of each circle; fold dough over filling to form semicircular turnovers. With moistened fingers, press edges of dough together to seal.

4. In large saucepan or dutch oven over high heat, bring 8 to 12 cups salted water to a rolling boil. Add pirogen and cook 3 to 5 minutes, until tender.

5. To serve, drain pirogen and toss with melted butter, if desired.

Potato Kneidlach

MAKES 6 TO 8 SERVINGS

This is a recipe I invented as a cross between matzoh balls and potato pirogen. These light potato balls can either be served in soup or sautéed with onions and mushrooms to serve as a savory addition to a dairy lunch.

5 potatoes, peeled, grated, and drained
2 eggs, lightly beaten
1 teaspoon salt
1 cup matzoh meal
3 tablespoons butter or margarine
1 medium onion, peeled and chopped
$\frac{1}{4}$ pound fresh mushrooms, sliced

1. In medium bowl, combine potatoes, eggs, and salt. Stir in matzoh meal until blended.

2. With hands form mixture into small balls. Set aside on waxed paper.

3. In large saucepan over high heat, bring 10 cups salted water to a

boil. Drop potato balls into boiling water; cover and reduce heat to medium. Simmer potato balls 1 hour. Remove from heat and drain well.

4. Meanwhile, in medium skillet over medium-high heat, melt butter or margarine. Add onion and mushrooms; sauté 5 minutes. Add drained potato balls; sauté 5 minutes longer, stirring gently. Serve hot.

N O T E : If using potato kneidlach in soup, omit Step 4; place drained balls directly into hot soup.

Wine note: How about these kneidlach on their own with a red wine as a lunch in itself? Pick any medium-bodied inexpensive red, preferably with a little fruit and less tannin—the proprietaries from Israel, the lesser Burgundies (Bourgogne) and Bordeaux, or a Rhône or Provençal wine. Then take a little snooze, as the wine and the weight of the kneidlach will demand it!

Rugelach

MAKES 4 DOZEN

Rugelach get their rich taste from a combination of either cream cheese or sour cream with the butter that forms the dough. These are a strictly dairy treat, best washed down with a good cup of coffee or hot tea. I fill rugelach with cinnamon, raisins, and nuts; apricot or raspberry jam is another option.

DOUGH
    2 cups all-purpose flour
    1 cup (2 sticks) sweet butter
One 8-ounce package cream cheese

FILLING
$\frac{1}{4}$ cup melted butter
$\frac{1}{2}$ cup granulated sugar
1 tablespoon ground cinnamon
2 cups finely chopped walnuts
1 cup currants or raisins

TOPPING
2 tablespoons confectioners' sugar, sifted

1. In medium bowl, combine all ingredients for dough; blend well with fingers. Divide dough into 4 sections; wrap each in waxed paper. Refrigerate at least 3 hours, or overnight.
2. Preheat oven to 350°F. Line cookie sheets with parchment paper or grease lightly.
3. On lightly floured surface with lightly floured rolling pin, flatten 1 section of dough. Continue rolling dough to form a circle about $\frac{1}{4}$ inch thick and 12 inches in diameter. (The larger the circle, the larger the rugelach will be.)
4. Brush 1 tablespoon melted butter evenly over surface of dough circle. Evenly sprinkle on a quarter of the granulated sugar and a quarter of the cinnamon. Sprinkle with a quarter of the nuts and a quarter of the currants or raisins.
5. With sharp knife, cut the dough circle into quarters; cut each quarter into 3 equal wedges. (You will have 12 wedges in all.) Starting at wide end, roll up each wedge to center point to form crescents. Place crescents on prepared cookie sheet.
6. Repeat rolling and filling with remaining dough, sugar, cinnamon, nuts, and currants or raisins.
7. Bake rugelach 30 minutes, or until golden brown. Remove to wire rack to cool. Before serving, dust lightly with confectioners' sugar.

Wine note: Just in case coffee or tea is not for thee, a Sauternes, Asti Spumante, or cream sherry might be.

Celebrations

*t*he international recipes we've presented in the preceding
pages are ideal for entertaining. Each menu is a full-course
meal around which a dinner party could easily be planned. As
a bonus, the menus were created to fit within the time frame
of a cooking class. In most cases, that means the preparation and
cooking can be completed in about two hours—a boon for the busy
host or hostess.

There are occasions, however, when a dinner party just doesn't fit
the bill. For that reason, we've included three alternatives for entertaining—a Mediterranean appetizer buffet, an English afternoon tea,
and a dazzling dessert party. A good deal of the food in these festive
menus can be prepared ahead, making them perfect for open-house
celebrations or more casual get-togethers.

MEDITERRANEAN APPETIZER BUFFET
(from Mimi Olanoff)

In several of the Mediterranean countries, dinner is not served until 9:00 or 10:00 P.M. To soothe hunger pangs till then, it's customary to nibble on savory appetizers while sipping an aperitif or a glass of wine. In Spain, these would be an assortment of bite-sized tapas; in Italy, antipasti; and in France, hors d'oeuvre.

Mimi Olanoff has assembled a spread that will take you on a journey along the Mediterranean coast, from Genoa to Gibraltar. All the recipes make the most of abundant local products—a variety of fresh vegetables and herbs, olive oil and many kinds of olives, different types of fresh seafood, and tree-ripened fruits picked no earlier than the previous day. Although these lend themselves well to a large buffet or cocktail party, you can also choose just a few to whet guests' appetites before dinner. The menu contains only pareve and meat ingredients. Much of the fare can be made in advance and/or served at room temperature, freeing the cook to enjoy the party, too!

Nice-style Salad—*Salade Niçoise*
Vegetable Omelet—*Frittata or Tortilla Espanola*
Marinated Anchovies with Dill and Pimiento
Spanish Sausage Stew—*Cazuelo de Chorizo*
Stuffed Mushrooms in the Style of La Varenne—
Champignons Farcis La Varenne
Meatballs on Toast—*Polpettoncini sui Crostone*
Nice-style Onion Tart—*Pissaladière*
Flaky Pastry

Nice-style Salad

Salade Niçoise

MAKES 8 SERVINGS

I once ate this colorful salad in an open-air dining room cantilevered over the Rhône River in the town of Villeneuve-les-Avignon, France. It was served in a deep glass bowl, allowing a full view of the beautiful contents. A good bit of the work for this salad can be done ahead, making it very easy to prepare and serve for company.

DRESSING

- $\frac{1}{2}$ cup wine vinegar
- 1 teaspoon salt
- 1 teaspoon dried basil
- 1 teaspoon dry mustard
- 1 small clove garlic, peeled and finely minced
- $\frac{1}{4}$ teaspoon freshly ground black pepper
- $\frac{3}{4}$ cup vegetable oil or olive oil

SALAD

- 6 medium potatoes (about $1\frac{1}{2}$ pounds)
  Salt to taste
- Two 10-ounce packages frozen whole green beans
- 1 cup vegetable broth
- 1 head Boston or red-leaf lettuce, separated into leaves
- 2 tablespoons chopped scallions
- Two 7-ounce cans solid-pack tuna, drained and separated into chunks
- 3 medium tomatoes, cut into wedges
- 2 hard-cooked eggs, quartered
- 24 pitted black olives, preferably niçoise
- 8 canned anchovy fillets, drained
- 3 tablespoons chopped parsley
  Fresh basil leaves (optional)

1. Prepare dressing: In small bowl, combine vinegar, salt, basil, mustard, garlic, and pepper; stir with wire whisk until blended. Slowly whisk in oil until well combined; set aside.

2. In large saucepan over medium-high heat, combine potatoes, salt to taste, and enough water to cover by 1 inch. Bring to a boil; boil 15 minutes, or just until tender. Drain; cool slightly. Peel potatoes and cut into slices about $\frac{1}{8}$ inch thick; place slices in medium bowl.

3. Stir dressing well; taste and adjust seasoning. Add about half the dressing to sliced potatoes. Let stand at room temperature until potatoes absorb dressing; refrigerate until ready to use.

4. In large saucepan over medium-high heat, bring green beans and broth to a boil. Cook 5 to 8 minutes, or until beans are tender; drain and cool. Refrigerate until ready to serve.

5. Just before serving, sprinkle or toss lettuce leaves with about $\frac{1}{4}$ cup dressing. Line serving platter with lettuce; heap potatoes to one side and sprinkle with scallions. Toss green beans with a little dressing; arrange beans in a mound behind potatoes. Place tuna chunks in a row where potatoes and beans almost meet.

6. Sprinkle tomato wedges with a little dressing. Distribute tomato wedges, egg quarters, and olives around outer edge of platter. Place an anchovy fillet across each egg quarter; sprinkle remaining dressing over all. Garnish with basil leaves, if desired.

Vegetable Omelet

Frittata or Tortilla Espanola

MAKES 8 SERVINGS

This puffy omelet-type dish is usually served at room temperature as a tapa in Spain, or for lunch or at a picnic in Italy. In Spain, it's sometimes referred to as the national dish when prepared with cooked potatoes and sautéed onions. The following recipe starts with raw vegetables and turns out more like a frittata.

$\frac{1}{2}$ pound small zucchini or thin asparagus (see Note)

$\frac{1}{4}$ cup all-purpose flour

$\frac{1}{2}$ teaspoon salt

6 eggs

Freshly ground black pepper to taste

$\frac{1}{4}$ teaspoon dry mustard

$\frac{1}{4}$ cup olive oil

1. Rinse zucchini and pat dry. Dice into $\frac{1}{2}$-inch pieces.

2. In plastic bag, combine flour and $\frac{1}{4}$ teaspoon salt. Add zucchini; close bag tightly, and shake until well coated with flour. Place vegetable pieces in strainer and shake out excess flour.

3. In medium bowl, combine eggs, 2 tablespoons water, black pepper to taste, mustard, and $\frac{1}{4}$ teaspoon salt; beat with fork just until combined.

4. In 10-inch nonstick skillet, heat oil over medium-high heat. Add zucchini; sauté 2 minutes, or until lightly browned, stirring frequently. Reduce heat to low; cover and cook 1 minute longer. Stir gently; cover and cook 1 minute longer.

5. Spread zucchini evenly in skillet. Restir eggs; pour over zucchini. Cook 10 to 15 minutes, or until eggs are set but still moist on top. With spatula, loosen edges of frittata from skillet. Cover with large plate and flip frittata out onto plate. Slide back into pan and cook on other side until firm but still slightly moist inside.

6. To serve, cut into small squares or wedges. Serve with toothpicks.

NOTE: If using asparagus, choose thin stalks. Trim bottom ends but leave stalks whole; flour and sauté as with zucchini, then arrange in skillet, spoke-fashion, before adding egg mixture.

Marinated Anchovies with Dill and Pimiento

This recipe can be made as early in the day as you wish—the longer it marinates, the better it tastes. I think flat-leafed Italian parsley has more flavor, but curly fresh parsley can be used as well.

Two 2-ounce cans flat anchovy fillets packed in oil
    Juice of 1 lemon
  1 teaspoon finely chopped shallot or onion
  ¼ teaspoon finely minced garlic
    Coarsely ground black pepper to taste
  1 tablespoon chopped fresh dill
  1 tablespoon chopped parsley
  1 teaspoon chopped chives or scallion greens (optional)
Two 4-ounce jars whole pimientos
    Toasted French or Italian bread slices

1. Prepare dressing: Drain oil from anchovies into small bowl. Add lemon juice, shallot, garlic, and pepper. With fork or wire whisk, beat until blended. Add dill, parsley, and chives; mix well. Add a little additional olive oil to achieve proper consistency, if necessary.
2. Set aside 1 whole pimiento; slice remaining pimientos into long, thin strips. In center of large round platter, place reserved whole pimiento. Arrange alternating strips of pimiento and anchovy fillets in spokes around whole pimiento.
3. Starting at outer edge, spoon dressing in concentric circles over anchovies and pimientos. Cover platter with plastic wrap and let stand at room temperature 1 hour or longer.
4. To serve, place platter of anchovies and pimientos in center of large round tray or lazy Susan. Arrange toasted bread slices all around. Spoon anchovies and pimientos onto bread.

Spanish Sausage Stew

Cazuelo de Chorizo

MAKES 8 SERVINGS

The original recipe for this stew calls for the Spanish sausages known as chorizo. Some cured kosher sausages made from beef come close in taste and are available in supermarkets. I've also prepared this dish with knockwurst and have been pleased with the results.

8 small red potatoes, unpeeled
7 links spicy beef sausage or knockwurst (about 1½ pounds)
3 tablespoon olive oil
1 medium onion, peeled and chopped
2 cloves garlic, peeled and finely minced
½ teaspoon chopped fresh thyme, or pinch of dried thyme
½ bay leaf
1 teaspoon paprika
1 teaspoon all-purpose flour
¼ cup dry white wine
⅓ cup tomato sauce
¼ cup chopped parsley

1. In large saucepan over medium-high heat, combine potatoes and enough water to cover; bring to a boil. Boil 10 to 15 minutes until tender; drain. Cut unpeeled potatoes into quarters; set aside.
2. Diagonally cut sausages into thin slices; set aside. In large skillet, heat oil over medium heat. Add onion, garlic, thyme, and bay leaf. Cook about 5 minutes, or until onion is translucent. Add sausage slices; cook about 4 minutes or until golden brown, stirring often.
3. Add paprika and flour; stir to coat sausages. Cook 2 to 3 minutes longer, stirring constantly. Add wine; cook 3 to 5 minutes, until wine evaporates.
4. Stir in tomato sauce and ⅓ cup water. Reduce heat to low; simmer, uncovered, 5 to 10 minutes, until hot and bubbly and slightly thickened. Remove bay leaf and sprinkle sausage mixture with parsley.

5. To serve, pour hot sausage mixture over quartered potatoes. Or add potatoes to skillet and cook briefly until they absorb some of the sauce.

Stuffed Mushrooms La Varenne

Champignons Farcis La Varenne

MAKES 8 SERVINGS

This recipe is based on one from the curriculum of the famous La Varenne Cooking School in France. It is said to be an old dish from the mid-seventeenth century. Instead of using a teaspoon to stuff the mushrooms, I sometimes form the mixture into small meatballs, and drop one into each mushroom cap.

1 pound large whole mushrooms
½ pound ground veal or chicken
2 tablespoons finely chopped chives or scallion greens
   Salt and freshly ground black pepper to taste
2 egg yolks
3 tablespoons margarine
1 to 2 teaspoons freshly squeezed lemon juice

1. Wipe mushroom caps clean and remove stems. Chop stems fine (a food processor does this quickly).
2. In medium bowl, combine veal or chicken, chives, chopped mushroom stems, and salt and pepper to taste; mix lightly to blend. Stir in egg yolks to bind mixture.
3. With teaspoon, press stuffing into mushroom caps, mounding slightly in center. Cover with plastic wrap and refrigerate 6 to 8 hours at this point, if desired.
4. Preheat oven to 350°F. In 12- by 8-inch baking dish, melt marga-

rine. Arrange mushrooms in dish, stuffing side up. Bake 25 to 30 minutes, or until mushrooms are tender and stuffing is browned, basting often with melted margarine.

5. Sprinkle with lemon juice and serve hot.

N O T E : For more even distribution of heat, place baking dish on a cookie sheet.

Meatballs on Toast

Polpettoncini sui Crostone

MAKES 8 SERVINGS

These tiny meatballs embody the flavors of the Italian Mediterranean area.

    1 pound ground beef
    2 large cloves garlic, peeled and minced
    1 teaspoon salt
      Freshly ground black pepper to taste
  $\frac{3}{4}$ cup canned crushed tomatoes, drained, or canned whole tomatoes, crushed and drained
    2 tablespoons dried oregano, or to taste
One 1-pound package firm white bread slices

1. In medium bowl, combine beef, garlic, salt, and pepper to taste. Add tomatoes; mix lightly.

2. Rub oregano between palms of hands to break up; add to meat mixture. With hands, blend lightly.

3. Trim crusts from bread slices, and discard crusts. Cut slices into 4 squares each; place on cookie sheet.

4. With wet hands, form meat mixture into walnut-sized balls. Place one meatball on each square of bread.

5. Preheat broiler. Broil meatballs 5 minutes, or until cooked through and edges of bread are toasted.

6. With spatula, remove bread squares from cookie sheet. Serve hot.

Nice-style Onion Tart
Pissaladière

MAKES 8 SERVINGS

This French "pizza" was created in the French town of Nice, but is served in other Mediterranean countries as well, such as Morocco. The word pissala means a purée of anchovies in French, hence its name. The crust is usually made with puff pastry, but for a pareve version, use a flaky pie crust made with vegetable shortening.

        Flaky Pastry (recipe follows)
    6 large onions, peeled and sliced
    4 to 6 tablespoons olive oil
        Salt and freshly ground black pepper to taste
    One 2-ounce can flat anchovy fillets, drained
    One 16-ounce can pitted black olives, drained

1. Preheat oven to 400°F. Prepare flaky pastry and fit into 12½- by 8½-inch foil rectangular baking pan. Or flatten pastry into a 12½- by 8½-inch rectangle on cookie sheet, forming edges into a slight rim. Bake 10 minutes, or until just set.

2. In large skillet, heat 4 or 5 tablespoons olive oil over medium heat until hot. Add onions; stir to coat well with oil. Reduce heat to low; cover and cook 15 to 20 minutes, until onions are golden and tender, stirring occasionally. Season with salt and pepper to taste.

3. Spread sautéed onions over partially baked crust. Arrange anchovy fillets over onions in a crisscross pattern, forming diamond shapes. Fill in center of each diamond with a black olive. Brush or drizzle top of tart lightly with olive oil.

4. Bake tart 10 to 15 minutes, until crust is golden and topping is piping hot. To serve, cut into squares.

N O T E : Cooking the onions slowly over low heat brings out their sweetness.

FLAKY PASTRY

MAKES ENOUGH PASTRY FOR 2-CRUST PIE

For pissaladière you will need only half this recipe. You may either prepare the whole recipe and save half, wrapped tightly, in the refrigerator or freezer for a later use, or you can cut the ingredient amounts in half to make enough pastry for a 1-crust pie.

> 3 cups all-purpose flour
> 1 teaspoon salt
> 1 cup vegetable shortening, chilled
> About $\frac{1}{2}$ cup ice water

1. In large bowl, combine flour and salt. Add shortening. With pastry blender or fingertips, lightly combine ingredients until mixture resembles coarse meal.

2. Sprinkle 6 tablespoons water over mixture; stir with fork until dough holds together to form a ball, adding more water, if necessary, 1 tablespoon at a time until proper consistency is reached.

3. Place ball of dough on large sheet of waxed paper; flatten slightly with palm of hand. Wrap tightly and refrigerate 30 to 40 minutes.

4. Cut dough in half. Place one half on lightly floured board or countertop. With lightly floured rolling pin, roll dough out from center to about $\frac{1}{8}$- to $\frac{1}{4}$-inch thickness. Fit into baking pan for pissaladière and proceed with recipe.

Wine note: Why not use this menu as an excuse for a kosher wine-tasting party? To carry out the theme, stick to wines grown and produced around the Mediterranean region. Bring out an assortment of fruity whites, light reds, rosés, and even sparkling wines from Italy, Spain, the south of France, and Israel. Then have a wonderful time nibbling and sipping with friends!

♦ ENGLISH AFTERNOON TEA ♦
(from Mimi Olanoff)

English afternoon tea has often been called the world's most civilized repast. Perhaps that is why this tradition is currently catching on here, as more and more Americans adopt the refined habit of taking tea. A number of hotels, restaurants, and even department stores in New York City and other metropolitan areas now offer tea as a refreshing pause in the day's activities—a chance to socialize, relax, and refuel at the same time.

Of course, afternoon tea encompasses much more than the beverage for which it's named. In English homes, hotels, inns, farmhouses, and shops where it originated, the typical tea includes a variety of small sandwiches, a basket of scones accompanied by clotted cream, butter, and/or jam, toasted teacakes, and pastries—served in that order with plenty of freshly brewed hot tea.

Tea is a delightful way to entertain, especially on a leisurely Sunday afternoon. It's a calmer, less pricey alternative to the cocktail party, at which energy and food costs can soar. And the all-dairy menu created here by Mimi Olanoff invites you to indulge in the creamy spreads, rich pastries, and buttery sandwiches that have made this custom justly famous.

English Tea Sandwiches
Tea Sandwich Fillings
Potted Fish
Lemon Curd or Lemon Cheese
Scones
Devonshire Cream
Irish Soda Bread
English Trifle

English Tea Sandwiches

MAKES 8 SERVINGS

The best way to prepare a batch of tea sandwiches is to arrange all the ingredients assembly-line style. Specific filling quantities are not provided, nor are they really needed—just gather several varieties and set to work.

2 loaves unsliced white bread
1½ cups (3 sticks) unsalted butter, softened
2 tablespoons heavy cream
½ teaspoon Dijon-style mustard
Juice of ½ lemon
Salt and ground white pepper to taste
Fillings (see below)

1. Chill bread for easier slicing. With long serrated knife, cut bread into very thin slices.
2. In medium bowl, combine butter, cream, mustard, lemon juice, and salt and pepper to taste until well blended. Spread butter mixture on one side of each bread slice.
3. Place or spread choice of filling between buttered bread slices right up to edges; trim off crusts.
4. Cut each sandwich into quarters, forming small squares, triangles, or strips. Or use cookie cutters to cut out small decorative shapes.
5. Wrap sandwiches in damp towel and refrigerate, or place on damp towel and cover tightly with plastic wrap until ready to serve.

N O T E : For easy identification, match a specific sandwich shape with a specific filling.

TEA SANDWICH FILLINGS

Cucumber: Thinly slice long, thin (preferably seedless) cucumbers into rounds. Let slices soak in white or cider vinegar 5 to 10 minutes; drain thoroughly. Season with salt and pepper to taste.

Watercress: Remove thick stems from 1 or 2 bunches watercress and finely chop leaves. In small bowl, combine chopped watercress with enough butter mixture or cream cheese to make of spreading consistency.

Egg: Finely chop hard-cooked eggs. Blend with melted butter or mayonnaise to a pastelike consistency. Season to taste with dry mustard, salt, and freshly ground white pepper.

Smoked Salmon: Thinly slice smoked salmon and cut into pieces to fit bread. Sprinkle with chopped chives, if desired.

Potted Fish

MAKES 1 CUP

Although small crocks of potted fish or meat are traditionally served at tea, you probably won't find my version in England or in a British cookbook. When I was a child, my father created it to use as a sandwich spread. I've found it to be very well suited to tea when placed in a small crock to spread on toast or when stuffed into hollowed-out cherry tomatoes.

One 4⅜-ounce can skinless, boneless sardines, drained
  1½ tablespoons mayonnaise
  1¼ tablespoons cream cheese, softened
  1½ tablespoons unsalted butter, softened
  1 teaspoon lemon juice, or to taste

In small bowl, mash together all ingredients until blended.

NOTE: To use as a stuffing for cherry tomatoes, cut bottom ¼ inch off tomatoes with serrated knife. With small pointed knife, carefully scoop out pulp and seeds. Sprinkle each tomato lightly with salt. Invert and place on paper towels to drain for 30 minutes. With teaspoon, fill each tomato with fish mixture. Garnish with a parsley leaf or caper.

Lemon Curd or Lemon Cheese

MAKES 1½ CUPS

The British use this spread on tea breads or in tarts. Use a glass or stainless-steel double boiler to prepare the mixture, since lemon juice will pick up the metallic flavor of aluminum or copper.

½ cup (1 stick) unsalted butter
1½ cups sugar
½ cup freshly squeezed lemon juice
2 teaspoons grated lemon peel (yellow part only)
3 whole eggs
3 egg yolks

1. In top of double boiler set over simmering water, melt butter. With wire whisk, stir in sugar, lemon juice, and lemon peel until sugar is dissolved.
2. In medium bowl with electric mixer at medium speed, beat eggs and egg yolks 2 minutes, until thick and blended. Whisk a little hot lemon mixture into eggs, stirring constantly until blended. Quickly transfer egg mixture into lemon mixture in top of double boiler and whisk to combine.
3. Cook over hot water about 15 minutes, or until mixture is very thick, whisking constantly.
4. Pour into glass jar or plastic container. Cover and refrigerate until well chilled.

Scones

MAKES 16 SCONES

Scones are small cakes that originated in Scotland. Unlike other tea cakes, they're usually shaped or cut into wedges, and are sometimes cooked on a griddle. They resemble American biscuits in texture and taste.

2 cups sifted all-purpose flour
2 tablespoons sugar
1 tablespoon baking powder
$\frac{1}{2}$ teaspoon salt
$\frac{1}{3}$ cup ($\frac{2}{3}$ stick) butter
2 eggs
About $\frac{3}{4}$ cup milk
Devonshire Cream (recipe follows) (optional)

1. Preheat oven to 425°F. Grease two 8-inch round baking pans or a large cookie sheet.

2. Into medium bowl, sift together flour, sugar, baking powder, and salt. With pastry blender or fingertips, cut in butter, tossing until particles resemble coarse cornmeal.

3. Add 1 beaten egg and about $\frac{1}{2}$ cup milk to flour mixture. With fork, stir quickly and lightly just until moistened. Add more milk, if necessary, to form a soft dough. (Mix only until no flour shows; overmixing will result in dense, tough scones.)

4. Turn dough out onto floured surface. Knead gently about 15 times.

5. Cut dough in half. Lightly shape each half into a ball. Pat each ball into a round about $\frac{1}{2}$ inch thick. Place rounds in prepared pans or on cookie sheet. With sharp knife dipped into flour, cut down into dough about $\frac{3}{8}$ inch deep, marking off into 8 wedges. (If using cookie sheet, separate dough into wedges; do not allow sides to touch.) Lightly beat the second egg and brush it on top of dough, if desired.

6. Bake about 12 minutes, or until golden brown. Cool slightly in pan. Split hot scones horizontally and serve with butter, jam, and a dollop of Devonshire cream, if you wish.

NOTE: You may prepare the dough ahead through Step 2, before adding any egg or liquid; cover and let stand at room temperature. Twenty minutes before you wish to serve the hot, fresh scones, continue to Step 3, then complete recipe. Baked scones can be wrapped tightly in aluminum foil and frozen, then reheated in the oven.

DEVONSHIRE CREAM

MAKES 1½ CUPS

True Devonshire cream is not available in the United States. However, this mock version makes an excellent substitute for the real thing.

One 3-ounce package cream cheese, at room temperature
¼ cup sour cream
¼ cup heavy or whipping cream
2½ tablespoons confectioners' sugar

1. In large bowl, combine cream cheese with sour cream. With electric mixer at medium speed, beat until light and fluffy. Beat in heavy cream and confectioners' sugar.
2. Cover mixture and refrigerate at least 1 hour.
3. Allow mixture to come to room temperature before using.

Irish Soda Bread

MAKES 1 LOAF

This quick bread comes out almost as high as a typical yeast bread, but requires no rising and only minimal kneading. It freezes well, too, and is quite good when lightly toasted.

1 teaspoon cornmeal or Cream of Rice cereal
3 cups all-purpose flour
½ cup sugar
2 teaspoons baking powder
1 teaspoon baking soda
1 teaspoon salt
¾ cup raisins

$\frac{1}{2}$ cup (1 stick) butter

2 teaspoons caraway seeds

$\frac{3}{4}$ cup sour cream

3 eggs

Additional granulated sugar (optional)

1. Preheat oven to 400°F. Grease an 8-inch round baking pan; sprinkle with cornmeal or Cream of Rice cereal.

2. In large bowl, combine flour, sugar, baking powder, baking soda, and salt; add raisins, tossing well. Set aside.

3. In medium saucepan, combine butter and $\frac{1}{4}$ cup water over medium heat; cook until butter melts. Add caraway seeds; heat about 2 minutes. Remove from heat and allow to cool slightly.

4. In small bowl with wire whisk or fork, beat together sour cream and 2 eggs. Add to warm butter mixture, mixing well.

5. Add liquid ingredients to flour mixture, stirring until well blended. (You will have a very soft dough.) Turn dough out onto lightly floured board and knead 4 or 5 times.

6. Shape dough into a large round loaf; place in prepared pan. With sharp knife, make a $\frac{1}{4}$-inch-deep X across top to keep bread from splitting during baking.

7. In cup, beat remaining egg with 1 tablespoon water; brush on top of bread. Sprinkle with a little sugar, if desired. Bake bread 30 to 35 minutes, or until toothpick inserted in center comes out dry. Remove to wire rack to cool.

8. Wrap bread in foil and let stand overnight for easier slicing. To serve, cut into slices.

English Trifle

A trifle dish is usually a footed, straight-sided glass bowl, but a 2-quart glass soufflé dish or compote dish will do nicely, too. The cake and custard should fill the bowl about two-thirds full.

Two 3-ounce packages ladyfingers, or one 16-ounce pound
    cake, thinly sliced
    About $\frac{3}{4}$ cup seedless raspberry jam
$\frac{1}{4}$ cup medium-sweet sherry
4 cups milk
6 egg yolks
$\frac{1}{2}$ cup granulated sugar
1 teaspoon vanilla extract
2 cups heavy or whipping cream
2 heaping tablespoons confectioners' sugar
    Crumbled almond macaroons or blanched sliced
    almonds for garnish (optional)

1. Split ladyfingers apart. Or cut pound cake slices in half. Spread ladyfingers or pound cake with raspberry jam and sandwich together. Line bottom of 2-quart glass bowl or dish with sandwiches, all running in the same direction; cut to fit corners, if necessary. Sprinkle half the sherry on top of ladyfingers or cake. Place a second layer of sandwiches over first, running in opposite direction; sprinkle with remaining sherry. Let stand 30 minutes.
2. Meanwhile, in medium saucepan over medium heat, heat milk until tiny bubbles form around the edges; keep warm. (Milk should come almost but not quite to a boil.)
3. In top of double boiler, off heat, beat egg yolks lightly; add granulated sugar. With wire whisk or electric mixer at medium speed, beat mixture 5 to 10 minutes, or until thick and lemon-colored. With wooden spoon, gradually and slowly stir in scalded milk.
4. In bottom of double boiler, heat water until simmering (tiny bubbles will form but water should not boil). Place top of double boiler

over simmering water; it should not touch the water. Cook egg mixture 10 to 20 minutes, until it forms a film or coating on the spoon and becomes slightly thickened, stirring constantly. Stir in vanilla.

5. Pour hot custard over ladyfingers, allowing it to seep down. Cover and refrigerate several hours or overnight, until well chilled.

6. In medium bowl with electric mixer at high speed, whip cream and confectioners' sugar until soft peaks form. Spread whipped cream on top of chilled custard. Garnish with macaroons or almonds, if you like.

NOTE: Sliced angel food cake or sponge cake can be substituted for the ladyfingers or pound cake. If using cake, make jam sandwiches by placing 2 thin slices together, then cut to fit into layers in bowl. If time is short, you may prepare 2 packages regular vanilla pudding as label directs, beating in 2 eggs for extra richness. This can be used instead of the cooked custard mixture.

Wine note: This is the time to get away from uncompromisingly dry wine. Afternoon tea, such a relaxing and pleasant occasion, needs the charm of wine of varying sweetness to raise it above the ordinary. Riesling, for instance, which except in its Alsace form is of various degrees of sweetness, would be delightful sipped with sandwiches. A sweeter Riesling would go best with sweeter fillings, and a drier Riesling with mustardy or peppery fillings, or those containing fish or meat. Sweet sherry or sweet Muscat would be heavenly with scones topped with cream and fruit. And don't forget some of the proprietary wines from Israel or France. The lightly sweet New York whites would add yet another fruit dimension. This is a category with which to have fun!

"Come for dessert and coffee" is always a tempting invitation, especially for those with a bit of a sweet tooth. Happily, an all-dessert party can actually be a relatively uncomplicated event to plan and execute. While it may take several hours to bake and assemble the sweets, much of the work can be done ahead. That leaves a good chunk of time to set the table with pretty china, silver, and flowers, gather an assortment of wines, liqueurs, and brandies, brew the coffee, and arrange the display of desserts.

The recipes here represent the best in European desserts, reminiscent of the treats served in cafés and coffeehouses from Budapest to Vienna to Paris. The finest chocolate, preserves, fruits, and other ingredients are used to create tortes, tarts, sorbets, and confections that will start your mouth watering. Try just one for a grand finale to a dinner party, or prepare several for an after-theater dessert extravaganza. Or you may want to do what André Balog did in one of his classes for chocolate lovers—present an all-chocolate feast.

Viennese Chocolate Cake—*Sachertorte*
Mousse-filled Meringues
Double-Chocolate Pecan Tarts
Exotic Fruit Coupe
Raspberry Sorbet
Double-Chocolate Truffles

Viennese Chocolate Cake

Sachertorte

MAKES 8 TO 10 SERVINGS

This chocolaty cake was created by Eduard Sacher, the pastry chef for Prince Klemens von Metternich of Austria. Eventually, the Sachers opened their own hotel in Vienna, and this popular torte was a main attraction. Another great Viennese bakery called Demel's made their own rendition of sachertorte, claiming it was the original. This duplication resulted in a lawsuit; ultimately both versions were permitted to be sold as sachertortes.

CAKE

- $6\frac{1}{2}$ to 7 ounces semisweet chocolate, broken into pieces
- $\frac{3}{4}$ cup ($1\frac{1}{2}$ sticks) butter or margarine
- $\frac{3}{4}$ cup sugar
- 8 egg yolks
- 1 cup all-purpose flour
- 10 egg whites
- 2 tablespoons fruit preserves (apricot, red currant, or raspberry)

ICING

- 1 cup sugar
- $\frac{1}{3}$ cup water
- 7 ounces semisweet chocolate

1. Preheat oven to 300°F. Grease 9-inch springform pan.

2. Prepare cake: In top of double boiler set over simmering water, melt $6\frac{1}{2}$ to 7 ounces chocolate, stirring until smooth and creamy. Add butter or margarine; stir until well blended. Add $\frac{3}{4}$ cup sugar; stir until sugar dissolves.

3. Remove from heat; transfer chocolate mixture to large mixing bowl and let stand several minutes until cool.

4. Add egg yolks to chocolate mixture, 1 at a time, blending well after each addition. Stir in flour; mix well.

5. In another large mixing bowl, beat egg whites with electric mixer at high speed until stiff peaks form. Gently fold beaten whites into chocolate mixture; do not overmix. Pour batter into prepared springform pan; smooth top with rubber spatula. Bake 1 hour, or until top springs back when lightly touched.

6. Remove sides of pan from cake. Let cake cool on wire rack. Meanwhile, prepare icing: In small saucepan over medium-high heat, combine 1 cup sugar and water; bring to a boil. Reduce heat to medium; stir until sugar dissolves. Remove from heat; immediately stir in 7 ounces chocolate until it is melted and smooth. If necessary, beat icing with wire whisk until it is very smooth. Set aside and let stand at room temperature until cool, stirring occasionally.

7. To assemble, split cake in half horizontally with long serrated knife. Spread preserves on cut sides; sandwich layers together with preserves in the middle. Spread icing on top, allowing some to drip down sides; smooth over sides with small spatula. Serve immediately.

Mousse-filled Meringues

MAKES 12 SERVINGS

These meringue shells can be baked and kept in an airtight container for several days. Embellish them with any number of sweet fillings instead of mousse—sorbet, ice cream, prepared chestnut purée, or sliced, sugared berries are some possibilities.

MERINGUES

3 egg whites

$\frac{1}{3}$ cup plus 2 teaspoons granulated sugar

$\frac{1}{2}$ cup confectioners' sugar

CHOCOLATE MOUSSE

8 to 9 ounces semisweet chocolate, broken into pieces
    5 eggs, separated
    2 tablespoons brandy (optional)
      Pinch of salt

1. Preheat oven to 250°F. Line cookie sheet with parchment or waxed paper.

2. Prepare meringues: In medium bowl, beat egg whites with electric mixer at high speed until soft peaks form. Gradually add 2 teaspoons granulated sugar; continue beating until stiff peaks form. Sift together remaining $\frac{1}{3}$ cup granulated sugar and the confectioners' sugar; gently fold into beaten whites until blended.

3. With a tablespoon, drop mounds of egg white mixture onto parchment-lined cookie sheet; spread into 2-inch rounds, indenting in center to form a slight rim around edge. Or fill a pastry bag fitted with a $\frac{1}{2}$- or $\frac{3}{4}$-inch-wide tip with egg white mixture; squeeze onto cookie sheet, coiling around to form a 2- by $\frac{1}{2}$-inch round.

4. Bake meringues $1\frac{1}{4}$ hours, or until completely dry on both top and bottom. (If they start to brown, reduce oven temperature.) Remove meringues to wire rack to cool.

5. Meanwhile, prepare mousse: In top of double boiler set over simmering water, melt chocolate with 2 tablespoons water, stirring occasionally until smooth. Remove from heat and let cool slightly.

6. Place egg yolks in large bowl; beat lightly with fork. With wire whisk, gradually stir in cooled melted chocolate, blending well. Stir in brandy, if desired.

7. In medium bowl, combine egg whites and salt. With clean beaters and electric mixer at high speed, beat until stiff peaks form. Add beaten whites to chocolate mixture, gently folding from bottom to top until loosely blended. Cover mousse and refrigerate 3 hours.

8. To serve, spoon mousse into meringue shells.

NOTES: Place dabs of beaten meringue mixture under corners of parchment paper or waxed paper to keep it stuck to the cookie sheet during baking.

For the mousse, use as fine a chocolate as your purse permits, preferably an imported brand.

Double-Chocolate Pecan Tarts

Chocolate in both crust and filling makes this dessert extrarich and delicious. Although the package isn't stamped, Hershey's unsweetened cocoa is an approved kosher brand, provided it is processed in the Hershey, Pennsylvania, plant. The location of the plant will be on the cocoa label.

FILLING
- 5 eggs, slightly beaten
- 1½ cups light corn syrup
- 1½ cups sugar
- ¼ cup melted butter or margarine
- 1½ teaspoons vanilla extract
- 2½ cups toasted pecan halves
- 3 tablespoons semisweet chocolate chips

TART SHELLS
- 1½ cups all-purpose flour
- 1 tablespoon unsweetened cocoa powder
- ⅛ teaspoon salt
- ½ cup (1 stick) butter or margarine, cut into 5 pieces and frozen
- ¼ cup ice water
- Vegetable cooking spray

1. Prepare filling: In medium bowl, combine eggs, corn syrup, sugar, melted butter or margarine, and vanilla; mix well. Stir in pecans and chocolate chips; set aside.

2. Prepare tart shells: In food processor, combine flour, cocoa powder, and salt; process to mix. Add frozen butter or margarine pieces; process until evenly blended but still lumpy, about 15 seconds. Add ice water, 1 tablespoon at a time, processing until dough forms a ball, about 45 seconds total. Remove dough from processor and divide in half. Refrigerate one half; place second half on lightly floured board.

3. With floured rolling pin, roll out pastry to a 10-inch circle about $\frac{1}{8}$ inch thick. Spray two 8-inch pie plates with vegetable cooking spray. Transfer dough circle to one pie plate, cutting excess dough away from edges. Place tart shell in freezer while rolling out and fitting second pastry half into second pie plate.

4. Preheat oven to 350°F. Evenly divide filling between tart shells. Bake 50 to 55 minutes, or until knife inserted 2 inches from edge of tarts comes out clean. Cool tarts slightly on wire racks. Serve warm or at room temperature.

Exotic Fruit Coupe

MAKES 8 SERVINGS

Fruit makes a refreshing counterpoint to an array of rich desserts. The rather unusual combination of fresh fruits and flavorings used in this recipe will surprise guests who are accustomed to ordinary fruit salads. If mangoes, passion fruit, and kiwis are not available, you may substitute other fresh seasonal fruits.

$\frac{3}{4}$ cup sugar
Grated peel of 2 limes
Grated peel of 2 oranges
Grated peel of $\frac{1}{2}$ lemon
$1\frac{1}{2}$ vanilla beans, split in half lengthwise
1 tablespoon chopped lemon grass (optional)
1 teaspoon chopped peeled fresh gingerroot
$\frac{1}{2}$ teaspoon Chinese 5-spice powder (see Note)
3 coriander seeds
1 whole clove
12 passion fruit, peeled and sliced
3 to 6 kiwis, peeled and sliced
1 mango, peeled, pitted, and cut into chunks
$\frac{1}{2}$ to 1 fresh pineapple, peeled, trimmed, cored, and cut into chunks
4 fresh mint leaves, cut into strips

1. In medium saucepan, combine first 10 ingredients; stir in 4 cups water. Place over high heat and bring to a boil, stirring to dissolve sugar. Remove immediately and let cool completely.
2. In compote dish or glass bowl, combine passion fruit, kiwis, mango, and pineapple. Strain cooled liquid from saucepan over mixed fruit. Cover and refrigerate at least 2 hours.
3. To serve, sprinkle mint strips on top of fruit.

NOTE: Chinese 5-spice powder is a mixture of ground star anise, cinnamon, fennel seeds, cloves, and Szechuan peppercorns. It's available in the oriental groceries section of many large supermarkets. Lemon grass is a type of fresh herb used in Thai and other oriental cooking; it can be found in specialty produce markets. It may be omitted.

Raspberry Sorbet

MAKES 8 TO 10 SERVINGS

The intense, pure flavor of the fruit shines through in this simple-to-make sorbet. Although an electric ice cream maker is handy to have for this recipe, it's not essential. You can freeze the raspberry mixture in a metal pan, break it into chunks, and whip it up in a food processor or with an electric mixer just before serving.

$2\frac{1}{4}$ cups sugar
2 pints fresh raspberries or two 10-ounce packages frozen unsweetened raspberries, thawed
Juice of $\frac{1}{2}$ lemon

1. In medium saucepan over medium-low heat, combine sugar and 4 cups water; bring to a boil, stirring to dissolve sugar. Remove from heat and cool.
2. In food processor or blender, purée raspberries. Place wire mesh sieve or strainer over medium bowl; pour raspberry purée into sieve. With wooden spoon, rub and stir raspberries in sieve to remove seeds and extract all juice into bowl.
3. To raspberry juice in bowl, add cooled sugar syrup and lemon juice; stir to blend well. Place mixture in container of ice cream maker; freeze according to manufacturer's directions.
4. To serve, scoop sorbet into individual dishes.

Double-Chocolate Truffles

MAKES 3 DOZEN

These luscious mouthfuls of chocolate will please the most discriminating chocoholic in your crowd. The two different types of chocolate—semisweet to form the body of the truffle, and cocoa to dust the surface—make these particularly intriguing.

- 9 ounces semisweet chocolate, broken into pieces
- 6 tablespoons ($\frac{3}{4}$ stick) butter or margarine
- 3 egg yolks
  About 1 teaspoon brandy, liqueur, or vanilla extract
- $\frac{1}{4}$ cup unsweetened cocoa powder

1. In top of double boiler over simmering water, melt the chocolate until completely smooth, stirring occasionally.
2. Remove from heat. With wire whisk, beat in butter or margarine until blended.
3. In small bowl, beat egg yolks with wire whisk. Whisk in about 1 tablespoon melted chocolate until blended; pour yolk mixture into chocolate mixture in double boiler, mixing well. Place top of double boiler over simmering water and stir constantly for 3 minutes. Stir in brandy; remove from heat. Remove top part of double boiler and place in bowl of ice water to cool mixture quickly.
4. When mixture is firm enough to hold its shape, drop 36 equal portions onto large sheet of aluminum foil, using a teaspoon. Let stand at room temperature 30 minutes until firmed up.
5. Place cocoa powder in shallow bowl. Roll truffles in cocoa until evenly coated; return to aluminum foil and let stand until very firm.
6. Store in tightly covered tin or container at room temperature 24 hours before serving. Or store in refrigerator up to 1 week; let stand at room temperature 1 hour before serving.

Wine note: The term *dessert wine* was coined for this category. But wait! Chocolate is not every wine's best friend. Few wines marry well with chocolate, although, perverse as it may seem, a stray Cabernet or two may do the trick; but trick it is, as who would want a dry Cabernet with a luscious chocolate dessert? Depending on the actual sweetness of the dessert and the palate's perception of sweetness, a cold cream sherry, Muscat, or even Kiddush-type wine might be an admirable choice. Keep the fruit wines in mind too—peach, black-berry, and elderberry are available. There also seems no limit on the fruits, berries, and nuts flavoring brandies and cordials—take in tiny sips as these meringues, tarts, sorbets, fruit coupes, and the like are nibbled.

Holiday Meals

*t*hrough years of persecution and dispersion, many Jewish food customs have survived surprisingly intact, but those surrounding the holidays seem to be the strongest and most enduring. These culinary traditions may vary a bit depending on a family's roots, notably between those of Sephardic and Ashkenazic descent. Nevertheless, certain foods are closely associated with certain holidays among most Jews. The recipes that follow cover five particularly food-oriented holidays in the Jewish calendar—Rosh Hashanah, Chanukah, Purim, Passover, and Shavuot.

Rosh Hashanah, the Jewish New Year, is ushered in by Jews everywhere with a festive holiday meal. As with the new year celebrations of other cultures, the foods served at this meal are rich in symbolism. In one way or another, the traditional Rosh Hashanah dishes represent the spiritual and material fortune that is hoped for in the coming year.

Honey, for example, shows up in several places—in honey cakes, fruit compotes, tzimmes (a carrot and sweet potato dish), and as a dip for sliced apples and/or bread. In all its guises, honey is meant to stand for a sweet new year ahead, as is the date syrup used by the Sephardim.

Raisins and carrots appear on Rosh Hashanah too, partly as a promise for a sweet year, and partly for other reasons. Some think that sliced carrots and golden raisins resemble gold coins—symbols of prosperity. And in Yiddish or German, the word for carrot is the same as the word for multiply or increase—a wish made by Jewish families in the past.

The challah baked on Rosh Hashanah is coiled into a round circle instead of a braid like that used on Shabbat and other holidays. Although explanations for this shape vary, the most common is that the roundness means time will roll on year after year like a circle, having no beginning or end. Others think a round challah looks like a crown and stands for the divine power of God. Still another explanation is that the spiral assures an ascent into heaven.

Fish is frequently served as a first course at Rosh Hashanah dinner, perhaps because of its status as a sign of fertility. Gefilte fish with horseradish is a typical dish for Ashkenazic Jews, while Sephardim might serve a whole cooked fish, the head of which would go to the head of the household. This probably dates back to the Sephardic practice of including ram's meat at the Rosh Hashanah meal, and presenting the head of the family with a stuffed ram's head.

Many homes place baskets of fruit on the table at the end of dinner, choosing those specifically mentioned in the Bible. These include grapes, pomegranates, dates, figs, and St. John's bread (carob). Pomegranates hold an immense quantity of seeds, believed by some to represent fertility, and by others the number of good deeds that will be undertaken in the coming year.

Nuts may be served along with the fruit in certain families, but not among Polish Jews. In Poland nuts were eschewed on this holiday because the Hebrew letters that make up the word add up to seventeen—the same numerical value as for the word "sin." By doing without nuts, Polish Jews feel they are refraining from sin.

The Rosh Hashanah menu that follows is largely Eastern European in origin, emphasizing those foods that were plentiful in that part of the world.

—*Gil Marks*

Round Challahs
Stuffed Cabbage
Chicken with Figs
Carrot, Apple, and Sweet Potato Tzimmes
Honey Cake
Almond Bread—*Mandelbrot*

Round Challahs

MAKES 3 BREADS

Challah has played an integral role in Jewish tradition since biblical times. Portions of bread dough, the challah, were given to the priests: "Of the first of your dough you shall set apart a cake for a gift" (Numbers 15:20). Since white flour was the choice of the wealthy, it was used in the Shabbat and holiday loaves.

Today, challah refers to the Sabbath loaves. To keep up with progress, this recipe was developed for the food processor to save time, but it can also be mixed in a large bowl.

> 2 packages active dry yeast
> 6 to 8 cups all-purpose flour
> $\frac{1}{2}$ cup sugar
> 1 tablespoon salt
> $\frac{1}{2}$ cup (1 stick) margarine, melted
> 5 eggs
> Poppy or sesame seeds (optional)

1. In container of food processor, combine yeast, 3 cups flour, sugar, and salt. In medium saucepan, combine $1\frac{3}{4}$ cups water and margarine over medium heat; heat to around 110°F on thermometer (liquid should feel hot but shouldn't burn your finger). Add warm liquid to yeast mixture in processor; cover and process until blended.
2. With machine running, add 4 eggs, 1 at a time, until blended. Gradually add enough remaining flour through the feed tube to form a ball of dough that cleans the sides of the container. Process dough around container 25 times.
3. On lightly floured surface, knead dough 10 to 15 times, until smooth and elastic. Place in greased bowl, turning to grease sides. Cover with towel and let rise about 1 hour, or until dough has doubled in size.
4. Punch dough down and divide into 3 pieces. Cover and let rest 10 minutes.
5. Roll each piece of dough into a rope about $1\frac{1}{2}$ inches in diameter

(fig. A). Coil each rope into a circle (fig. B). Place coiled circles on greased cookie sheets; cover and let rise about 45 minutes, or until doubled in size. (Or cover and let rise overnight in refrigerator.)
6. Preheat oven to 350°F. In small bowl, beat remaining egg with 2 tablespoons water. Brush challahs with egg mixture; sprinkle with poppy or sesame seeds, if desired. Bake challahs 40 to 50 minutes, until golden brown and hollow-sounding when tapped with fingers. Remove to wire racks to cool.

NOTE: To make challah rolls, divide dough into small balls and shape into coils or braids (see illustrations). Bake on greased cookie sheet, spaced at least 2 inches apart, at 375°F for 20 to 25 minutes.

Wine note: Challah is a fine foil for any number of spreads with which wine is an easy companion. However, round challah on the holiday calls for something special. A wine of ancient origin called variously med, mehd, mead, or simply honey wine, is made from honey. Pair it with a fig spread or sweet poppy paste on challah and serve as appetizer or dessert with chicken with figs. Challah by itself is also enjoyable with honey wine. To return to grape wine and yet to add extra glitter to the occasion, a sparkling Vouvray Moelleux from the Loire Valley of France would be most appropriate and delicious.

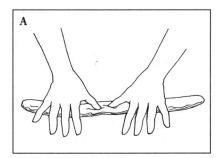 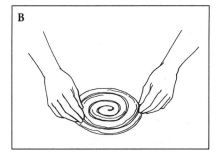

ROUND CHALLAHS

Stuffed Cabbage

MAKES 8 SERVINGS

The sweet-sour taste makes this a Russian-style stuffed cabbage. Instead of vinegar or lemon juice, old-time Jewish cooks used sour salt (citric acid) to impart a sour taste. For Rosh Hashanah, some families, however, completely omit any sour ingredient for fear it will spoil the sweetness of the new year. This recipe can be prepared either way, and also is a fitting dish for Succot—the harvest holiday that follows closely behind Rosh Hashanah.

1½ pounds ground beef
½ cup cooked rice
1 medium onion, peeled and finely chopped
1 egg
1 teaspoon salt
¼ teaspoon freshly ground black pepper
8 to 10 large green cabbage leaves, blanched (see Note)
One 16-ounce can (2 cups) tomato sauce
¼ cup packed brown sugar
¼ cup golden raisins
3 tablespoons vegetable oil
2 tablespoons vinegar or lemon juice
1 bay leaf

1. Preheat oven to 350°F.
2. In medium bowl, combine beef, rice, onion, egg, salt, and pepper; mix well. In center of each cabbage leaf, place a mound of beef filling. Fold sides of cabbage leaf over filling, then roll up, jelly roll style, completely enclosing beef mixture.
3. In large deep baking dish or dutch oven, arrange cabbage rolls, seam side down, in a single layer. In medium bowl, combine tomato sauce and remaining ingredients; pour over cabbage rolls. Cover and bake 1 hour, or simmer over low heat 1 hour until cabbage is soft and beef is cooked through. To serve, remove bay leaf.

NOTE: To facilitate removal of cabbage leaves, and to make them more pliable for rolling, place head of cabbage in boiling water. Remove supple outer leaves, then repeat the blanching process until you have as many leaves as you need.

Wine note: The tastes in this dish would seem to call for a low-key wine, something more to wash the food down than anything else. In red, something fruity and light-bodied, such as a Beaujolais-Village or one of the lesser coteaux of France, a Valpolicella from Italy, or one of the lighter and less expensive Israeli proprietaries. In white, Soave from Italy, or Sauvignon Blanc, French Colombard, or an Emerald Riesling from Israel. There are also some lovely rosés from California worth matching with this dish.

Chicken with Figs

MAKES 4 TO 6 SERVINGS

This easy Middle Eastern–style recipe blends figs and honey, two typical Rosh Hashanah ingredients. For a large holiday dinner, this recipe can be easily doubled.

 One 3 to 3½-pound chicken, cut into pieces
  12 ounces Greek-style dried figs, soaked and drained
   1 cup dry white wine
   ¼ cup honey
   1 teaspoon ground cinnamon
   1 teaspoon ground coriander
   ½ teaspoon salt
   ¼ teaspoon freshly ground black pepper

1. Preheat oven to 375°F.

2. Arrange chicken pieces in large deep roasting pan. In medium bowl, combine figs and remaining ingredients, stirring to dissolve honey. Pour mixture over chicken.

3. Bake chicken about 1 hour, or until tender and browned, turning once and basting occasionally with pan juices.

Wine note: Given that this dish includes dry white wine as an ingredient, key on it. Riesling would be superb, either the very dry versions from Europe or the less dry from New York and California. Dry sparkling wine with some fruitiness would match well also, perhaps something from the Touraine of France, or a dry Italian Spumante. As a kick, a dry Gewürztraminer would stand up well. See, too, the wine note for challah, page 341.

Carrot, Apple, and Sweet Potato Tzimmes

MAKES 6 SERVINGS

Among Ashkenazic Jews, carrots are traditionally served on Rosh Hashanah because they are one of the few sweet root vegetables that have always grown abundantly in the colder climates where these Jews settled. Combined with sweet potatoes and apples in tzimmes, they promise a sweet new year.

- 3 large carrots, peeled and sliced
- 4 sweet potatoes, peeled and sliced
- $\frac{1}{2}$ cup packed brown sugar
  Salt and freshly ground black pepper to taste
- 3 tablespoons margarine
- 3 tart apples, peeled, cored, and sliced

1. Preheat oven to 350°F.

2. In large saucepan over high heat, combine carrots, potatoes, and enough water to cover by 1 inch; bring to a boil. Reduce heat to medium; cover and cook 15 to 20 minutes, until tender; drain.

3. In 2½-quart baking dish, layer carrot slices to cover bottom; sprinkle one-third the brown sugar, salt, and pepper on top, and dot with 1 tablespoon margarine. Continue layering with potatoes, then apples, until all ingredients are used up, sprinkling one-third the brown sugar, salt, and pepper on each layer and dotting with 1 tablespoon margarine. Pour 1 cup water over mixture.

4. Cover and bake about 30 minutes, or until apples are tender. Uncover and bake 5 minutes longer, or until top is golden brown.

Wine note: For this sweet, hearty vegetarian dish, go for one of the lesser sparkling wines, perhaps from New York or, in red, a fruity big-bodied wine from one of the smaller wine houses of Israel. Rosé from California or Israel would do admirably, too.

Honey Cake

MAKES 10 SERVINGS

Many early cakes were made with honey to mask the flavor of the wood ash in which they were baked. Later on, only the wealthy could afford sugar. Therefore, honey cakes evolved into a popular dessert among the Jewish peasants, and became an anticipated item on the Rosh Hashanah table.

2 tablespoons dry bread crumbs
2 tablespoons instant coffee
2¼ cups all-purpose flour
2 teaspoons ground cinnamon
¾ teaspoon baking powder
¾ teaspoon baking soda
½ teaspoon salt
½ teaspoon ground allspice (optional)
3 eggs
¾ cup packed brown sugar
3 tablespoons margarine, melted
¾ cup honey
   Grated peel of 2 oranges

1. Preheat oven to 350°F. Grease 9- by 5-inch loaf pan and dust with bread crumbs.
2. In small bowl, dissolve coffee in ¾ cup hot water; cool.
3. In medium bowl, sift together flour, cinnamon, baking powder, baking soda, salt, and allspice, if desired; set aside.
4. In large bowl with electric mixer at medium speed, lightly beat eggs and brown sugar; beat in margarine and honey. Add half the flour mixture, stirring to combine. Gradually stir in coffee; blend in remaining flour mixture. Stir in orange peel.
5. Pour batter into prepared pan. Bake about 1¼ hours, or until top springs back when lightly touched. (If cake begins to brown too much on top, cover loosely with foil.)
6. Cool cake in pan on wire rack 10 minutes. Remove from pan and cool completely on wire rack.

NOTE: To measure honey, grease the measuring cup beforehand—the honey will then flow out easily.

Wine note: Honey wine would seem the perfect answer but don't believe it—that's too much of the same sweetness and taste. Instead, opt for one of the Israeli dessert wines, an Asti Spumante, a cream sherry from Spain, or even a very sweet fruit wine or nut liqueur.

Almond Bread

Mandelbrot

MAKES 4 DOZEN SLICES

More a cookie than a bread, this is so named because the dough is formed into a loaf, baked, then sliced into cookies. For a crisper product, you may then rebake the cookie slices briefly.

- 2 cups all-purpose flour
- 1½ teaspoons baking powder
- ¼ teaspoon salt
- ⅔ cup plus 2 teaspoons sugar
- ⅓ cup vegetable oil, shortening, or softened margarine
- 2 eggs
- 2 tablespoons brandy or water
- 1 teaspoon almond extract
- 1 teaspoon vanilla extract
- ⅔ cup chopped almonds
- 1 teaspoon ground cinnamon

1. Preheat oven to 325°F. Grease and flour two 8- by 4-inch loaf pans.

2. In medium bowl, combine flour, baking powder, and salt. In large bowl with electric mixer at low speed, or with wooden spoon, blend ⅔ cup sugar, oil, shortening, or margarine, eggs, brandy or water, and extracts. Stir in flour mixture until blended; add almonds, stirring to combine.

3. Form mixture into two 1-inch thick loaves. Place in prepared pans or on ungreased cookie sheet, smoothing tops. In cup, combine remaining 2 teaspoons sugar and cinnamon; sprinkle over loaves.

4. Bake 30 to 45 minutes, until light brown. While still warm, cut loaves crosswise into ½-inch-thick slices. Bake slices 5 minutes longer, or until golden, if desired. Cool completely on wire racks.

VARIATIONS: For marble mandelbrot, mix 2 tablespoons unsweetened cocoa powder into $\frac{1}{2}$ cup batter and swirl into batter before shaping.

For chocolate chip mandelbrot, add $\frac{1}{2}$ cup semisweet chocolate chips to batter.

Wine note: A sipping wine is needed for this nibble. Sherry would be ideal; so would a Muscat from Israel or Italy. Fruit-flavored wines would be interesting alternatives, as would a fruit-flavored liqueur or brandy.

With its exchange of gifts, dreidel games, and lighting of the menorah, Chanukah is a holiday well loved by children. Therefore, it's no surprise that the story behind the Chanukah celebration is ingrained in Jewish memories early.

The story begins with the ascent of King Antiochus to the throne of Syria in 175 B.C. At that time, the largest, most splendid temple the Jews had ever built stood in Jerusalem, part of the vast Syrian kingdom. Antiochus's soldiers denigrated this stately and cherished building by placing a Greek statue inside and destroying a number of its religious articles. In addition, they ordered the Jews to practice Greek religious customs, prohibiting them to study the Torah or observe their holidays.

A small group of Jewish villagers, led by Mattathias, finally protested these ordinances openly and began a rebellion, retreating to the hills to fight the Greeks in a type of guerrilla warfare. About a year after the fighting began, Mattathias put his son, Judah Maccabee, in charge. Under his brave command, the small Jewish army eventually pushed the much larger Greek force back to Syria.

After this victory, Judah and his soldiers returned to the temple to assess the damage. They spent many days cleaning and repairing the building, after which they planned a dedication ceremony. For this celebration, they wanted to light the large gold menorah that was one of the temple's proudest possessions. The menorah could only be lit with pure oil, which the soldiers finally located in a small sealed container. Although the tiny amount inside looked barely enough to last one day, it miraculously kept the menorah lit for eight days straight!

Chanukah, or dedication, is now celebrated for eight days and nights. To recall the miracle of the burning oil, foods fried in oil are traditional Chanukah fare. These include potato latkes, or pancakes, popularized by Eastern European Jews, and sufganiyot, or fried doughnuts, prepared by cooks in Israel and those of Sephardic ancestry. Naturally, each family has its own favorite Chanukah menus, and there are many alternatives in this book for those who are inspired to broaden the scope of their holiday table. Latkes and sufganiyot will be festive additions to the celebration.

—*Gil Marks*

Potato Pancakes—*Latkes*
Applesauce
Jelly Doughnuts—*Sufganiyot*

Potato Pancakes

Latkes

MAKES 16 PANCAKES

Everyone looks forward to crispy potato latkes at Chanukah time. This foolproof recipe will turn out perfect pancakes. For a home-made touch, try the easy applesauce recipe that follows; it complements the latkes nicely.

3 to 4 large baking potatoes (about 3 pounds), peeled
1 small onion, peeled and minced
2 eggs, beaten
$\frac{1}{3}$ cup matzoh meal or all-purpose flour
1 teaspoon salt
$\frac{1}{4}$ teaspoon baking powder
Dash of freshly ground black pepper
Vegetable oil for frying

1. Grate potatoes, coarse or fine, into bowl of cold water. Drain and squeeze out liquid.
2. In medium bowl, combine grated potatoes, onion, eggs, matzoh meal or flour, salt, baking powder, and pepper; mix well.
3. In large skillet, heat $\frac{1}{2}$ inch oil over medium-high heat until very hot. Drop potato mixture by tablespoonfuls into hot oil, a few at a time, flattening each with a spatula. Cook 2 to 3 minutes on each side, until browned and crisp, turning once and reducing heat slightly if necessary.

4. Remove cooked latkes to paper towels to drain. Repeat frying with remaining potato mixture, adding more oil, if necessary. Serve hot, with applesauce or sour cream.

VARIATION: For sweet potato latkes substitute $1\frac{1}{2}$ pounds sweet potatoes, peeled and grated, for half the white potatoes; add a dash of ground cinnamon, nutmeg, or ginger.

Applesauce

MAKES 4 CUPS

This version of homemade applesauce turns out chunky. For a smoother product, purée in a food processor or push through a food mill.

> 6 cooking apples (about 2 pounds), peeled, cored, and sliced
> $\frac{1}{2}$ cup apple cider or water
> 1 to 2 tablespoons lemon juice
> $\frac{1}{4}$ teaspoon ground cinnamon, or $\frac{1}{2}$-inch cinnamon stick (optional)
> About $\frac{1}{2}$ cup granulated or brown sugar, to taste

1. In large saucepan over high heat, combine apples, cider or water, lemon juice, and cinnamon; bring to a boil. Reduce heat to low; cover and simmer 15 to 20 minutes, until apples are soft, stirring occasionally and adding more cider or water, if necessary.
2. Stir in sugar; simmer 2 to 3 minutes longer, until juice becomes syrupy. Cool slightly before using.

VARIATIONS: For raspberry applesauce, add 2 cups puréed raspberries along with apples. To make cranberry applesauce, add 8 ounces fresh cranberries with apples and increase sugar to 1 cup. Add 4 ounces soaked dried apricots with apples for apricot applesauce. Add $\frac{1}{2}$ cup raisins with sugar to make raisin applesauce.

Beverage note: There is yet to be a wine devised for latkes with sour cream or applesauce except, possibly, apple wine. A kosher version of that should be next to impossible to find, but there are kosher apple ciders, including several varietals such as McIntosh, Granny Smith, and Northern Spy. They're made from Vermont apples and should be fun to try.

Jelly Doughnuts

Sufganiyot

MAKES 14 TO 16 DOUGHNUTS

These fluffy yeast-raised doughnuts are deep-fried in oil to carry on the Chanukah tradition. Israelis eat these or cheese pancakes rather than latkes in celebration of the holiday.

- 2 packages active dry yeast
- $\frac{1}{3}$ cup granulated sugar
- 1 teaspoon salt
- $\frac{1}{2}$ cup milk or liquid nondairy creamer
- $\frac{1}{3}$ cup butter or margarine, melted
- 3 eggs, separated
  About $3\frac{3}{4}$ cups all-purpose flour
  About $\frac{1}{3}$ cup jelly or jam (any flavor)
  Vegetable oil for frying
  Confectioners' sugar or granulated sugar for dusting (optional)

1. In large bowl, dissolve yeast in $\frac{1}{2}$ cup warm water (105°F to 115°F); stir in $\frac{1}{3}$ cup granulated sugar and salt. With wooden spoon, blend in

milk or creamer, butter or margarine, egg yolks, and 2 cups flour. With spoon or electric mixer at low speed, beat in enough remaining flour to form a smooth, soft dough. Cover and let rise about $1\frac{1}{2}$ hours, or until doubled in size.

2. Punch down dough. On lightly floured surface, knead about 12 times, until smooth and elastic.

3. With floured rolling pin, roll out dough $\frac{1}{4}$ inch thick. With $2\frac{1}{2}$- to 3-inch round biscuit cutter or glass, cut dough into circles.

4. In center of each of half the dough circles, place a teaspoonful of jelly. Lightly blend reserved egg whites; brush edges of dough circles with beaten whites and top each with another dough circle, pressing edges to seal. Place filled dough circles on lightly floured cookie sheet; cover and let rise about 1 hour, or until doubled in size.

5. In large heavy saucepan or deep-fat fryer, heat 2 inches oil over medium heat until it reaches 370°F on deep-fat or candy thermometer. With spatula, carefully lift doughnuts and drop them, 3 or 4 at a time, top sides down, into hot oil. Fry 3 to 5 minutes, until golden brown on all sides, turning occasionally. (Make sure the temperature of the oil doesn't drop below 350°F.)

6. With slotted spoon, remove doughnuts to paper towels to drain. Repeat frying remaining doughnuts, a few at a time, draining on paper towels.

7. Before serving, dust with sifted confectioners' sugar or roll in additional granulated sugar, if desired.

NOTE: If you do not have a deep-fat or candy thermometer, you can test the temperature of the oil by dropping in a cube of soft bread; it should brown in 35 seconds when the temperature reaches 370°F.

The derivation of the word Purim explains, in large part, how the holiday came to be. Purim is the plural of the Hebrew word *pur*, which translates to "lot." In this case, lot refers to determination by chance, which is how Haman (the wicked adviser to an ancient Persian king) decided to choose the date on which the Jews in his kingdom would be killed. To commemorate the fact that this mass destruction never took place, Purim is now celebrated every year, usually falling sometime in March to coincide with the fourteenth day of Adar, the day after which Haman had set his decree.

The story of Haman and the other characters involved in Purim is written in the Megillah or Megillat Esther, the scroll of Esther. She was the Jewish wife of that Persian king, Ahasuerus. When Esther's uncle, Mordecai, found out about Haman's plan to kill the Jews, he asked Queen Esther to intervene and save her people. She devised her own plan, which turned the king's sentiment against his evil adviser and resulted in the execution of Haman instead.

Today, Purim takes place in a carnival atmosphere in many congregations. Children dress up in costumes, plays relating the Purim story are performed, and noisemakers called greggers are sounded whenever the name of Haman is mentioned during the reading of the Megillah.

The main Purim meal is usually eaten in the afternoon, but the foods served are not as steeped in tradition as they are at other holidays. Nevertheless, a number of Jews consider kreplach a Purim dish, and many bakeries and cooks turn out dozens of hamantaschen for dessert. The latter are triangular-shaped pastries named after Haman and heralding his downfall. In some Sephardic families, swirls of fried pastry resembling Haman's ears are more commonly served than hamantaschen.

Hamantaschen are often included in the sweets and baked goods that Jews traditionally send to relatives and friends during Purim. This exchange evolved through Mordecai, who instructed Jews to celebrate their liberation with feasting and gladness, and "by sending portions (*mi'sholach manot*) one to another and gifts to the poor."

The words *mi'sholach manot* developed into "shalachmones" by the Yiddish-speaking Jews, and basketfuls and platters of goodies are still sent at Purim by many contemporary families.

The recipes here offer an assortment of homemade treats that can make up a delicious and hospitable shalachmones basket for a lucky recipient. All can be prepared with either butter or margarine, providing the choice of a dairy or pareve selection of baked goods.

—*Gil Marks*

Poppy Seed Bread
Hamantaschen
Poppy Seed Filling
Monster Chocolate Mint Sandwich Cookies
Rum Balls
Lace Roll-ups
Butter Cookies

Poppy Seed Bread

MAKES 2 LOAVES

In Yiddish or German, the word for poppy seeds is mohn—*similar in pronunciation to the name Haman. Perhaps that is the reason poppy seeds are frequently used in baked goods during Purim. This quick bread is really more like a loaf cake, and improves in flavor if left to stand overnight.*

    $2\frac{1}{4}$ cups all-purpose flour
    $1\frac{1}{2}$ cups sugar
    $\frac{3}{4}$ cup poppy seeds
    1 tablespoon baking powder
    3 eggs, beaten
    $1\frac{1}{4}$ cups milk or water
    $\frac{3}{4}$ cup vegetable oil
    1 teaspoon freshly squeezed lemon juice
    1 teaspoon vanilla extract
    1 teaspoon grated lemon or orange peel

1. Preheat oven to 350°F. Grease and flour two 9- by 5-inch loaf pans.
2. In large bowl, combine flour, sugar, poppy seeds, and baking powder. In small bowl, beat eggs, milk or water, oil, lemon juice, vanilla, and lemon or orange peel. Stir egg mixture into flour mixture just until evenly moistened. Do not overmix.
3. Fill prepared loaf pans two-thirds full of batter. Bake 50 minutes to 1 hour, or until toothpick inserted in center of each loaf comes out clean.
4. Cool breads in pans on wire rack 15 minutes. Remove from pans and cool completely on wire racks.
5. Wrap loaves in foil and let stand overnight, if possible, for better flavor.

Hamantaschen

MAKES 3½ DOZEN

Literally translated, hamantaschen *means "Haman's pockets." According to one legend, these pastries were baked to remind the Jews that this villain's pockets were filled with bribe money. Others believe* hamantaschen *are shaped in a triangle to resemble Haman's three-cornered hat. Whatever the story, they are traditionally made on Purim and filled with either poppy seed, prune, or apricot filling.*

    ⅔ cup (1⅓ sticks) butter or margarine, softened
    ½ cup sugar
    1 egg
    3 tablespoons milk or water
    ½ teaspoon vanilla or almond extract
    ¼ teaspoon salt
    2¾ cups all-purpose flour
    2 cups Poppy Seed Filling (recipe follows), prune butter, or apricot preserves

1. In medium bowl with electric mixer at medium speed, cream butter or margarine with sugar 5 to 10 minutes, until light and fluffy. Beat in egg until well mixed. Add milk or water, vanilla or almond extract, and salt, beating to mix well. Stir in flour until dough forms.

2. Form dough into a ball and wrap in plastic wrap. Refrigerate at least 2 hours or overnight, until firm.

3. Preheat oven to 375°F. Divide dough into 4 equal portions. On lightly floured surface with floured rolling pin, roll out each dough portion $\frac{1}{8}$ inch thick. With 2- to 3-inch round cookie cutter or glass, cut dough into circles (figs. A, B).

4. Place 1 teaspoon filling in center of each dough circle (fig.C). With fingers, pinch dough together at 12, 4, and 8 o'clock to form a triangle (fig. D).

5. Place triangles on cookie sheet and bake 10 to 15 minutes, until golden. Remove to wire racks to cool.

NOTE: For more texture, add chopped nuts to apricot preserves or prune butter (lekvar).

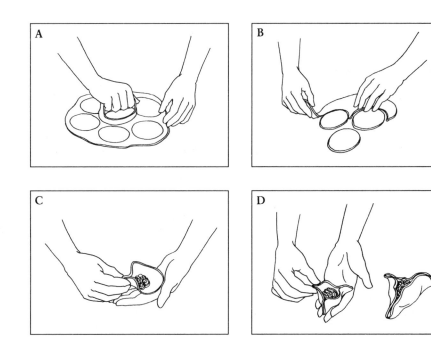

HAMANTASCHEN

MAKES 2 CUPS

$\frac{1}{2}$ pound poppy seeds ($2\frac{1}{4}$ to $2\frac{1}{2}$ cups)
$\frac{1}{2}$ cup honey
2 tablespoons butter or margarine
2 teaspoons freshly squeezed lemon juice
Grated peel of 1 lemon
$\frac{1}{2}$ cup raisins (optional)

1. In food grinder or food processor, finely grind or process poppy seeds. Transfer to medium saucepan; stir in 1 cup water, honey, butter or margarine, lemon juice, and lemon peel. Place over low heat and simmer 10 minutes, until thickened, stirring frequently.
2. Remove from heat; stir in raisins, if desired. Let cool to room temperature.

Wine note: To accompany hamantaschen, choose a late harvest Riesling, fruit wines such as plum or peach, amaretto or hazelnut liqueur —or how does a date liqueur sound?

Monster Chocolate Mint Sandwich Cookies

MAKES 2 LARGE SANDWICH COOKIES

These oversized cookies should make a big hit with the kids on Purim.

$1\frac{3}{4}$ cups all-purpose flour
2 teaspoons baking soda
1 teaspoon ground cinnamon
$\frac{1}{4}$ teaspoon salt
$\frac{2}{3}$ cup vegetable shortening

$\frac{1}{2}$ cup granulated sugar

1 egg

One 6-ounce package semisweet chocolate chips, melted

$\frac{1}{4}$ cup light corn syrup

Granulated sugar for coating

$\frac{1}{4}$ cup ($\frac{1}{2}$ stick) butter or margarine

$\frac{1}{4}$ teaspoon peppermint extract

2 cups confectioners' sugar

2 to 3 tablespoons milk or nondairy creamer

1. Preheat oven to 350°F.

2. In medium bowl, combine flour, baking soda, cinnamon, and salt. In large bowl with electric mixer at medium speed, beat shortening, $\frac{1}{2}$ cup granulated sugar, and egg 5 minutes, or until light and creamy. With mixer at low speed, blend in melted chocolate and corn syrup. Gradually add flour mixture, stirring until blended.

3. Divide dough into 4 equal portions; shape each into a ball. Roll each ball in granulated sugar until well coated.

4. On large cookie sheet, arrange balls of dough 4 inches apart. Bake cookies 25 minutes, or until lightly browned. (They will spread out into large, flat cookies during baking.) Remove to wire racks to cool.

5. Meanwhile, in medium bowl with electric mixer at medium speed, cream butter or margarine with peppermint extract. Gradually beat in confectioners' sugar until blended. Beat in milk or creamer until frosting mixtue is of spreading consistency.

6. Spread the frosting on tops of 2 cookies; press unfrosted cookies on top to form sandwiches. Cut into wedges for serving.

Rum Balls

MAKES 50

This recipe requires no baking, but the balls should be stored in a covered container and left to stand for several days to mellow the flavor.

2½ cups vanilla wafer or graham cracker crumbs
1 cup finely chopped nuts
1 cup confectioners' sugar
2 tablespoons unsweetened cocoa powder
¼ cup rum or bourbon
3 tablespoons light corn syrup
Confectioners' sugar, chopped nuts, or grated chocolate (optional)

1. In medium bowl, combine cookie crumbs, finely chopped nuts, sugar, and cocoa. Stir in rum or bourbon and corn syrup until well blended.
2. With hands, shape mixture into 1-inch balls. Roll in additional confectioners' sugar, chopped nuts, or grated chocolate, if desired.
3. Store in airtight container at room temperature for several days, if possible.

NOTE: Each sealed package of graham crackers will yield about 1¼ cups crumbs.

Lace Roll-ups

MAKES 20

The whipped cream filling makes these delicate cookies inappropriate for a shalachmones basket, but they are a marvelous addition to the Purim table.

$\frac{1}{2}$ cup all-purpose flour
1 teaspoon ground ginger
Dash of salt
$\frac{1}{2}$ cup (1 stick) butter or margarine
$\frac{1}{2}$ cup sugar
$\frac{1}{3}$ cup molasses or dark corn syrup
1 teaspoon freshly squeezed lemon juice
$\frac{1}{2}$ teaspoon vanilla extract
1 cup heavy or whipping cream

1. Preheat oven to 325°F. Grease large cookie sheets.
2. In medium bowl, sift together flour, ginger, and salt. In large saucepan over medium heat, melt butter or margarine with sugar and molasses or corn syrup; stir to blend. Remove from heat and stir in flour mixture. Add lemon juice and vanilla, stirring to blend.
3. Drop batter by teaspoonfuls, about 5 inches apart, onto prepared cookie sheets. Bake 7 to 8 minutes, until golden brown.
4. With spatula or sharp knife, immediately remove cookies, 1 at a time, from cookie sheet. Roll each around the handle of a wooden spoon to form cylinders. Slip cookies off spoon handle and cool completely on wire racks.
5. Meanwhile, in small bowl with electric mixer at high speed, whip cream until soft peaks form. To serve, pipe or spoon whipped cream into cookie cylinders.

NOTE: Once they spread out, only 4 or 5 cookies will fit on one cookie sheet at a time. If cookies set before you can roll them around spoon handle, reheat in the oven for a few seconds.

Wine note: A rich wine with a strong acid structure is needed to stand up to this rich confection. Several would provide felicity—sweet Chenin Blanc or sweet Gewürztraminer from California, a late-harvest Johannisberg Riesling (also from California), or, from Israel, a dessert Muscat.

Butter Cookies

MAKES 4 DOZEN

This versatile dough can be shaped and flavored many ways to produce several variations on the traditional butter cookie.

1 cup (2 sticks) butter or margarine, softened
$\frac{2}{3}$ cup sugar
2 eggs or egg yolks, at room temperature
1 teaspoon vanilla or almond extract
   Pinch of salt
2 cups all-purpose flour

1. In medium bowl with electric mixer at medium speed, cream butter or margarine, sugar, eggs or egg yolks, vanilla or almond extract, and salt about 4 minutes, or until very light and fluffy. Lightly stir in flour until blended. Wrap dough in plastic wrap and refrigerate 1 hour.
2. Preheat oven to 375°F.
3. Place chilled dough in pastry bag fitted with star tip; pipe onto ungreased cookie sheets into small rounded stars. Or roll dough into small ropes or circles; place on cookie sheets. Bake 8 to 10 minutes, until lightly browned.
4. Cool cookies on cookie sheets about 1 minute or until set. Remove to wire racks to cool completely.
5. Store cookies in airtight containers at room temperature for 1 to 2 days. For longer storage, wrap carefully and place in freezer.

VARIATIONS: *Chocolate-dipped Butter Cookies:* Melt 8 ounces semisweet chocolate; dip baked cookies in melted chocolate and place on waxed-paper-lined cookie sheets. Let stand until set.
Butter Cherry Cookies: Shape dough into 1-inch balls; press halved candied cherries in center of each. Bake as above.
Thumbprint Cookies: Shape dough into 1-inch balls. With thumb, press down center of each; fill each indentation with $\frac{1}{2}$ teaspoon jam.

Modern Jews the world over celebrate Purim similarly. The Megillah is read in the temple, children dress up in costumes, and pageants are staged to reenact the story of Queen Esther, King Ahasuerus, Mordecai, and Haman. In my birthplace, Iran, originally Persia and the setting of the Purim story, we had a couple of other customs as well. One I particularly remember from my childhood was a trip with my family to Hamadan, the place where Mordecai and Esther are buried. After what seemed like a very long journey, we arrived at the burial site, left a burning candle, and quietly thought about the significance of Purim.

Special foods also commemorated Purim for us. Persian Jews follow the Sephardic tradition, and our typical Purim dishes differ from the baskets of baked goods exchanged by the Ashkenazim. Rice is one of the staples of Iranian cuisine, and for festive occasions, it's combined with other ingredients to form a variety of sweets. On Purim, I always make a rice halvah (a thick puddinglike confection) and rice-flour cookies. In other Sephardic homes as well as mine, it's also customary to prepare coco sabzie, a crustless vegetable pie made with an assortment of spring greens.

Now that I live in New York City, I try to preserve my heritage by cooking these and other traditional dishes at Purim and other holidays. The large Iranian-Jewish population in my area makes this easier. Ingredients are relatively simple to find in the Middle Eastern groceries, and family members and friends are nearby to help me recall the foods I knew as a young Jewish girl growing up in Iran.

—*Nahid Noorani*

Nahid Noorani

Born in Teheran, Iran, Nahid came to the United States at eighteen to attend college. Two of her brothers were already in New York City, and Nahid lived in their Queens apartment while she studied interior design at the New York Institute of Technology.

During her third year of college in 1979, the Iranian revolution took place, and political circumstances made it impossible for her to return home. Soon thereafter, more family members left their native land; Nahid's parents, another brother, and a sister joining the others in the states. Today, all live within blocks of each other in Manhattan.

Nahid was brought up in a kosher home in Teheran and was able to practice most Jewish customs. As a child, she attended synagogue and learned Hebrew in school, but was later sent to a Moslem high school in accordance with national policy. Although she was always interested in food, Nahid didn't cook much herself until she came to New York. With her mother as her teacher, she soon learned how to make the traditional Sephardic dishes she had enjoyed during her childhood. Now Nahid is a whiz in the kitchen, preparing everything from family Shabbat dinners to gala parties for more than a hundred guests.

Nahid's busy days are filled with her work as an interior designer and full-time mother. She also assists in the activities of the Sephardic Society of America—a group with a very large following among the members of the Persian-Jewish community in the New York metropolitan area.

Rice Halvah
Rice-Flour Cookies—*Nanbrangi*
Vegetable Pie—*Coco Sabzie*

Rice Halvah

For this traditional Purim sweet, the rice goes through several preparation steps—it's soaked, washed, dried, ground, roasted, and boiled. The cooked dish resembles cream of wheat, but after it's thoroughly cooled, this confection is sturdy enough to cut into squares as you would fudge. Rosewater, saffron, and almonds give the halvah its characteristic Middle Eastern accent.

  2 cups raw long-grain rice
  $\frac{1}{3}$ cup vegetable oil
  1 teaspoon ground turmeric
   About 1$\frac{1}{2}$ cups sugar
   Large pinch of crushed saffron
  1 to 2 tablespoons hot water
  1 tablespoon rosewater
  $\frac{1}{4}$ teaspoon ground cardamom
  $\frac{1}{4}$ cup toasted slivered almonds

1. In medium bowl, combine rice with 2 cups cold water. Let soak 30 minutes.

2. Drain rice, rinse in water, and drain again. Spread washed rice on paper towels and pat dry. (Do not dry thoroughly; rice should be a little damp.)

3. In blender or food processor, grind rice until the grains are about the size of large sand particles.

4. In large saucepan, toast ground rice over medium heat 3 to 5 minutes, until lightly browned, stirring constantly. Add oil and turmeric; toss to coat rice well with oil. Continue cooking 1 to 2 minutes longer, stirring constantly.

5. In cup, combine 1 teaspoon sugar and saffron. Add hot water and stir to dissolve. Stir saffron mixture into toasted rice; add 1 cup sugar (or more to taste) and 4 cups cold water.

6. Increase heat to medium-high; cook rice mixture, stirring constantly, until most of the water is absorbed and rice no longer sticks together.

7. Reduce heat to medium-low; cover and simmer 30 minutes, or until thick and creamy, adding more water if necessary and stirring occasionally. Remove from heat; stir in rosewater and cardamom. Let rice mixture cool 2 minutes.

8. Pour into glass serving dish or individual dessert dishes. Sprinkle almonds on top. Let stand at room temperature or refrigerate until completely cool and set.

9. Serve at room temperature, with spoons, or cut into squares.

Beverage note: Sweets for the sweet—try an amaretto cordial to lengthen the slivers of toasted almond.

Rice-Flour Cookies

Nanbrangi

MAKES 3 DOZEN

Almost every Iranian-Jewish family I know serves these cookies on Purim. Many bake them on Passover as well, since rice flour is an ingredient permissible in Sephardic households during that holiday. The dough is quite soft, so handle it with care.

1 to 2 eggs
    1 cup sugar
    1 cup vegetable oil
    2 tablespoons rosewater
       About $1\frac{1}{2}$ cups rice flour (see Note)
       Poppy seeds

1. Preheat oven to 350°F. Line cookie sheets with parchment paper or aluminum foil.

2. In medium bowl, combine eggs and sugar with wire whisk or electric mixer at low speed. Whisk or beat until pale yellow. Stir in oil, then rosewater, until blended. Stir in rice flour until soft dough forms, adding additional flour, if necessary.

3. With hands, form dough into rounds about $1\frac{1}{2}$ to 2 inches in diameter. Place rounds on prepared cookie sheets. With teaspoon, make an indentation on top of each; sprinkle poppy seeds into indentations, making designs, if desired.

4. Bake cookies 15 to 20 minutes, until very lightly browned. With spatula, remove from cookie sheets and let cool on wire racks.

NOTE: To make rice flour, rinse long-grain rice in cold water, drain, and dry on paper towels. Place dried rice grains in container of blender or food processor. Blend or process very well; rice should be finely ground, almost like flour.

Vegetable Pie

Coco Sabzie

MAKES 6 SERVINGS

Although the rough translation of this Persian recipe is "pie," it's actually cooked in a skillet and turns out looking more like an Italian-style frittata. While this dish is typically served on Purim, many Jews also prepare it to bring to a family that is sitting shiva, the week-long mourning period following a death. If the coco sabzie is being prepared for a shiva call, it is customary for the cook to say the name of the person who died after breaking each egg that goes into the recipe.

Vegetable oil for cooking
2 tablespoons chopped onion (optional)
1 bunch celery, finely chopped
$\frac{1}{2}$ pound fresh spinach, rinsed, dried and finely chopped
1 bunch scallions, finely chopped (green tops only)
$\frac{1}{2}$ cup chopped fresh dill
3 to 4 large eggs
Pinch of ground turmeric
Salt and freshly ground black pepper to taste
Plain yogurt

1. In 10-inch skillet, heat 2 teaspoons oil over medium heat. Add chopped onion; sauté 5 minutes, or until tender. Remove from heat.
2. In large bowl, combine cooked onion, celery, spinach, scallions, and dill. With spoon, beat in eggs, turmeric, and salt and pepper to taste, until mixture is well blended and creamy.
3. In same 10-inch skillet, heat $\frac{1}{4}$ inch oil over medium-high heat until hot. Spread egg mixture evenly in skillet. Cover and cook about 10 minutes, or until underside is set.
4. Loosen egg mixture from skillet with spatula and invert onto large plate. Slide back into skillet and continue cooking on other side 5 to 10 minutes longer, until completely set.
5. To serve, flip onto serving plate and cut into wedges. Top each serving with a dollop of yogurt.

NOTE: For speedy preparation, the vegetables for this recipe can be chopped in the food processor.

The holiday of Passover marks the exodus of the Jews from Egypt more than three thousand years ago. It always falls in the spring and is celebrated for eight days, beginning at sundown with a seder-night dinner. At the seder, which means "order" in Hebrew, the story of the exodus is retold, as all those sitting around the table read responsively from the haggadah. This reading is followed by a succession of ceremonial foods.

The culinary customs surrounding Passover are probably the most complex of all those for Jewish holidays, and the only ones based on a different set of dietary restrictions. Because the Jews were forced to leave Egypt in a hurry, they couldn't wait for their bread dough to rise. They took the dough with them as they began their long journey, but it stayed flat and thin, never rising into light, airy loaves. This unleavened bread, or matzoh, often called "the bread of affliction," is still the focal point of Passover cuisine.

In observant Jewish homes, the weeks before Passover are filled with preparations. All leavened products *(hametz)* must either be given away, discarded, or burned, and the kitchen scrubbed from top to bottom to rid it of any lingering crumbs. The separate Passover dishes, cutlery, and cooking utensils are taken out of storage and cleaned for the holiday. Special kosher-for-Pesach groceries (manufactured under strict rabbinical supervision) are purchased, and baked goods are prepared with matzoh meal or cake meal. The day of the first seder is spent cooking dinner and preparing the seder plate—a large, divided plate holding the foods that symbolize the Passover story. These include *maror* (bitter herbs such as pure horseradish) to remind the Jews of their years of suffering; *charoset* (usually an apple-wine-nut mixture) to resemble the mortar used by Jewish slaves to build the palaces and pyramids in Egypt; *z'roah* (roasted shank bone) to represent the sacrifice of the Paschal Lamb; *baytzah* (roasted egg) to symbolize the burnt offerings brought to the temple on festival days; and *karpas* (parsley, lettuce, or celery), a springtime symbol to be dipped in salt water for recalling the tears shed by the Jews under Egyptian bondage.

The Passover food customs of the Ashkenazic and Sephardic Jews have evolved somewhat differently. Starting with the seder plate, many Sephardim substitute lemon juice for salt water; date syrup or a dried fruit mixture for the apple-based charoset; and romaine lettuce for parsley. In addition, the Ashkenazic Jews forbid any grain or grain product that might ferment, including barley, wheat, rye, oats, and rice. Among the Sephardim, however, rice is considered kosher for Passover and is a staple on this holiday.

Of the two menus that follow, one illustrates the Ashkenazic tradition, the other, a Sephardic-style Passover. Since the holiday is a springtime celebration, many of the ingredients used are seasonal and fresh. Although matzoh is a mainstay of the diet during Passover, it doesn't have to be included in every recipe, as demonstrated by the updated, lighter dishes presented here.

—*Gil Marks, Ashkenazic Passover*
—*Esther Shear, Sephardic Passover*

Passover Mina
Passover Brown Eggs
Charoset Sephardic Style
Shoulder of Lamb Roast
Artichokes Sephardic Style
Walnut Clusters—*Moustachudos*

Passover Mina

MAKES 8 SERVINGS

The word mina *means "mine" in Spanish. This matzoh, meat, and egg dish was probably named mina because it's rich, like a gold mine. At the seder, it would be served as a first course after the soup. But it also makes an excellent lunch entrée during the Passover week.*

$\frac{1}{4}$ cup vegetable oil
1 medium onion, peeled and chopped
1 pound ground beef
   Salt and freshly ground black pepper to taste
6 matzohs
$\frac{3}{4}$ cup chopped parsley
3 to 4 scallions, chopped
6 to 7 eggs, well beaten
1 medium potato, cooked and mashed (optional)

1. In large skillet, heat oil over medium-high heat. Add onion; sauté 5 to 10 minutes, until golden brown. Add ground beef; sauté 5 minutes longer, or until it loses its red color. Add $\frac{3}{4}$ cup water and salt and pepper to taste; reduce heat to low. Cover and simmer 10 minutes or until beef is tender. Remove from heat and let cool.
2. Preheat oven to 400°F. Grease 13- by 9-inch baking dish.
3. Dip matzohs in water until wet but not soaked: Squeeze out excess

water and break matzohs into pieces. In large bowl, combine matzohs, beef mixture, parsley, scallions, 6 eggs, and salt and pepper to taste; mix well and transfer to prepared baking dish.

3. In small bowl, blend mashed potato with remaining egg; spread evenly over meat mixture, if desired. Bake 45 minutes, or until golden brown.

NOTE: Ground beef mixture can be cooked ahead of time and refrigerated until you are ready to prepare mina.

Passover Brown Eggs

MAKES 1 DOZEN

In Sephardic homes, these hard-cooked eggs always accompany mina. The eggs should be cut in half when served—whole eggs are used only during mourning periods.

  12 eggs, at room temperature
   1 large yellow onion with peel
   1 tablespoon vegetable oil
   1 teaspoon salt
   1 teaspoon freshly ground black pepper

1. In large enamel or stainless-steel saucepan or dutch oven, place eggs and enough cold water to cover. Add onion and remaining ingredients. Bring to a boil over high heat. Reduce heat to low; cover and simmer $2\frac{1}{2}$ to 3 hours. (The longer the eggs cook, the browner they will become.)

2. To serve, peel eggs and cut in half. Serve warm.

NOTE: Be sure to leave the onion unpeeled. The onion skin imparts the characteristic brown color to the egg shells.

Charoset Sephardic Style

MAKES 2 CUPS

On the island of Rhodes and in other Sephardic communities, it was typical to prepare charoset with dates as well as apples. The fruit was cooked, and the resulting mixture truly resembled the mortar used by the Jewish slaves to hold the Pharaoh's bricks together in ancient Egypt. On our Passover table, the charoset was always served in a glass bowl placed on the seder plate, accompanied by chicory or lettuce leaves to symbolize the bitter herbs (no horseradish was available in our part of the world); a lamb shank bone; and a hard-boiled egg.

8 apples, peeled and cored
$1\frac{1}{2}$ pounds pitted dates
$\frac{1}{4}$ cup sugar
2 cups finely chopped walnuts
$\frac{1}{2}$ cup sweet wine
$\frac{1}{4}$ cup wine vinegar

1. Cut apples into chunks; place in large saucepan with 2 cups water, dates, and sugar. Bring to a boil over high heat. Reduce heat to low; cover, and simmer 20 to 30 minutes, until apples are tender.
2. Drain fruit well in colander; discard liquid. Let fruit cool to room temperature.
3. In food processor, blender, or food mill, purée fruit mixture. Transfer to medium bowl; stir in walnuts, wine, and vinegar. Refrigerate to allow flavors to blend. Charoset will keep in the refrigerator for at least 2 weeks.

Shoulder of Lamb Roast

MAKES 8 SERVINGS

Lamb is abundant in the Mediterranean lands settled by the Sephardim, especially in the springtime when Passover arrives. It was only natural, then, for roasted lamb to become a tradition in our family during this holiday.

One 3½- to 4-pound shoulder of lamb, preferably with shank attached
5 to 6 cloves garlic, peeled and halved
3 tablespoons vegetable oil
1 teaspoon crushed dried rosemary or oregano
Salt to taste
Freshly ground black pepper to taste
Juice of 1 large lemon

1. Preheat oven to 350°F.
2. Trim all excess fat from lamb; wash meat thoroughly. With sharp knife, prick or slit lamb in several spots. Insert half a garlic clove in each slit.
3. With palm of hand, rub oil over surface of meat. Sprinkle evenly with rosemary or oregano, salt, and pepper.
4. Place seasoned lamb in roasting pan or baking dish; cover tightly with foil. Bake about 1 hour.
5. Remove foil from pan and pour in ½ cup water. Continue baking, uncovered, 1 hour longer, or until lamb is nicely browned and tender. Just before removing from oven, squeeze lemon juice over meat.
6. To serve, carve lamb into slices and serve with pan juices, seasoned to taste.

Artichokes Sephardic Style

The special way these artichokes are cut and prepared is Jewish in origin. Since artichokes are in season during Passover, this recipe is perfect for a seder meal. As a bonus, it can be served hot, cold, or at room temperature.

    4 large artichokes
       Juice of 3 lemons
    2 tablespoons vegetable oil
       Salt to taste
       Iceberg lettuce leaves

1. Rinse artichokes and snap off outer leaves, leaving only the fleshy edible parts (figs. A, B). With sharp knife, cut off top third of each artichoke and most of stem (fig. C). With teaspoon, remove fuzzy part of choke (fig. D). Scrape edges of artichokes and remaining stems until smooth and clean (fig. E).

2. In large bowl, combine cleaned artichokes with juice of 1 lemon and enough salted water to cover; set aside.

3. In large saucepan or dutch oven, combine 3 cups water, juice of 2 lemons, oil, and salt to taste. Bring to a boil over high heat. Drain artichokes and drop into boiling liquid; cover with lettuce leaves. Reduce heat to medium; cover pan and continue boiling 30 to 40 minutes, until artichokes are tender.

4. Serve artichokes hot, cold, or at room temperature, with some of cooking liquid spooned on top; discard lettuce.

NOTE: The lettuce leaves keep the artichokes moist and prevent discoloration during cooking.

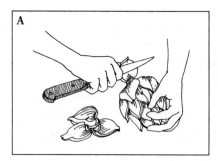

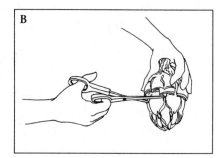

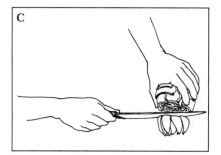

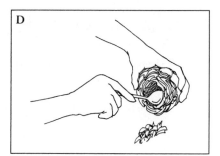

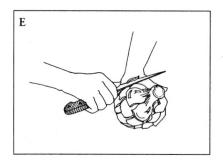

ARTICHOKES SEPHARDIC STYLE

Walnut Clusters

Moustachudos

MAKES 4 DOZEN

The translation of moustachuds *is "mustaches"—the name given to these cookies because the eater ends up with a powdered-sugar mustache! If you can't find kosher-for-Pesach confectioners' sugar, combine granulated sugar with a little potato starch in a blender or food processor, then grind together until a fine powder forms.*

1 pound shelled walnuts, ground (4 cups)
3 eggs, beaten
1 cup granulated sugar
3 tablespoons matzoh meal
1 teaspoon ground cinnamon
1 teaspoon ground cloves
   Confectioners' sugar for sprinkling

1. Preheat oven to 350°F. Line cookie sheets with aluminum foil; grease foil.

2. In large bowl, combine all ingredients except confectioners' sugar. With spoon, stir until mixture forms a pastelike consistency.

3. With tablespoon, drop dough into small, rough stacks on prepared cookie sheets (stacks should not be rounded on top). Bake 10 to 12 minutes until golden.

4. Let cool slightly on cookie sheets. Sprinkle with confectioners' sugar while still warm. Remove to wire racks to cool completely.

5. Place cookies in airtight container and store in freezer or refrigerator to preserve their chewy texture; do not store at room temperature.

Mushroom Pâté or Duxelles
Matzoh Balls—*Knaidlach*
Stuffed Roast Chicken
Fruit Stuffing
Matzoh Stuffing
Vegetable and Fruit Kugel
Matzoh Pancakes in Honey Sauce—*Chremslach*

Mushroom Pâté or Duxelles

MAKES 6 SERVINGS

This appetizer makes an elegant vegetarian substitute for chopped liver. Chop the mushrooms and shallots in the food processor, if possible, to conserve time and energy.

$\frac{1}{4}$ cup ($\frac{1}{2}$ stick) margarine
1 pound fresh mushrooms, finely chopped
2 shallots, peeled and finely chopped
   Salt and freshly ground black pepper to taste
   Matzoh or assorted cut-up raw vegetables

1. In medium skillet, melt 2 tablespoons margarine over medium-high heat. Sauté mushrooms and shallots in hot margarine about 10 minutes, or until moisture has evaporated.
2. In blender or food processor, purée mushroom mixture with remaining margarine and salt and pepper to taste until it reaches a spreading consistency, scraping down mixture with rubber spatula.
3. Transfer to small bowl or container; cover and refrigerate at least 1 hour for flavors to blend. To serve, spread on matzoh or raw vegetables.

Matzoh Balls

Knaidlach

MAKES 10 BALLS

The secret to perfect matzoh balls is to steam them in boiling salted water. Add these to your favorite homemade chicken soup or canned chicken broth for a Passover treat the whole family will enjoy.

    2 eggs, at room temperature
    2 tablespoons chicken fat or vegetable oil
    $\frac{1}{2}$ cup matzoh meal
    1 teaspoon salt
    $\frac{1}{4}$ to $\frac{1}{3}$ cup chicken broth
      Dash of freshly ground black pepper
      Dash of ground ginger, or 2 tablespoons chopped
        parsley (optional)
      Hot chicken soup

1. In medium bowl, beat eggs with chicken fat or oil. Stir in matzoh meal and salt until blended. Stir in 2 tablespoons broth. Let mixture stand at room temperature 15 to 20 minutes, or refrigerate 1 hour.
2. Stir 2 to 3 tablespoons additional broth into matzoh meal mixture, until it feels light. With wet hands, form mixture into walnut-sized balls; set aside.
3. In large saucepan or dutch oven, bring 2 quarts salted water to a boil over high heat. Reduce heat to medium or medium-low; drop in matzoh balls. Cover and simmer gently for 20 to 30 minutes, until fluffy and tender. (Do not uncover pot for at least 20 minutes, and do not boil or balls will fall apart.)
4. With slotted spoon, remove balls and add to hot soup.

Stuffed Roast Chicken

MAKES 6 SERVINGS

A mixture of margarine and seasonings inserted between the skin and flesh of the chicken imparts a unique juiciness and flavor.

Fruit Stuffing or Matzoh Stuffing (recipe follows)
½ cup (1 stick) margarine, softened
4 cloves garlic, peeled and minced
1 scallion, minced
2 to 3 tablespoons chopped fresh parsley, basil, oregano, and/or tarragon
½ teaspoon salt
Dash of freshly ground black pepper
One 4- to 5-pound whole roasting chicken, rinsed and patted dry

1. Prepare fruit stuffing or matzoh stuffing. Remove giblets from cavity of chicken; fill cavity with stuffing, packing loosely. Tie or skewer cavity closed.
2. Preheat oven to 375°F. In small bowl, combine margarine, garlic, scallion, chopped herbs, salt, and pepper. With hands, carefully loosen skin from breast side of chicken, creating a pocket without breaking the skin. Spread herbed margarine mixture evenly under skin.
3. Place chicken, breast side up, on rack in shallow baking pan. Roast, uncovered, basting occasionally with pan drippings, 1½ to 2 hours, or until golden brown and thigh meat registers 185°F on meat thermometer, and thigh juices run clear when pierced with a fork. Cover loosely with foil and let stand 10 minutes before carving.
4. To serve, spoon stuffing from cavity into serving bowl; carve chicken into slices.

NOTE: Instead of a rack, you can roast chicken on a layer of cut-up vegetables such as potatoes, carrots, and/or turnips.

FRUIT STUFFING

3 tablespoons vegetable oil
1 medium onion, peeled and chopped
½ cup chopped dried apricots
½ cup chopped pitted dried prunes
½ cup whole or slivered almonds
¼ cup golden raisins
1 teaspoon dried tarragon, or 1 tablespoon chopped fresh tarragon
½ teaspoon dried thyme, or 1½ teaspoons chopped fresh thyme
Dash of ground cinnamon
Salt and freshly ground black pepper to taste

1. In medium skillet, heat oil over medium heat. Sauté onion in hot oil 5 to 10 minutes, until soft and translucent.
2. Stir in remaining ingredients; sauté 5 to 10 minutes longer, until fruit begins to soften. Cool slightly before using.

MATZOH STUFFING

If you prefer a starchy stuffing, try this matzoh version as an alternative to the fruit stuffing.

5 matzoh, broken into small pieces
3 tablespoons vegetable oil
1 medium onion, peeled and chopped
3 ribs celery, chopped
2 eggs, beaten
1 tablespoon chopped parsley
1 teaspoon salt
Dash of freshly ground black pepper

1. In large bowl, soak matzoh in 1 cup warm water until soft. Drain and squeeze out water.

2. In medium skillet, heat oil over medium heat. Sauté onion and celery in hot oil 5 to 10 minutes, until soft and translucent. Add matzoh; sauté 5 minutes. Remove from heat and stir in eggs, parsley, salt, and pepper. Cool slightly before using.

Vegetable and Fruit Kugel

MAKES 6 TO 8 SERVINGS

The type of pudding known as kugel has been an integral part of Eastern European Jewish cuisine for generations. It can be made with vegetables, fruits, noodles, and other starchy ingredients. This particular recipe uses matzoh cake meal and margarine instead of eggs to bind it.

1 cup matzoh cake meal
1 teaspoon ground cinnamon
1 teaspoon baking soda
1 teaspoon salt
$\frac{1}{4}$ teaspoon ground nutmeg or allspice
1 cup (2 sticks) margarine
$\frac{1}{2}$ cup sugar
1 medium apple, peeled, cored, and grated
1 large carrot, peeled and grated
1 medium sweet potato, peeled and grated
$\frac{1}{2}$ cup raisins

1. Preheat oven to 325°F. Grease a 12- by 8-inch baking pan.
2. In medium bowl, combine matzoh cake meal, cinnamon, baking soda, salt, and nutmeg or allspice. In large bowl with electric mixer at medium speed, cream margarine and sugar until light and fluffy. Stir in cake meal mixture until blended. Add apple, carrot, sweet potato, and raisins, stirring to combine.

3. Pour mixture into prepared pan. Cover with foil and bake 45 minutes.

4. Increase oven temperature to 350°F. Uncover and bake 15 minutes longer, or until golden. Cut into squares and serve warm.

Matzoh Pancakes in Honey Sauce

Chremslach

MAKES 3 DOZEN PANCAKES

This nostalgic recipe is true comfort food, always evoking fond memories of my childhood seders. Every year at Passover, I travel back to my family's home in Richmond to celebrate the holiday and help with the cooking. Chremslach is one dish that I always prepare for the seder table.

    1 cup matzoh meal
    $\frac{1}{2}$ cup chopped almonds
    1 teaspoon ground cinnamon
    1 teaspoon sugar
    $\frac{1}{4}$ teaspoon salt
    $\frac{1}{8}$ teaspoon ground ginger
    1 cup sweet wine or water
    4 eggs, beaten
    Vegetable oil for frying
One 12-ounce jar honey

1. In medium bowl, combine matzoh meal, almonds, cinnamon, sugar, salt, and ginger. Stir in wine or water and eggs until well blended. (If mixture looks too thin, let stand about 10 minutes to thicken.)

2. Coat bottom of large skillet with about $\frac{1}{4}$ inch oil; place over medium-high heat and heat until hot. Drop batter by tablespoonfuls

into hot oil to make pancakes about 1 inch in diameter. Fry pancakes, a few at a time, for 5 to 8 minutes, until brown on both sides, turning once. Drain on paper towels. Repeat with remaining batter until all is used up.

3. In medium saucepan, bring honey to a boil over medium-high heat. Remove from heat; add pancakes, stirring to coat all with honey. Serve warm. Store leftovers in refrigerator.

Wine note: Wine takes on special significance at Passover, yet debate is renewed each year as to what to drink for the ritual four cups and what change, if any, to make for the wine that accompanies the meal. Tradition holds that the finest red wine fill the four cups. Wine buffs might contend that "fine" means dry and expensive. But those who wish to drink the familiar sweet Concord wine for the ritual four cups need have no fear that palate memory somehow will ruin the taste of dry wine with the meal. For the menus here, start off with a dry Riesling, perhaps from Alsace. Riesling, the king of white wine, contains layer upon layer of complexity and richness and would serve admirably to the end of the meal, were it not for the lamb. Lamb deserves a fine, aged red wine; the chicken dish wouldn't suffer with that, either. Fine burgundies now are available—genuine ones from France. Deep and delicious Bordeaux reds are multiplying on the shelves as well. Cabernets from the Golan Heights, also known as Mount Hermon, are making their mark around the world. Chianti? Certainly. It might not be a bad idea to buy twice as much as necessary, laying down the extra wine in the coolest, darkest, least-used spot in the house to mature until next Passover. If the wine does not live up to expectation at the seder, drink the extra ration within the next few months.

Shavuot, the Hebrew word for "weeks," falls seven weeks after the first day of Passover. What the name doesn't reveal, however, is that this early-summer celebration actually has three derivations.

Originally an agricultural holiday, Shavuot marked the beginning of the wheat harvest. In ancient days, Jews baked two loaves of bread from flour milled from the first wheat and took them to the temple as offerings of gratitude. Shavuot also occurred around the time of the first fruit harvest in Israel, so many farmers took their newly ripened fruits along with their loaves of bread.

Among modern American Jews, the agricultural roots of Shavuot are largely overshadowed by its significance as the holiday on which the Jewish people received the Torah. It was on this day that God spoke to the Jews from Mount Sinai, declaring the Ten Commandments. In Israel, however, farming is an important part of life today, and the holiday has regained its agricultural aspects.

Dairy foods are the most popular fare on Shavuot, and menus based on cheese, milk, and ice cream have evolved. Several reasons have been given for the prevalence of dairy dishes, the most common being that milk represents purity and reinforces the holiness of the Torah. Other sources claim that after spending so much time on Mount Sinai, the Jews found that their milk had soured and had to be turned into cheese. Still another explanation is that the giving of the Torah initiated the custom of keeping kosher. Having only one set of utensils, Moses and his people chose to eat dairy foods.

Whatever its origin, a dairy meal is the order of the day on Shavuot. Often it includes cheese blintzes or kreplach filled with cheese, and cheesecake or ice cream for dessert. Assorted fresh seasonal fruits are usually served as well, carrying out the harvest theme. The menu here combines both these categories, resulting in a light but traditional Shavuot meal.

—Gil Marks

Cherry Soup
Lasagne Rolls with Spinach-Cheese Filling
Cheese Blintzes
New York–style Cheesecake

Cherry Soup

MAKES 6 TO 8 SERVINGS

The inhabitants of Hungary, Czechoslavakia, and other Eastern European countries are particularly fond of fruit soups. This one makes the most of fresh cherries, in season during Shavuot. To prepare the soup at other times of the year, simply substitute canned cherries with their liquid, decreasing the amount of water from 4 cups to 3 cups.

2 pounds pitted sweet red cherries (4 cups), or two 16-ounce cans dark sweet pitted cherries, undrained
One 2-inch cinnamon stick
2 tablespoons freshly squeezed lemon juice
1 strip lemon peel
1 cup dry red wine
1 tablespoon cornstarch
$\frac{1}{4}$ cup sugar, or to taste (use less for canned cherries)

1. In large saucepan, combine 3 cups cherries, 4 cups water, cinnamon, lemon juice, and lemon peel. Place over high heat and bring to a boil. Reduce heat to low; cover and simmer 10 minutes for canned cherries and 15 minutes for fresh cherries, or until tender.
2. In food processor or blender, purée cherry mixture. Add wine; blend well and return to saucepan. In small bowl, blend cornstarch with 2 tablespoons cold water; stir in a little cherry mixture and return all to saucepan.

3. Place saucepan over high heat and bring to a boil. Stir in sugar; reduce heat to low and cook 4 to 5 minutes, until slightly thickened. Stir in reserved 1 cup whole cherries. Serve soup warm, or refrigerate to serve chilled.

Lasagne Rolls with Spinach-Cheese Filling

MAKES 6 SERVINGS

Although not a typical Shavuot dish, this Italian-inspired recipe makes an attractive entrée for an all-dairy meal. Another plus: The rolls can be made ahead and refrigerated till baking time.

$1\frac{1}{2}$ cups tomato sauce or spaghetti sauce
2 cups ricotta cheese or small-curd cottage cheese
One 10-ounce package frozen spinach, thawed and squeezed dry
$\frac{3}{4}$ cup grated Parmesan cheese
2 eggs, slightly beaten
$\frac{1}{2}$ teaspoon freshly ground black pepper
10 to 12 lasagne noodles, cooked and drained
$\frac{1}{2}$ pound mozzarella cheese, shredded (optional)

1. Preheat oven to 350°F. In large oblong baking dish, spread a thin layer of sauce.
2. In medium bowl, combine ricotta or cottage cheese, spinach, $\frac{1}{2}$ cup Parmesan cheese, eggs, and pepper; mix well. On each lasagne noodle, evenly spread 5 to 6 tablespoons cheese mixture. Starting at narrow end, roll up noodles, jelly roll style, enclosing cheese. Place lasagne rolls over sauce in baking dish.
3. Cover lasagne rolls with remaining sauce; top with mozzarella, if desired, and sprinkle with remaining Parmesan cheese. Cover with foil and bake 40 minutes, or until bubbly. (Uncover and bake 10 minutes longer until lightly browned, if using mozzarella.) Serve hot.

Wine note: Dairy normally doesn't demand wine, but the ingredients here could well be paired with an Italian red wine, such as Barbera, Chianti, or Valpolicella.

Cheese Blintzes

MAKES 18 BLINTZES

These blintzes are baked instead of fried, cutting down a bit on the calories and cleanup.

CRÊPES

    3 eggs, at room temperature
    1 cup milk or water
    2 tablespoons melted butter or margarine
    $\frac{1}{4}$ teaspoon salt
    $\frac{3}{4}$ cup all-purpose flour
    Oil or butter

CHEESE FILLING

    2 cups creamed cottage cheese, drained,
      or mashed farmer cheese
    1 egg
2 to 4 tablespoons sugar, or to taste
    1 tablespoon butter, melted
    1 teaspoon freshly squeezed lemon juice (optional)
    $\frac{1}{2}$ teaspoon vanilla extract or ground cinnamon
    $\frac{1}{2}$ teaspoon salt

1. Prepare crêpes: In medium bowl, beat eggs, milk or water, melted butter or margarine, and salt. Add flour; stir to make a smooth, thin batter. Cover and refrigerate at least 30 minutes.
2. Place a 6-inch nonstick skillet over medium-high heat. Add enough oil or butter to lightly coat bottom and sides; heat until hot.

Pour in 1 to 2 tablespoons crêpe batter, tilting pan until batter coats bottom evenly. Cook about 1 minute, or until edges of crêpe begin to brown. Flip crêpe over and cook several seconds on other side, until set.

3. Line plate with waxed paper; put cooked crêpe on plate. Repeat with remaining batter, stacking crêpes between sheets of waxed paper.

4. Prepare cheese filling: In medium bowl, combine cottage or farmer cheese and remaining ingredients; blend well.

5. Preheat oven to 350°F. Grease oblong 13- by 9-inch baking dish.

6. In center of each crêpe, place a heaping tablespoon cheese filling. Fold 2 opposite sides of crêpe in to meet in center, covering filling; fold in remaining 2 sides to enclose filling and form a pocket-shaped blintz.

7. Place blintzes, seam side down, in greased baking dish. Bake 15 to 20 minutes, until heated through.

NOTE: To fry, melt 2 tablespoons butter or margarine in large skillet. Add blintzes, seam side down; fry until golden on both sides, turning once. It should take 5 to 10 minutes per batch.

New York–style Cheesecake

Cheesecake is the most traditional Shavuot dessert. For more color and flavor, you may add sliced berries, peaches, or other seasonal fruit over the sour cream topping.

CRUST
- 1½ cups graham cracker crumbs
- 2 tablespoons sugar
- ½ teaspoon ground cinnamon
- ¼ cup (½ stick) butter or margarine, melted

FILLING
- Three 8-ounce packages cream cheese, softened
- 4 eggs
- One 16-ounce container sour cream (2 cups)
- 1½ cups sugar
- 2 tablespoons cornstarch
- 1 tablespoon freshly squeezed lemon juice
- 2 teaspoons vanilla extract

TOPPING
- One 16-ounce container sour cream (2 cups)
- 3 tablespoons sugar
- 1 teaspoon vanilla extract

1. Prepare crust: In medium bowl, combine graham cracker crumbs, sugar, and cinnamon. Stir in melted butter or margarine until blended. Press mixture into bottom and 1 inch up sides of 9-inch springform pan. Refrigerate while preparing filling.

2. Preheat oven to 350°F. Prepare filling: In medium bowl with electric mixer at medium speed, beat cream cheese until fluffy. Beat in eggs, sour cream, sugar, cornstarch, lemon juice, and vanilla until blended. Pour filling into prepared crust.

3. Bake cheesecake about $1\frac{1}{4}$ hours, or until firm around the edges and lightly browned, but still soft in center. Turn off oven, open door, and let cheesecake stand in oven 30 minutes longer.

4. Remove from oven and cool completely on wire rack.

5. Prepare topping: In small bowl, stir together sour cream, sugar, and vanilla. Spread over top of cooled cheesecake. Refrigerate until ready to serve.

Wine note: Why not a New York wine to go with New York cheesecake? While a New York port may be nothing like the real thing, cheesecake will smooth it out. How about an additional taste, such as plum? Not bad! From further fields, cream sherry would slide down easily, and there is a wide range of sweet wines from Israel, including Muscat. Many flavored liqueurs can also be sipped pleasurably with this cheesecake.

Kosher and/or Ethnic Shopping Sources

DIRECTORIES/GUIDES

Kosher Club
18 Davidge Rd.
Middletown, NY 10940
1-800-3-KOSHER
or 914-344-1933
    Guidebooks listing kosher
    markets and restaurants
    around the country; newsletter
    for travelers and shoppers

Kof-K Kosher Supervision
1444 Queen Anne Rd.
Teaneck, NJ 07666
201-837-0500
    Guide to Kashrus publications
    (quarterly) listing new and
    unusual kosher products;
    hotline for questions on kosher
    certification

SUPERMARKETS

Supersol
220 Central Ave.
Lawrence, NY 11559
516-295-3300

Kosher City
1590 Ralph Ave.
Brooklyn, NY 11236
718-763-4992

Ben David
24–28 Fair Lawn Ave.
Fair Lawn, NJ 07410
201-794-7740

Pathmark Supermarkets
(Eastern United States)

Waldbaum's Supermarkets
(Greater New York Metropolitan
area)

SUPERMARKETS

Amira's Kosher Market
1351 Altamonte Dr.
Altamonte Springs, FL 32701

East Side Kosher Deli
5600 East Cedar Ave.
Denver, CO 80216

DISTRIBUTORS *(can either sell
product directly or provide
information on where to buy
product)*

Prime Kosher Food Inc.
Turkey Hollow Rd.
Donora, PA 15033
412-379-5506
Gourmet and specialty items

Twin City Poultry & Kosher
3855 Beau D'rue Dr.
Eagen, MN 55122
612-454-8177
Gourmet and specialty items

Central Kosher Sales Inc.
3450 West Lake Ave.
Glenview, IL 60025
708-657-7770
Gourmet and specialty items

Nobil House Foods
2826 East First St.
Los Angeles, CA 90033
Gourmet and specialty items

Prestige Foods Ltd.
5818 Lance St.
San Diego, CA 92120
619-265-1709
Gourmet and specialty items

Giamboi Kosher Distributors
117 White Oak Lane
Old Bridge, NJ 08857
201-679-4443
Imported olive oil, dried pasta,
pasta sauces

Sinai Kosher Food Corporation
1000 West Pershing Rd.
Chicago, IL 60609
312-927-2810
Kosher sausages and cold cuts;
wide selection of kosher meat
cuts

Lieber's Kosher Food Specialties
142 44th St.
Brooklyn, NY 11232
718-499-0888
Assorted packaged goods, such
as spices, seasonings, etc.

Paprikas Weiss
1572 Second Ave.
New York, NY 10028
212-288-6117
Herbs, spices, Hungarian
staples and condiments

Gel Spice Company
48 Hook Rd.
Bayonne, NJ 07002
1-800-922-0230
  Spices, herbs, and seeds

Atlantic Processing Co.
150 Varick Ave.
Brooklyn, NY 11200
  Spices and herbs

Yoni's
15 Drake Ave.
New Rochelle, NY 10805
914-576-7030
  Frozen pasta

Eden Foods Inc.
701 Tecumseh Rd.
Clinton, MI 49236
1-800-248-0301
  Japanese ingredients and
  organic products

China Pack Company
4 Division St.
Tarrytown, NY 10591
  Chinese sauces and condiments

China Bowl Trading Company,
Inc.
80 Fifth Ave.
New York, NY 10011
212-255-2935
  Oriental ingredients

Pacific Trader
Central Square
Chatham, NY 12037
518-392-2125
  Japanese, Middle Eastern,
  Chinese, and Korean products

Far East Flavors
8547 E. Arapahoe Rd.
Suite J205
Greenwood Village, CO 80111
303-290-0575
  Thai, Chinese, Vietnamese,
  Japanese and Indian
  ingredients

Azteca Milling Company
501 West Chapin
Edinburgh, TX 78540
  Corn flour (masa) for tortillas

Tia Mia
P.O. Box 685
4501 Anapra Rd.
Sunland Park, NM 88063
  Mexican ingredients including
  chile peppers and spices (not
  all certified; consult with
  rabbi)

Romanoff International Inc.
11111 Carmel Commons Blvd.
Suite 100
Charlotte, NC 28226
  Fish roe, sauces, salad
  dressings

DISTRIBUTORS

Rokeach/Mother's
South 61 Paramus Rd.
Paramus, NJ 07652
201-587-1199
 A variety of ethnic products,
 including those used in Italian,
 Mediterranean, and French
 cooking

Season Products Corp.
34 Laretto St.
Irvington, NJ 07111
201-923-1818
 Caviar, canned fish, oriental
 vegetables

Kirsch Mushroom Company
920 Longfellow Ave.
Bronx, NY 10474
 Dried mushrooms

Famous Specialties Company
55 B Saratoga Blvd.
Island Park, NY 11558
 Strudel leaves

ETHNIC FOOD STORES
Cheese Shops

Miller's Cheese
13 Essex St.
New York, NY 10002

Miller's Cheese
2192 Broadway
New York, NY 10024

Hungarian/Eastern European

Paprikas Weiss Importer (see
distributors list)

Middle Eastern

Sunflower Imports
97-22 Queens Blvd.
Rego Park, NY 11374

Nader International Foods
1 East 28th St.
New York, NY 10016

Sahadi Importing Company
187 Atlantic Ave.
Brooklyn, NY 11238

International Grocery Store and
Meat Market
529 Ninth Ave.
New York, NY 10018

Kosher International
169 Locust Ave.
West Long Branch, NJ 07764
908-870-8777

Adriana's Bazaar
2152 Broadway
New York, NY 10024
212-877-5757

Indian

Little India Stores
128 East 28th St.
New York, NY 10016

ETHNIC FOOD STORES

Annapurna Emporium
126 East 28th St.
New York, NY 10016

Kalustyan Orient Export Trading
Company
123 Lexington Ave.
New York, NY 10016

Indian Spice World
168-37 Hillside Ave.
Jamaica, NY 11432

Shah Groceries
56-11 Junction Blvd.
Elmhurst, NY 11372

Patel Brothers
37-54 74th St.
Jackson Heights, NY 11372

*Oriental (Thai, Vietnamese
Japanese and/or Chinese)*

Katagiri and Company
224 East 59th St.
New York, NY 10022

Kam Man Food Products
200 Canal St.
New York, NY 10007

Sam Bok
127 West 43rd St.
New York, NY 10036

Poo Ping Grocery
81A Bayard St.
New York, NY 10007

Siam Grocery
790 Ninth Ave.
New York, NY 10036

Thailand Food/Sunflower
Grocery
2445 Broadway
New York, NY 10025

Sharmas Oriental and Domestic
Foods
197 Atlantic Ave.
Brooklyn, NY 11238

Caribbean/Hispanic

Moore Street Retail Market
Moore and Humboldt streets
Brooklyn, NY 11211

Note: Some of the shopping
sources listed here sell both
kosher and non-kosher products.
If you have any question about
the purity of a product or
ingredient, consult with your
rabbi. These sources are not
endorsed by Rabbi Gorelick.

Index

Achiote seeds:
in recado rojo (red seasoning), 259
Alexander, Linda, 146, 147
Alle belle, 68–69
Almond(s):
in baklava (syrup-soaked pastry)
baklowa, 142
bread *(mandelbrot)*, 347
chocolate chip (variation), 348
marble (variation), 348
flan *(flan Yucateco or queso de Napoles)*, 261–62
in fruit stuffing, for chicken, 381
in Indian pareve dessert *(suji halwa)*, 79
in matzoh pancakes in honey
sauce *(chremslach)*, 383–84
in nut pastries *(malfuf)*, 135–36
paste, 102–103
in pine nut confections *(bouchées aux pignons)*, 180
in stuffed crêpes *(alle belle)*, 68–69
in stuffing, for dried fruit *(noix et dates fourées)*, 102–3
Alsatian noodles, 19
Anchin, Steve, 93
Anchovies:
with dill and pimiento, marinated, 310
and olives, roasted peppers with *(peperoni arrostiti con acciughe)*, 226–27
Apio con zanahorias, 112
Appetizers:
anchovies with dill and pimiento, marinated, 310
artichokes with beets and beet
greens, braised, 24–26
avocado dip *(guacamole)*, 242–43

chopped liver *(gehakte leber)*, 290–91
vegetarian, 299
corn fritters *(khao pud tod)*, 157–58
cucumber salad, spicy *(thangua dong)*, 152
fish roe dip *(tarama)*, 115–16
hot cigars *(garros)*, 85–87
lentil cakes *(vadas)*, 58
lime chicken brochettes *(ga nuong voi)*, 276–77
meatballs on toast *(polpettoncini sui crostone)*, 313–14
mushroom pâté or duxelles, 378
Nice-style salad *(salade Niçoise)*, 307–8
onion tart, Nice-style *(pissaladière)*, 314–15
"pigeon" pie *(pastilla)*, 94–95
pita crisps, 243
potato balls *(bondas)*, 54–55
puffy Tunisian omelet *(maakoude de poisson)*, 177–78
sausage stew, Spanish *(cazuelo de chorizo)*, 311–12
sesame paste dip *(tahini dip)*, 137
stuffed grape leaves *(dolmahs)*, 130–31
stuffed mushrooms *(shiang dong-gu)*, 212–13
La Varenne *(champignons farcis La Varenne)*, 312–13
vegetable fritters *(pakoras)*, 53–54
vegetable omelet *(frittata or tortilla Espanola)*, 308–9
Apple(s):
cake, 296–97
carrot, and sweet potato tzimmes, 344–45

bananas in coconut milk *(khrow buad chi)*, 165
black bean *(che dau den)*, 283
double-chocolate pecan tarts, 330–31
double-chocolate truffles, 334
English trifle, 324–25
fried plantains *(plantanos fritos)*, 248–49
fruit compote *(kompót)*, 196
fruit coupe, exotic, 332–33
gratin of fresh peaches and bananas *(gratin de pêches et bananes)*, 26–27
hamantaschen, 356–58
hazelnut torte *(magyoró torta)*, 190–91
Indian pareve *(suji halwa)*, 79
jelly doughnuts *(sufganiyot)*, 352–53
lemon tart *(torta di limone)*, 235–36
lime and coconut pie *(pay de limon y coco)*, 268–69
mousse-filled meringues, 328–29
noodle pudding *(lokshen kugel)*, 295
noodles with poppy seeds *(makos metelt)*, 197
nut pastries *(malfuf)*, 135–36
pancakes for sweet fillings *(palacsinta)*, 194–95
pastry horns *(travados)*, 123–24
pastry turnovers, sweet *(empanandes de dulce)*, 249–50
peaches poached in wine scented with pepper and bay leaf (variation), 14
pears poached in wine scented with pepper and bay leaf *(les poires au vin de poivre et de laurier)*, 14
pine nut confections *(bouchées aux pignons)*, 180
raspberry sorbet, 333
rice halvah, 365–66
rice pudding with apricots, sweet *(khow neeow sum)*, 156
rugelach, 302–3
stuffed dates *(dattes farcies)*, 176
stuffed dried fruit *(noix et dates fourée)*, 102–3
vegetable and fruit kugel, 382–83
whipped wine custard *(zabaglione)*, 230
see also Cake(s); Cookies
Devonshire cream, 322
Dill and pimiento, marinated anchovies with, 310
Dips:
avocado *(guacamole)*, 242–43
fish roe *(tarama)*, 115–16
ranch sauce *(salsa ranchera)*, 267
sesame paste *(tahini)*, 137
Directories/guides, 393
Distributors, 394–96
Dolmahs, 130–31
Double-chocolate pecan tarts, 330–31
Double-chocolate truffles, 334
Doughnuts, jelly *(sufganiyot)*, 352–53
Dua cai, 280
Dun hwa tong, 204–5

Egg(s):
drop soup, new-style *(dun hwa tong)*, 204–5
filling, for tea sandwiches, 319
Passover brown, 372
in puffy tunisian omelet *(maakoude de poisson)*, 177–78
in vegetable omelet *(frittata or tortilla Española)*, 308–9
in vegetable pie *(coco sabzie)*, 367–68
Eggplant:
and beef casserole *(engreyee)*, 138
braised (variation), 112
fritters, 54
salad, 91–92
Empanades de dulce, 249–50
Engel, Brian, 6–7
English afternoon tea, 317–25
English trifle, 324–25
Engreyee, 138
Epazote, 264
Ethnic food stores, 396–97
Ethnic foods, permissible, xxxiv–xxxv
Exotic fruit coupe, 332–33

Gram flour: *See* Besan flour
Grated carrot salad *(salada de chizo)*, 91
Gratin de pêches et bananes, 26–27
Gratin of fresh peaches and bananas *(gratin de pêches et bananes)*, 26–27
Green beans: *See* Beans, green
Greens:
   beet, braised artichokes with beets and, 24–26
   mustard, pickled *(dua cai)*, 280
Groats and noodles *(kasha varnishkes)*, 293–94
Ground beef salad *(lap nuea)*, 158–59
Guacamole, 242–43

Hamantaschen, 356–58
Hand-rolled cone *(temaki)*, 42–43
Harira, 97–98
Harissa, 100
Hazelnut torte *(mogyoró torta)*, 190–91
Heavy cream:
   in Devonshire cream, 322
Herring, smoked:
   for sushi, 35
Herzog, Ernest, xxxviii
Hirsch, Leila, 287–88
Honey, 338
   cake, 345–46
   measuring, 346
   sauce, matzoh pancakes in *(chremslach)*, 383–84
Hong sau gee, 208
Hot cigars *(garros)*, 85–87
Hout metbuch, 88
   in red sauce, 96
Hungarian cuisine, 181–83

Indian cuisine, 49–51
Indian pareve dessert *(suji halwa)*, 79
Iraqi cuisine, 125–27
Iraqi-style rice, 139
Irish soda bread, 322–23
Isserles, Moses, xxxviii
Italian cuisine, 221–24

Japanese cuisine, 29–31
Jelly doughnuts *(sufganiyot)*, 352–53

Ka-ti, 151
Kachumber, 73
Kapama, 116–17
Kasha, 293
   and noodles *(kasha varnishkes)*, 293–94
Keftes de prasa, 113
Khao pud tod, 157–58
Khow neeow sum, 156
Khow phat pong kali, 164
Khrow buad chi, 165
Kirschenbaum, Levana Levy, 83–84
Knaidlach, 379
Köménymagos leves, 186–87
Kompót, 196
Korabies, 114
Kosher foods, shopping for, xxxii–xxxiv
Kosher Gourmet magazine, 7
Kubba bamish, 129–30

Lace roll-ups, 360–61
Lamb:
   in lentil soup, Moroccan *(harira)*, 97–98
   permitted, xxxii
   prohibited, xxxii
   shoulder roast, 374
   in stuffed vegetables *(mahasha)*, 140–41
   see also Beef; Veal
Lap nuea, 158–59
Lasagne rolls with spinach-cheese filling, 387
Latkes, 350–51
   sweet potato (variation), 351
Lattanzi, Paolo, 223, 224–25
Laws of kashrut, xxvii–xxviii, xxix–xxxv
   and guide to kosher meats, xxxi–xxxii
   permitted foods, xxix–xxx
   prohibited foods, xxx
   and ritual slaughter and koshering of meat, xxx–xxxi

Morels: *See* Mushroom(s)
Moroccan cuisine, 81–83
Moroccan lentil soup *(harira)*, 97–98
Moros y cristianos, 245–46
Mousse-filled meringues, 328–29
Moustachudos, 377
Mung dal, 70–71
Mushroom(s):
  barley soup, 289–90
  black dried
    and rice in a clay pot *(com nam huong)*, 282
    stuffed *(shiang dong-gu)*, 212–13
  fritters, 54
  morels
    about, 13
    asparagus with *(asperges et morilles)*, 12–13
    pâté or duxelles, 378
  shiitake
    soup *(sopa de hongos)*, 255–56
    turnovers *(quesadillas de hongo silvestre)*, 264–66
  stuffed, La Varenne *(champignons farcis La Varenne)*, 312–13
Mustard:
  okra with *(subzi)*, 74
  sauce
    sea bream with spinach and, 9–10
    veal chops with *(veau au moutarde)*, 18
Mustard greens: *See* Greens

Nam jim gai yang, 163
Nam prik kaeng dang, 150–51
Nanbrangi, 366–67
Nash, Helen, 203
New-style egg drop soup *(dun hwa tong)*, 204–5
New York-style cheesecake, 390–91
Newsday (newspaper), 288
Nice-style onion tart *(pissaladière)*, 314–15
Nice-style salad *(salade Niçoise)*, 307–8
Nigiri sushi, 36–37
Noix et dates fourées, 102–103
Noodle(s):
  Alsatian, 19

bean thread
  about, 160
  stir-fried *(pad woon sen)*, 160–61
  with poppy seeds *(makos metelt)*, 197
  pudding *(lokshen kugel)*, 295
  and vegetables, stir fried *(yaki soba)*, 45–46
  see also rice noodles
Noorani, Nahid, 363–64
Nori, 32
Nuea pad prik, 160
Nuoc cham (hot sauce), 273
Nuoc mam (fish sauce), 272–73
Nuoc tuong, 277–78
Nut(s), 339
  cookies *(korabies)*, 114
  pastries *(malfuf)*, 135–36
  stuffed (variation), 103
  see also individual names

Oil, testing temperature of, 353
Okra *(bamias)*, 117–18
  and chicken casserole *(ganaouia au poulet)*, 178–79
  with mustard *(bhindi-subzi)*, 74
Olanoff, Mimi, 240, 241, 306, 317
Olive(s):
  butter, salmon with *(salmon au beurre d'olive en papillote)*, 23–24
  potatoes, and tomatoes, chicken tagine with *(bel btata)*, 90
  roasted peppers with anchovies and *(peperoni arrostiti con acciughe)*, 226–27
Omelets:
  puffy Tunisian *(maakoude de poisson)*, 177–78
  vegetable *(frittata or tortilla Espanola)*, 308–9
Onion(s):
  in cream of carrot soup *(potage Lorraine)*, 16–17
  fritters, 54
  red
    roasted, Yucatan style *(cebollas asadas à la Yucateca)*, 260
  steaming, 188
  in stir-fried noodles and vegetables *(yaki soba)*, 45–46